TOWARD AN ANTI-CAPITALIST COMPOSITION

TOWARD AN ANTI-CAPITALIST COMPOSITION

JAMES RUSHING DANIEL

UTAH STATE UNIVERSITY PRESS
Logan

© 2022 by University Press of Colorado

Published by Utah State University Press
An imprint of University Press of Colorado
245 Century Circle, Suite 202
Louisville, Colorado 80027

All rights reserved

 The University Press of Colorado is a proud member of the Association of University Presses.

The University Press of Colorado is a cooperative publishing enterprise supported, in part, by Adams State University, Colorado State University, Fort Lewis College, Metropolitan State University of Denver, University of Alaska Fairbanks, University of Colorado, University of Denver, University of Northern Colorado, University of Wyoming, Utah State University, and Western Colorado University.

ISBN: 978-1-64642-241-8 (paperback)
ISBN: 978-1-64642-242-5 (ebook)
https://doi.org/10.7330/9781646422425

Library of Congress Cataloging-in-Publication Data

Names: Daniel, James Rushing, author.
Title: Toward an anti-capitalist composition / by James Rushing Daniel.
Description: Logan : Utah State University Press, [2022] | bibliographical references and index.
Identifiers: LCCN 2022017915 (print) | LCCN 2022017916 (ebook) | ISBN 9781646422418 (paperback) | ISBN 9781646422425 (ebook)
Subjects: LCSH: English language—Rhetoric—Study and (Higher)—Economic aspects. | English language—Rhetoric—Study teaching (Higher)—Political aspects. | Academic writing—Study teaching—Economic aspects. | Academic writing—Study teaching—Political aspects. | Capitalism and education. | BISAC LANGUAGE ARTS & DISCIPLINES / Writing / Composition
Classification: LCC PE1404 .D359 2022 (print) | LCC PE1404 (ebook) | 808/.0420711—dc23/eng/20220601
LC record available at https://lccn.loc.gov/2022017915
LC ebook record available at https://lccn.loc.gov/2022017916

Cover photograph © hrui/Shutterstock.

CONTENTS

Acknowledgments   *vii*

Introduction: Money Changes Everything   3

1. Gathering   29
2. Debt   61
3. Work   88
4. Data   121
5. Action   149

Coda   179

Notes   185
References   193
Index   217
About the Author   225

ACKNOWLEDGMENTS

Writing a book often feels like taking on a second job. You constantly struggle to carve out time away from teaching, grading, and your personal life to do a bit of writing. The feeling is compounded, of course, when the writer is a scholar off the tenure track. I've accordingly been fortunate to receive extensive support and encouragement from colleagues, friends, and family in bringing this book into the world.

I am grateful to my colleagues at the University of Washington who read drafts, advised me on publication, and otherwise helped me find my footing. Thank you to Anis Bawarshi, Nancy Bou Ayash, Megan Callow, Eva Cherniavsky, Juan C. Guerra, Amy Hagopian, Gillian Harkins, Katie Malcolm, Carrie Matthews, Candice Rai, Stephanie L. Kerschbaum, Josephine Walwema, John Webster, and Marc Zachry. A special thanks goes to Jessica Burstein, who offered enormously helpful and supportive feedback.

Thanks also to Mike Baccam at the University of Washington Press for his advice and encouragement.

I also wish to thank Bruce Horner and Tony Scott for their generous feedback on the proposal.

I'm indebted to my professors at the University of Wisconsin–Madison for their advice and support over the years. Morris Young graciously allowed me into his graduate seminar to workshop an early draft of the proposal. Thanks as well to Michael Bernard-Donals and to B. Venkat Mani.

Erik Olin Wright, also at the University of Wisconsin–Madison, passed away while this manuscript was in preparation. While I only met Erik once, attending a lecture by Alain Badiou, whom Erik had brought to campus, I'm immensely indebted to his formidable scholarship and for his establishment of the Havens Center (now the Havens Wright Center). His posthumously published text, *How to Be an Anticapitalist in the Twenty-First Century* (2019), inspired my title and has hugely propelled my thinking on labor, class, and economic inequality.

Two chapters in the text are adapted from journal articles and benefitted from the generous guidance of journal editors Jonathan

Alexander and Laurie Gries. Portions of chapter 2 were previously published in *College Composition and Communication*, volume 70, issue 2. Chapter 3 was originally published in issue 30 of *enculturation: A Journal of Rhetoric, Writing, and Culture* (February 2020) (http://enculturation.net/Burning_Out). They are used with permission.

Thank you also to Rachael Levay, Darrin Pratt, Beth Svinarich, Laura Furney, Dan Pratt, and the rest of the staff at Utah State University Press.

I'm especially thankful for the friendship and intellectual support of William Banks. This book owes a tremendous debt to his tireless reading, advice, and insight.

My family has been a constant source of support and encouragement throughout some long years in the dark forest of academia. Robert, Daphne, and Diana, thank you so very much.

Last, and most of all, I want to thank my partner, Vlada.

TOWARD AN ANTI-CAPITALIST COMPOSITION

Introduction
MONEY CHANGES EVERYTHING

Riders taking the Megabus out of New York line up along West Thirty-Fourth Street. During my days as an adjunct, I was there a few times a week. Back then, the area held little of interest beyond a bar called the Frying Pan. Now the towers of Hudson Yards loom above the neighborhood, the tallest rising 1,296 feet. At a cost of $20 billion, the site is the largest private real-estate project in US history (Wirthman 2018). In addition to nearly four thousand apartments (Nonko 2018) and 1.5 million feet of office space (Palmer 2019), the complex also boasts the largest Equinox health club in the world (Lushing 2019); the Shed, where avant-garde artists like Arca and Tomás Saraceno showcase new work; and Vessel, Thomas Heatherwick's interactive sculpture the *New Yorker*'s Alexandra Schwartz (2019) called a "shawarma-shaped stairway to nowhere." At the cost of an additional billion dollars, 30 Hudson Yards also offers Edge (see figure 0.1), a 1,100-foot-high, cantilevered observation deck where visitors can look down on tenth Avenue and "sip champagne in the sky" (Hudson Yards n.d.). Apartments at the site went on the market in 2016 and were listed in the "relatively modest" (Plitt 2016) price range of $2 million to $32 million.

Just across the Hudson and the Passaic lies Newark, New Jersey, a majority Black city (United States Census Bureau n.d.) recently ranked the third neediest in the country (O'Sullivan 2018). The site of a brutal six-day race riot in 1967 sparked by the beating of John Smith, an African American, by white police (Mitter, *Guardian*, July 11, 2017), the city has endured decades of disinvestment, job flight, and political corruption (Newman 2004). The city also remains embroiled in an extended water contamination crisis that has drawn comparisons to Flint, Michigan. For years, city officials were aware lead had been leaching from the city's aging pipes into its water supply but had few financial resources to address the problem (Corasaniti, Kilgannon, and Schwartz, *New York Times*, September 23, 2019). The cascading failures resulting from subsequent cheap fixes are almost too calamitous to be believed. As a stopgap

Figure 0.1. Hudson Yards and Edge (Photograph by Rhododendrites. Licensed under the Creative Commons Attribution-Share Alike 4.0 International license. https:// creativecommons.org/licenses/by-sa/4.0/deed.en.)

measure, the city added sodium silicate to its water, but a 2015 decision to lower the pH levels of the city's water supply to reduce carcinogens neutralized the effects of the chemical; in 2016, elevated lead levels were found in half the city's public and charter schools. In an alternative solution, the city distributed faucet filters designed to remove lead from drinking water, but in 2018 the filters were found to be defective and the city was forced to distribute bottled water (Corasaniti, Kilgannon, and Schwartz, *New York Times*, September 23, 2019).

    This brief sketch of these two radically distinct urban sites just thirteen miles apart dramatizes the conditions many of us currently live in, places where wealthy white enclaves bask in luxury and where racial minorities and other marginalized populations face a diminishing quality of life. Yet while I have depicted what may appear to be multiple crises—institutional racism, privatization, the neglect of infrastructure, and poverty in the midst of enormous privilege—these share a common relation insofar as they are all either deepened by or the direct consequence of capitalism. Capitalism, in these and other sites across the world, creates, maintains, and intensifies economic and racial inequality; incentivizes and protects political corruption; restricts opportunity; and hastens the developing climate crisis. As sociologists Mathieu Desan and Michael A. McCarthy (2018) contend, "Capitalism is the chief source of human suffering today and a system that promotes the worst of human behaviors." In their view, capitalism's production of hierarchy, its remapping of the world as a place of strife rather than kinship, its degradation of the climate, and its capacity to impoverish are fundamental to its project. They are features, not bugs.

Building on this assertion, this book advocates the adoption of an anticapitalist approach in the field of composition. My contention is that only by becoming an explicitly and avowedly anticapitalist field can composition hope to conceptualize, let alone confront, the enormity of capitalism's contemporary harms and prepare students to encounter and resist them. While some in the discipline have long made similar claims,[1] for many of us, this shift would entail significant changes to our research practices, administrative work, and pedagogy. With respect to our research, we must strive to map the landscape of twenty-first-century capitalism, identify its relationship to writing and to the composition classroom, and isolate means of resisting this influence while abandoning support, both explicit and implicit, for unbridled and unregulated capitalist growth. We must approach our institutional work with the similar understanding that capitalist logics of austerity, casualization, and exploitation must be opposed through unionizing, fighting for secure positions and fair wages, and protecting faculty governance. We must additionally be fearless in our classrooms about tracing the history and effects of capitalism, teaching writing as a technology entangled in the global economy, and orienting our students toward analyzing and confronting capitalist hegemony. We must also not be content to limit our work to the university but must engage with broader publics on issues of economic inequality, austerity, and related social justice concerns.

My framing of this work as *anticapitalist* is a deliberately ambiguous gesture intended to signify a general critique of capitalism irrespective of credo and, accordingly, to offer compositionists a broad array of methods, texts, and theories to inform their work. Rather than bind myself or the field to a single tradition, I adopt an expansive approach that unites numerous perspectives in the critique of capitalism and aim to build upon the disparate murmurs of economic dissatisfaction heard across the world. Because of this approach, I do not attempt to offer a precis of anticapitalist thought, leaving that to others,[2] but rather strive to begin a disciplinary conversation on anticapitalism rooted in contemporary conditions, activism, and theoretical interventions. In understanding emergent articulations of anticapitalism as rendering this conversation especially necessary, I follow David Harvey (2020), who observes a common critique emerging among unaffiliated movements: "What we now see is perhaps the beginnings of the coming together of all those who feel that there is something wrong with the basic economic model" (8). Anticapitalism, however, is not simply an ethos or position but, rather, following sociologist Erik Olin Wright (2019), "a practical stance toward building an alternative toward greater human flourishing" (3). It is, in other words, an active and engaged orientation contending that capitalism, as a set of material processes and conditions, an ideology, a constellation of arguments, and a litany of effects, must be broadly resisted, even from the marginal position of composition, and that such opposition is not simply an ethical obligation for those of us who teach writing but a practical means of improving local and global conditions. While many in composition are sympathetic to these concerns, our discipline, in general, has not evinced a strong anticapitalist position for some time. Despite our support of equality, social justice, and students' well-being, composition, with some notable exceptions, has been quiet about capitalism's demonstrable harms and has typically shied away from, as Geoffrey Clegg (2019) frames it, teaching students "to resist neoliberal policies of capitalist assent" (160).

I am certainly aware my advocacy of an anticapitalist approach in the field may raise questions. To what extent is composition capable of becoming anticapitalist? If composition is indeed concerned with preparing students to, as David Smit (2007) contends, realize "their purposes outside the classroom in the larger 'marketplace'" (156), how can it reasonably oppose capitalism? Why should it? Furthermore, why is capitalism, of all potential issues, the one the field should devote itself to? And if anticapitalism is indeed the right direction for the field, what figures or critiques should orient this work?

The following pages attempt to answer these questions in calling for an anticapitalist (re)awakening in our discipline.

CAN COMPOSITION BE ANTICAPITALIST?

Some readers might reasonably suggest that composition—because of its strict commitments to teaching the craft of writing—can simply not be anticapitalist. Such critics might argue that because composition has a defined set of obligations, many of them directly capitulating to the needs of the professional world, reconceptualizing the field as anticapitalist would be an ultimately untenable contradiction. Such a position is effectively evinced, often implicitly, by proponents of writing about writing (WAW), a position that advocates importing composition research into course curricula as a means of engaging students in the task and discipline of writing. In the introduction to their 2019 collection *Next Steps: New Directions for/in Writing about Writing*, Barbara Bird, Doug Downs, I. Moriah McCracken, and Jan Rieman defend the WAW approach, arguing that writing itself must be the subject of the composition classroom insofar as "it is in wrestling with writing concepts . . . that students think deeply about what writing is, does, and means to them, and it is in writing about these concepts that students form their writer identities and develop deep writing knowledge" (3). A parallel approach in the field, that of threshold concepts, similarly contends writing courses are obligated to introduce students to the common understandings, ideas, and assumptions that undergird writing. As Linda Adler-Kassner and Elizabeth Wardle (2015) argue, threshold concepts are "concepts critical for continued learning and participation in an area or within a community of practice" (2). As with WAW, threshold concepts are promoted as content, a subject of explicit inquiry, allowing writers to gain fluency with the norms and conventions of interpretive communities. As Adler-Kassner noted in her 2017 CCCC chair's address, "Writers must recognize that to produce what's considered 'good writing' requires the ability to analyze expectations in specific locations. To do this, writers must approach writing as a subject of study and an activity" (332).

While I am far from opposed to introducing composition theory into the classroom, and indeed believe introducing students to examples of disciplinary scholarship specifically concerned with labor, precarity, and social class (Carter et al. 2019b; Kahn, Lalicker, and Lynch-Biniek 2017; Welch and Scott 2016) could achieve some of the same learning outcomes I advocate here—the work of this book is consistent with several threshold concepts, particularly Tony Scott's (2016b) notion that "Writing Enacts and Creates Identities and Ideologies" (48)—I depart from the restrictiveness of several of the positions described above. With other scholars of the field's social turn, I conceptualize composition as a field with profound and undeniable linkages to social and political concerns. In my view, composition, as Bruce Horner (2015) frames it, is a "material social practice" (451) rather than a defined set of aptitudes or, as Horner characterizes David Smit's (2007) position, "information or skill transfer . . . knowledge as commodity" (457). Following Horner, I conceptualize composition as a site where an exploration of social and material conditions must be staged if students are to confront the real operation of language and, indeed, the ways language is entangled in social, political, and economic phenomena. WAW and threshold concept advocates, by contrast, often imply that the writing classroom, by focusing exclusively on the task and theory of writing, is, in some respects, capable of being bracketed from larger social and political concerns. In the preface to *Writing about Writing: A College Reader*, Wardle and Downs (2011) note, "In conventional composition courses, students are too often asked to write about an arbitrary topic unrelated to writing" (v). I question how Wardle and Downs can make such distinctions when social and material forces—white racial habitus (Inoue 2019), ableism (Kerschbaum 2014), and, indeed, capitalism—are so profoundly imbedded in all writing, language, and university instruction as to trouble any demarcation of writing's boundaries. As Christian Marazzi (2011) contends, language in the post-Fordist context has become territorialized by capitalism's unbridled expansion. As he claims, "The dichotomy between the instrumental and the communicative sphere has been upended" (41). The consequence of this blurring, for Marazzi, is that language no longer simply reflects and participates in the economic sphere but rather is itself a site of economic production. Following Marazzi's logic, to exclude political economy from course content is to neglect the ways language and writing perpetuate, embody, and enact capitalism. Abandoning direct attention to language, I believe, positions students to be less cognizant of capitalism's power and its role in the professional and social worlds.

Composition's positionality as a paradigmatic site of economic exploitation offers further justification that the field is available to (and spectacularly in need of) anticapitalist intervention on the subject of labor. Marc Bousquet (2002) notoriously made this critique twenty years ago in his controversial article "Composition as Management Science: Toward a University without a WPA." In the text, Bousquet critiques the extent to which "managerial subjectivity" (494) permeates the field and equates WPAs to "members of the working class whose particular labor is to directly administer the labor of other members of their class at the frontline of the extraction of surplus value" (498). While Bousquet acknowledges most WPAs wish to improve conditions for their mostly contingent employees, he notes that, due to their own fidelity to the organizational system, they "understand that there is little they can do about the labor system" (507). He hence advocates the abolition of the WPA and the raising of class consciousness among exploited composition instructors. Bousquet's article certainly impacted the disciplinary conversation (Abraham 2016), but the changes he advocates have not been implemented and the field continues to be a site of enormous precarity (Daniel 2017). While Seth Kahn (2020) acknowledges labor issues have become more prominent in composition scholarship in recent years—in addition to Kahn's work, the contributions of Randall McClure, Dayna V. Goldstein, and Michael A. Pemberton (2017), Deborah Mutnick (2016), and Nancy Welch and Tony Scott (2016) bear this out—he contends composition teaching continues to be underpaid and intellectually undervalued, even *and especially* by compositionists themselves (Kahn 2020, 606). Following both Kahn and Bousquet (2002), I argue composition remains in need of anticapitalist intervention.

Some might also suggest that by advocating an anticapitalist writing pedagogy, I am untenably asking that writing instructors acquire and teach a secondary body of knowledge. My view, however, is that virtually any instructor with an interest in economic inequality or, for that matter, with the experience of precarity will be able to do this work. Beyond the fact that many in composition come to the field from working-class backgrounds, the pervasive precarity of writing instruction as a profession means this includes most of us. Those who patch together "scraps of teaching" (Clare 2020) certainly understand economic inequality and can begin an impactful anticapitalist conversation based solely on their experience. While some have cautioned that students may be resistant to such topics (Strickland 2007) or that such conversations have little relevance to composition's learning goals, the experiences of Josh Carmony (2021), a college student and essential worker, may be illustrative. In a recent article for *Contingent Magazine*, Carmony describes shock at realizing what little job security his history professor had: "One of the most impactful and inspiring professors at my college was on the verge of unemployment, with seven students and a three-credit course on Vietnam separating her from delivering food for Grubhub." This encounter with faculty precarity led Carmony to a broader realization of the culture of precarity operative in contemporary capitalism.

> My college was hiring one full-time instructor in each department (perhaps more in some of the larger departments) and then filling in the remaining classes with adjuncts—often three, four, or more in a single

department. It was a carbon copy of the corporate work-around that I experienced in the airline industry, where businesses exploit labor to avoid paying dignified wages and benefits.

For Carmony, making connections between the adjunct crisis at his university and the broader conditions of the casualization of work led to deeper and more critical thinking on labor and twenty-first-century capitalism. In concluding his article, he notes, "As for students, I think it's past time that we get a radical." From Carmony's testimony, it should be clear substantive knowledge of political economy on the part of instructors is not necessary to engage students in a critique of political economy. Moreover, such conversations are not ancillary to the work of writing. Just as Carmony's realization of his teacher's precarity extended his thinking on labor, the university, and contemporary capitalist conditions, anticapitalist inquiry offers to enhance students' critical capacities.

WHAT'S SO WRONG WITH CAPITALISM?

Some who accept composition is at least nominally capable of adopting an anticapitalist position may question why such a turn is necessary. Those asking such a question may be attuned to issues of social justice but not necessarily convinced capitalism is acutely problematic or, indeed, the chief crisis our field must attend to. They may argue, for instance, that alternate issues—racism, genderism, homophobia, ableism, authoritarianism, declining democracy—are more significant and more worthy of our attention. I certainly don't dispute the importance of these concerns. My response, however, is that capitalism also presents its own set of inimitably grave concerns and, more significantly, that capitalism plays a crucial role in deepening and sustaining virtually all other crises and inequities. In this section, I first discuss three of capitalism's most pressing effects—economic inequality, the cultivation of human misery, and the degradation of the environment—before turning to a discussion of the ways capitalism intensifies ostensibly noneconomic forms of inequality. This discussion aims to illuminate that while numerous crises mark our era, capitalism is both the most significant and the most expansive.

One of the most visible crises of the last several decades is rising economic inequality (Piketty 2014, 2015, 2020; Milanović 2018). As economist Thomas Piketty (2014) contends, US inequality was high prior to World War II, with the top decile claiming 45–50 percent of national income between 1910 and 1930 (32), but fell significantly after the war, with the wealthiest decile claiming only 30–35 percent of national income between 1950 and 1970 (32). Inequality, however, has exploded since 1980, with the top decile garnering nearly 50 percent of national income by 2018 (21). While, as Piketty argues, this surge in inequality was accompanied by enormous advancements in global wealth that have had some positive consequences—global life expectancy rose from twenty-six in 1820 to seventy-two in 2020 (16), the general health of the global population is now at its peak (17), and per capita income is ten times what it was in the 1900s (18)—these advancements have come at an enormous cost, particularly to the poorest 50 percent of the global population (21). The federal minimum wage "in real terms" (34) is below what it was in 1980, resulting in "the declining position of low wage workers" (531) and "decreased worker bargaining power" (531). Access to higher education in the United States has likewise become increasingly unequal (34) and is directly tied to parental income (535). Women and minority populations are also uniquely affected. Gender inequality, while declining, remains significant in economic terms (689). Racial inequality also remains stark. The Black poverty rate is more than twice that of white Americans (22 percent versus 9 percent, respectively), while the median household wealth of Black Americans is one-tenth that of white Americans (Rosalsky 2020).

A second deeply significant consequence of capitalist expansion is the rise in mortality among certain low-income population segments in the United States. In *Deaths of Despair and the Future of Capitalism*, economists Anne Case and Angus Deaton (2020) investigate the declining life expectancy of high school-educated, white, working-class Americans due to suicide, drugs, and alcohol, consequences propelled by economic inequality. As they detail, the United States is an increasingly unequal place where those without a college degree face a greater risk of death, a lower quality of life, "increases in their levels of pain, ill health, and serious mental distress, and declines in their ability to work and to socialize" (3). They cite a complex constellation of capitalist and social forces as responsible. Union membership has declined across the country, precipitating the decline of the working class (4). Workers have been both exploited by the US healthcare system (9) and overprescribed pain killers, leading to a devastating opioid epidemic (10). Perhaps most profoundly, Case and Deaton detail how the power of corporations has vastly outstripped workers, who have been variously consolidated and disempowered (10), finding themselves without agency or recourse in the twenty-first-century economic landscape. This is, crucially, not to suggest white people are unique in facing increased suffering in the twenty-first century. As Michelle Alexander (2019) argues, the abuses of the Jim Crow era continue through juridical racism and the criminalization of Blackness. As she writes, "Once you're labeled a felon, the old forms of discrimination . . . are legal" (2), specifically "employment discrimination, housing discrimination, denial of the right to vote, denial of educational opportunity, denial of food stamps and other public benefits, and exclusion from jury service" (2). Capitalism, of course, also plays a role here, as I discuss later in this introduction.

As troubling as these conditions are, capitalism's environmental impact is arguably its most expansive and catastrophic effect. As environmental activist Paul Fleckenstein (2019) argues, "Rapidly changing climate conditions threaten to radically disrupt the plant, insect, and soil ecologies that make agriculture possible." The role of capitalism in these events is increasingly impossible to deny. Indeed, some seeking to emphasize capitalism's links to planetary harm have employed the term "the Capitalocene," an alternative to the Anthropocene, to emphasize capitalism's unique role in driving the new geologic era and inaugurating novel relations among humans, nonhumans, and the Earth. As Jason W. Moore (2016a) theorizes, the Capitalocene, "an ugly word for an ugly system" (5), strives to respond to the unanswered questions raised by the Anthropocene: "questions of power, capitalism, and class, anthropocentrism, dualist framings of 'nature' and 'society,' and the role of states and empires" (5). The term, he elaborates, "signifies capitalism as a way of organizing nature—as a multispecies, situated, capitalist world ecology" (6). For Moore (2016b), coming to terms with capitalism's harmful relation to the planet entails a different order of anticapitalist solutions than have previously been proposed, namely combatting the "Cheap Nature strategy" (113), the notion that the world's abundant natural resources are, indeed, free and available for exploitation without consequence. The term "Capitalocene" hence names and critiques capitalism's absolute and catastrophic transformation of the physical world.

In addition to crises directly linked to its dominance, capitalism also plays a significant role in creating, deepening, and sustaining seemingly noneconomic forms of inequality. Disability, an issue extensively taken up in composition (Dolmage 2017; Kerschbaum 2014; Simpkins 2018), is one of many forms of inequality capitalism, in generally unacknowledged and invisible ways, informs. Disability rights activist Marta Russell and professor of law and rehabilitation sciences Ravi Malhotra (2019) critique the inadequacy of "the *minority* model of disability, which views it as the product of a disabling social and architectural environment" (2). Disability, in their view, is not an objective state but rather "a socially created category derived from labor relations, a product of the exploitative economic structure of capitalist society" (2). They further assert that the most significant component of the subordination and marginalization of disabled people is their exclusion from the workforce (2) and not, as alternate models contend, "prejudicial and discriminatory attitudes" (2). They additionally argue disability, as a category, emerged in the context of industrial capitalism, in which those "who did not conform to the standard worker's body and whose labor-power was effectively erased" (3) were barred from working and labeled a "social problem" (3). To be clear, I do not employ this critique to deny the enormous significance of prejudice. Rather, my purpose is to illustrate the extent to which capitalism is operative in all forms of social inequality and hence must be centered in our disciplinary work.

BUT HAVEN'T WE DONE THIS ALL BEFORE?

Some readers at this point may contend that while capitalism may be a significant concern, composition has already explored the subject and, indeed, done so extensively. They might further note that critics in composition continue to take up issues of capitalism in their work and that, because of this attention, the field should continue to expand its purview into previously unexplored areas. Such a criticism would not be inaccurate—composition scholars, particularly in the 1980s and 1990s, engaged in an explicit and censorious critique of capitalism. A critique of capitalism, likewise, continues in the field in the work of Bruce Horner, Tony Scott, Nancy Welch, and many others. However, as I discuss, attention to and interest in this critique have declined over recent decades, with scholars increasingly moving into other areas, often situating themselves within critiques of identity with nominal relation to capitalism. This decline is occurring in the context of capitalism's continued expansion and against a background of reawakening public sentiment recognizing that, as Katrina vanden Heuvel (*Washington Post*, December 19, 2019) argues, "capitalism as we've known it doesn't work." As I maintain, such conditions demonstrate that capitalism remains relevant and that the field faces a unique opportunity to engage students in criticism of twenty-first-century political-economic conditions.

In US popular culture and public discourse, socialism and Leftist ideas—once prominent in the flourishing American Communist Party in the 1940s and 1950s (Gornick 2020) and with the evanescent and embattled radicalism of the 1960s and 1970s (Davies 2017; Rosenfeld 2013)—are once again becoming normalized. In part thanks to the prominence and popularity of Bernie Sanders as a candidate for the

2020 Democratic presidential nomination and the role of progressive congresswomen like Alexandria Ocasio-Cortez, Ilhan Omar, Rashida Tlaib, and Ayanna Pressley, proposed policies like Medicare for All, student debt cancellation, and the Green New Deal, while they have not become policy, have nevertheless become mainstream. *Teen Vogue*, first with Elaine Welteroth and later with Lindsay Peoples Wagner and Versha Sharma, has become a prominent Leftist platform. Prominent celebrities like Lil Yachty, Cardi B, and Kim Gordon publicly defend Leftist ideas. Television shows like *Squid Game* and *The Dropout* and films such as *Judas and the Black Messiah*, about Black Panther Party chairman Fred Hampton (King 2021), are mainstream fare. Anticapitalist discourses have become particularly prominent during the COVID-19 crisis; strikes by essential workers at Amazon, McDonalds, Instacart, Whole Foods, and numerous other sites (Read 2020) have underscored the exploitation of workers and a growing willingness to organize. Several crucial union votes have been successful at Starbucks locations across the country and at an Amazon fulfillment center on Staten Island (Rosenblatt, *New York Times*, April 1, 2022). This radicalism, however, remains largely the province of the young and exists in the context of deepening conservatism and strengthening capitalist power. Donald Trump, among countless offenses, implemented policies favorable to the wealthiest Americans, while Republican leaders abdicated their role in checking his power (Chait 2017; Krugman, *New York Times*, April 22, 2019). Sanders, of course, lost the Democratic nomination to the far more moderate Joe Biden.[3] Hate crimes and racist rhetoric continue to proliferate (Gerstmann 2020; Hassan, *New York Times*, November 12, 2019), notably with the killing of George Floyd by Minneapolis police, an event that sparked massive BIPOC liberation protests that roiled cities in the United States and across the world in May and June of 2020 (Booker et al. 2020). Hence, while radicalism and anticapitalist ideas are increasingly prominent in US and global life, their emergence coincides with the strengthening of capitalism and conservatism.

While academia, particularly the discipline of composition, remains engaged, often profoundly, with a variety of progressive issues, it appears increasingly ambivalent about anticapitalism. As previously noted, this ambivalence was not always the case. Several of composition's leading figures from the late 1970s to the 2000s—most centrally Richard Ohmann (1996, 1978, 1985), John Trimbur (1989, 1997, 2000), and James A. Berlin (2003)—were not only critical of capitalism's effects but frequently defended explicitly anticapitalist pedagogical stances in their work. Though diverse in their interests, they took up such related concerns as social class, cultures of work, political conservatism, and technology, evincing a consistent and unambiguous critique of capitalism as antagonistic to critical thought and political life. They frequently framed writing as a highly political and critical enterprise. Ohmann in particular consistently declaimed the dangers of capitalism's postwar ascendency and defended the writing classroom's potential to support class consciousness and critique. In *English in America: A Radical View of the Profession*, Ohmann (1996) offers a fervent attack on English departments' capitalist capitulation. Advancing a critique that remains relevant today, he excoriates the MLA as a politically reactionary "meritocracy of scholarship" (29), laments the banishment of Marxist literary criticism (89), and frames first-year composition as cultivating the language skills of "a governing class" (134). In his view, the way forward lies in revolutionary politics: "Much of what's wrong in the profession reflects the needs of advanced capitalism and is remedial only through deep social change" (304–305).

Scholars such as Nancy Welch, Seth Kahn, Marc Bousquet, Tony Scott, Deborah Mutnick, and Bruce Horner have continued to work in the anticapitalist tradition, though their critiques occupy a smaller corner of the field than similar work once did. Scott's *Dangerous Writing: Understanding the Political Economy of Composition* (2009) is a particularly essential text devoted to exploring the financial conditions of the scene of composition, specifically the political economy of textbook publishing and the realities of students who toil in part-time positions. Framed largely in response to critics of politicized writing like Joseph Harris, the work defends an approach to composition rooted in political economy, political engagement, and a politicized understanding of the social. Welch's *Living Room: Teaching Public Writing in a Privatized World* (2008) similarly considers the regime of privatization following the events of 9/11 and responds by theorizing a working-class pedagogy grounded in social action and public discourse primed to support students' agency. Welch and Scott's coedited collection (2016) likewise explores the impact of neoliberal policies and narratives, austerity specifically, on the scene of composition. In recent years, there have also been several notable engagements with the political economy of composition (Abraham 2016; Cox et al. 2016; Horner, Nordquist, and Ryan 2017; Kalbfleisch and Abraham 2016; Mutnick 2019b; Sano-Franchini 2016), many of which adopt an anticapitalist stance.

The field has also engaged in numerous valuable critiques of the capitalist foundations of contemporary higher education and academic labor (Bousquet 2002, 2008; Bousquet, Scott, and Parascondola

2003; Kahn, Lalicker, and Lynch-Biniek 2017; McClure, Goldstein, and Pemberton 2017). Foremost among these critics is Bousquet, whose *How the University Works: Higher Education and the Low-Wage Nation* (2008) critiques the trend of underpaid and disposable academic labor, noting that "the university under managerial domination is an accumulation machine" (7). Bousquet's most scathing remarks are reserved for the rhetorical construction of the job market; he argues that the capitalist logics favoring cheap labor and a disposable workforce have come to govern graduate education: "In the full ripening apogee of second-wave knowledge, the system of graduate education is no longer understood as being 'like' a market; it is generally understood, simply and self-evidently, that graduate education *is* a market" (206).

Another valence of this critique is the field's attention to the way US colleges and universities have expanded across the globe and extended their financial project in often destructive and exploitative ways. In Rebecca Dingo, Rachel Riedner, and Jennifer Wingard's (2015) article "Disposable Drudgery: Outsourcing Goes to College," the authors use the case of the University of Houston's outsourcing of grading to an offshore company (265) to explore the ways the global university relies on devalued labor. In his article "'Globalist Scumbags': Composition's Global Turn in the Time of Fake News, Globalist Conspiracy, and Nationalist Literacy," Christopher Minnix (2017) contrasts the expanding educational scope of the university "aimed at preparing students for disciplinary, vocational, ethical, and political participation in an era of globalization" (64) with isolationist reactionaries. Insofar as these critics have employed the term *globalism* to critique the liberal perspective, Minnix writes that "globalism becomes, in its more extreme versions, indicative of a Leftist conspiracy to promote a one-world government" (64).

Relatedly, scholars have also sought to understand the capitalist valence of the spread of English education globally and, concomitantly, the maintenance of Standard English. LuMing Mao (2014), for example, has argued capitalism is behind both the global spread of English and the emergence of Chinese "cultural nationalism" (87), a form of "indigenous rhetoric" (82) that "stakes out an explicit claim to recover and reconstitute 'native knowledge' or what has been referred to as 'national learning'" (79) and engages with a variety of other forms of contemporary discourse (79). In a similarly critical analysis, Min-Zhan Lu (2005) critiques the capitalist valence of monolingual ideology, the result of "the global extension of market modes of operation and of the logic of flexible accumulation to all areas of life" (20). Countering essentialist definitions, Lu defines English as an unstable territory existing in the conflict "between and across English and diverse languages (peripheralized by the power of English under fast capitalism) and between and across diverse standardized englishes and their Othered, peripheralized englishes" (24).

In the last few years, there have also been a number of direct, albeit sporadic, engagements with composition's relation to political economy. *Economies of Writing: Revaluations in Rhetoric and Composition* (Horner, Nordquist, and Ryan 2017) makes important strides in highlighting the significance of structural and material concerns in composition. As the editors acknowledge, there is a need in the field for scholarship exploring "how the economic defines, limits, and thereby shapes the work we do, how we do it, and to what ends and with what effects we do it" (3). *Writing Democracy: The Political Turn in and Beyond the Trump Era* (Carter et al. 2019a) even more vehemently argues for a disciplinary critique of neoliberalism. As the authors note, neoliberalism "strips 'democracy' of values such as the 'public good,' human and civil rights, and relative economic equality" (5). They exhort "left-leaning scholars and activists who may have renounced Marxism to reconsider a historical materialist perspective" (3). In constructing my own anticapitalist critique, I particularly respond to the call for a composition that "explains and continues to investigate historical material realities in all forms and across disciplines, including the current crises of overaccumulation, environmental devastation, and intensifying global inequality" (Mutnick et al. 2019, 261).

Despite these works' persuasive call for greater attention to political economy in the context of teaching writing, in recent years many in the field have turned their attention to other matters, namely the experiences, values, and discourses of marginalized subjects, while often glossing over the economic conditions that contribute to such marginalization. While identity is an important construct for understanding and combatting inequality and is a crucial means of uniting mass movements, scholars in composition have tended to individualize identity in ways that sideline rather than promote substantive engagement with political economy. While this is visible in many areas, the discipline's encounter with social class is particularly guilty of this tendency.[4]

In discussing how composition pedagogy might better attend to social class, Irvin Peckham (2010) employs Pierre Bourdieu to make several generalizations about working-class identity, detailing how working-class students feel, think, and act in order to make characterizations about what they need. He writes, "Working-class people value predictable and traditional gender roles. Men are supposed to be men and women, women. . . . Labor means physical work, which in turn means muscle, masculinity" (121). This portrayal supports an argument against critical pedagogy on the grounds that such a focus is dissonant, and paternalistic, with respect to working-class values: "Working-class students, in particular, do not expect and may not appreciate attempts to get them to rethink their religious, social, and political convictions" (142). James T. Zebroski (2017) similarly characterizes the working class by way of cultural generalizations, observing how English departments tend to denigrate or ignore working-class values (331). He likewise recounts how some working-class students have been alienated by his department's focus: "Some of them tell me they do not feel comfortable with the culture of the department and what they see as its embrace of elite values" (333).

The point I wish to make here is not about the accuracy or validity of these characterizations of the working class[5] but rather about the tendency of both Peckham (2010) and Zebroski (2017) to frame social class by way of identity and individual experience rather than as a product of economic inequality. To better understand class and how economically disadvantaged students might be better served by our pedagogy, we must turn to and engage in the kind of historical class analysis sociologist Göran Therborn (2012) offers in his *New Left Review* article "Class in the Twenty-First Century." In the text, Therborn traces the long decline of working-class power, from a time in the twentieth century in which "working people who lacked property became a major and sustained political force" to the current period of poverty and political marginality. For Therborn, modern Left-wing political parties, while they may offer marginal progressive goods, have sided with capitalists, undermined the political potency of the working class, and "essentially capitulated to liberalism of one kind or another in the field of economic policy." Therborn notes that the twentieth-century working class was once able to draw upon an "extensive pre-industrial literacy and craft traditions of guild organization" but that it now faces "soaring inequality and recurrent economic crises" as well as the reproduction of "capitalist exploitation and imperialism." In the realm of composition, such conditions cannot be neglected as the field considers how to better meet the needs of working-class students. Likewise, issues of capitalism and political economy must also be considered when the field addresses other areas of exclusion and inequality insofar as capitalist conditions are indispensable when attempting to understand contemporary sites of inequality. This is, of course, not to suggest that all forms of inequality are due entirely to capitalism or that individual experiences should be neglected but, rather, to insist the kind of analysis Therborn engages in cannot be written out of any substantive consideration of composition's role, particularly when it comes to identity.

In the following section, I approach this issue through the framework of race, arguing the field's movement toward antiracism has often served to deprioritize political economic critique.

WHAT ABOUT ANTIRACISM?

Over the past several years, disciplinary attention to race and antiracism has become one of the most animated areas of composition. Antiracist theory (Condon and Young 2017; Inoue 2015, 2017, 2019; Inoue and Poe 2012), analysis of whiteness (Kennedy, Middleton, and Ratcliffe 2017; Ratcliffe 2005), and studies of racial justice activism (Epps-Robertson 2018; Hurlbert 2012; Kynard 2013; Lamos 2011) have been extensive and are increasingly central in the field. Regarding these interventions, while many may be persuaded that concern for political economy should inform composition's engagement with identity more substantively, they may nevertheless argue that our primary responsibilities lie with responding to racism and militating against the "White racial habitus" (Inoue 2019, 360) that courses through higher education and attitudes towards language more generally. Many may indeed argue composition holds a responsibility to attend to race *prior* to any additional social justice concerns and may, relatedly, believe that adopting an anticapitalist stance would unacceptably relegate race to a secondary concern. With rampant police violence against minorities and the proliferation of hate crimes and white supremacist groups (Porterfield 2020), the necessity of confronting racism and racist violence is abundantly clear. Nevertheless, the belief that race must somehow take precedence over the concerns of class difference and political economy, implicit in much of contemporary antiracist discourse, neglects the extensive role that political economy plays in deepening racial inequality. While the contemporary discourse of antiracism has, at times, gestured toward such a materialist critique,[6] its general disinterest in economic inequality has, at others, diluted its impact.

There are, importantly, scholars beyond the field who have given equal attention to racism and economic inequality.[7] Keeanga-Yamahtta Taylor's *Race for Profit: How Banks and the Real Estate Industry Undermined Black Homeownership* (2019) critiques racism while exploring the decimation of Black wealth by way of predatory banking and lending practices. As Taylor details, the move of the Federal Housing Administration (FHA) to end redlining and promote Black homeownership in the 1970s, an ostensibly progressive and empowering change, heralded a more pernicious policy of "predatory inclusion" (5) in which "homebuyers were granted access to conventional real estate practices and mortgage financing, built on more expensive and comparatively unequal terms" (5). As Taylor notes, these policies had the dual function of legitimizing racism and exposing Black homeowners to capitalist predation (6). Such a study demonstrates the complex and deep linkages between capitalism and race—economic exploitation can frequently serve to excuse and intensify racism while racism is consistently enacted through economic means. The centering of the entanglement of racism and capitalism present in Taylor's work, however, is typically absent in composition studies. While scholars in this area certainly acknowledge structural racism, many, not unlike the field's critics of social class, tend to subordinate relevant political-economic issues.

To begin with a prominent example, in the introduction to their edited collection *Performing Antiracist Pedagogy in Rhetoric, Writing, and Communication*, Frankie Condon and Vershawn Ashanti Young (2017) contend the pervasive disregard of racism in the context of higher education underscores the need for antiracist interventions in the teaching of writing. They specifically exhort readers to pay attention to conservative currents in US political discourse that seek to "de-trope race, to unlink remarks, policies, perceptions, and practices clearly designed to stigmatize, berate, and oppress people of color from the perpetuating legacies of white privilege" (11). Such an approach implies that in addition to racist discourses, minorities are harmed by a specific set of practices and policies that can be read as racist (and combatted) after cutting through conservative discourses with an antiracist lens. This is, at least in part, the case with respect to such issues as high minority incarceration rates (Leonhardt, *New York Times*, June 3, 2020). Such a critique, however, neglects how capitalism broadly functions to subordinate minorities in ways not legible to antiracist critique or responsive to antiracist action. The decline of unions and the stagnant minimum wage are examples of policies that disproportionately harm minority populations but are not necessarily legible as racism. Rather, insofar as these comprehensive economic policies impact white workers as well as minority populations, they require a political-economic lens.

In his 2019 CCCC chair's address, "How Do We Language So People Stop Killing Each Other, or What Do We Do about White Language Supremacy?," Asao B. Inoue more conspicuously rejects the lens of political economy in exhorting compositionists to interrogate the structures of white supremacy that undergird language and the work of writing instruction. Inoue specifically calls for revising our models of assessment to combat the racism implicit in our language and disciplinary practices: "If you use a single standard to grade your students' languaging, you engage in racism" (359). One method of such work, for Inoue, lies in labor-based grading contracts insofar as they address "teachers who are by necessity steeped in a White racial habitus" (360). More expansively, he argues this work requires an aggressive process of self-interrogation insofar as instructors, particularly white instructors, must understand how they have benefitted from and perpetuate white supremacy. This process, he cautions, is a matter of public as well as individual change, arguing we must transform "the way power moves through White racial biases, through standards of English that make White language supremacy" (364).

Inoue's argument is undercut by an uncompromising and, at times, ungenerous rejection of political-economic perspectives. In one significant argument, Inoue glosses the Left's critique of the political economy of racial inequality: "many White folks wish to make the racist problems we experience, such as prison and educational racism, and the White bias of those systems, as about something else, about mostly economics, laziness, or bad values" (354). In this assessment, while he does acknowledge that prison and educational racism are "are interconnected and intersectional dimensions" (354), Inoue nevertheless rejects perspectives based in economic exploitation and economic inequality, suggesting that racism must be the dominant lens though which racial inequality is understood. In this assertion, Inoue conflates the Left's long-standing criticism of the prison-industrial complex with the reactionary arguments of such figures as Daniel Patrick Moynihan (Geary 2015), who rationalize minority poverty as a defect of Black culture. Such a conflation unfairly mischaracterizes the work of many leading Leftist scholars and activists and, moreover, suggests that tracing the economic roots of social and political problems is simply the self-serving project of white people.[8] On this point, we should remember the work of activist and academic Angela Y. Davis, the keynote presenter at CCCC 2014. For Davis, prisons are an economic *and* racial formation. As she argues, prisons remove "the responsibility of seriously engaging with the problems of our society, especially those produced by racism and, increasingly, global capitalism" (2003, 16).

Inoue deemphasizes potential links between race and political economy elsewhere in his address, even in instances where resonances between the two are palpable and ready-to-hand. He references Max Weber's "iron cage" metaphor from *The Protestant Ethic and the Spirit of Capitalism* (2002), a concept Weber employs to refer to capitalism's coercive power. Inoue uses Weber's concept to argue white supremacy functions analogously, as an economy in the context of language: "The market I call your attention to today is the market of White language preferences in schools, although it is also not hard to find the connections between it and the flows of capital" (2019, 354). Here, Inoue contends that white language preferences function as a market but only alludes to the further point that white language preferences and white supremacy are deepened and sustained by literal market forces.[9] Later in the address, Inoue turns to Marx in a further indictment of white supremacy's systems of valuation, asking, "Who owns the means of opportunity production in the classroom?" (367). As Inoue notes, teachers perpetuate racist systems of valuation when they tell students who "may be starving with pockets and purses full of useless coins in the bustling market of your classrooms" (367) to adopt white language practices. As with his previous reference to Weber, Inoue uses Marx to highlight the devaluation of nonwhite discourse practices in the context of the classroom but brackets Marx's larger critique of capitalist exploitation. In so doing, he neglects capitalism's role in devaluing nonwhite language practices or, more extensively, in exploiting minority workers.[10] Despite utilizing Weber and Marx to discuss race, Inoue fails to address how capitalism itself is disempowering to minorities.

Beyond this critique of disciplinary limitations, I further argue, controversially perhaps, that anticapitalism offers the most significant and emancipatory potential for marginalized populations and, accordingly, should occupy a much more central position in composition's social justice efforts. While minority populations experience a broad array of harms not all primarily or necessarily economic, either in nature or in cause, one aspect of inequality affects all minority populations with devastating consequences—economic inequality. Black and Hispanic workers report significantly lower income than white workers and are more likely to live in poverty than whites or Asian Americans (Wilson 2020). The inequality African Americans experience, as Taylor (2016) contends, is largely the product of "government policy and private institutions that not only impoverish African Americans but also demonize and criminalize them." While Taylor acknowledges that racism, in its entanglement with capitalism, is also secured by belief, she nevertheless claims political-economic interventions are vital for redressing many of the causes of racial inequality and the lived realities of minority populations, particularly the ways centuries of racism and predatory economic practices have created chronic—and deepening—wealth and wage gaps. I likewise contend studying and responding to the political-economic conditions that created and maintain these inequities is one of our most pressing tasks.

In an October 25, 2020, *New York Times* article, economists Ellora Derenoncourt and Claire Montialoux similarly claim that raising and expanding the minimum wage will substantively narrow the wage gap among white and minority workers. Touré F. Reed (2020) likewise argues that solutions to racial inequality lie in the institution of a "public-good model of governance" (14), noting that "those of us who want to eliminate contemporary black poverty and inequality must insist on addressing the material sources of poor and even working-class African Americans' disadvantage" (171–172). This is also the position Heather McGee (2021), former president of Demos, defends in *The Sum of Us: What Racism Costs Everyone and How We Can Prosper Together*, a text decrying the pervasive and racist "zero-sum story" (xxi) that reductions in racism will entail fewer opportunities for everyone. According to McGee, racism not only harms minorities but also disadvantages "non-wealthy white Americans" (38) by reducing their support for programs they would benefit from and motivating them to vote for politicians whose policies do not align with their class interests (38). As a solution, McGee contends we need to cultivate "a new formula of cross-racial solidarity" (xxii) that will "refill the pool of public goods, for everyone" (271).

In addition to holding broad capacity to address the marginalization of all minority populations, anticapitalism also has an expansive potential to attract and unite excluded and marginalized subjects into a single political struggle. Political scientist Adolph L. Reed Jr. (2000) offers such an assessment: "The goal of building a mass movement ... requires proceeding from those identities that unite as much of the society as possible around a vision and program that most directly challenge the current power relations" (xxvii). For Reed, issues of economic marginalization, regardless of race, gender, or other markers of difference, are comprehensively disempowering and thus most capable of being framed as sites of collective struggle. "For the vast majority of people in this country," he writes, "the common frame of reference is the employment relation, the fact of working, or being expected to work, a job" (xxvii). He argues that economic struggles associated with the essential act of working—"finding, keeping or advancing in a job with a living wage, keeping or attaining access to decent healthcare, securing decent, affordable housing ... being able to seek or keep the protection of a union, having time for quality of life" (xxvii)—are universal desires affecting the broadest swath of people. These amount, for Reed, to "a concrete, material basis for solidarity" (xxvii). Importantly, while Reed certainly acknowledges the stain of racism and racist violence—and indeed discusses its personal impact in his autoethnography on growing up in Louisiana during the Jim Crow era (2022)—he nevertheless defends an expansive materialist framework for conceptualizing race:

> Defeating the white supremacist regime was a tremendous victory for social justice and egalitarian interests. At the same time, that victory left the undergirding class system untouched and in practical terms affirmed it. . . . The larger takeaway from this reality is that a simple racism/antiracism framework isn't adequate for making sense of the segregation era, and it certainly isn't up to the task of interpreting what has succeeded it or challenging the forms of inequality and injustice that persist. (140)

Regarding Reed's defense of unions, many have additionally argued that unions and labor activism directly combat racism. As Paul Frymer and Jacob M. Grumbach (2021) found in a study of union membership, white members of unions are "less racially resentful" (233) than nonunion members. Such a finding supports the argument of *Jacobin* associate editor Meagan Day (2020), who contends unions are a crucial means of opposing racism. As she writes, unions offer "opportunities for people of different racial backgrounds and identities to not merely work side by side . . . but to *work toward a common goal* together." It is important to note here that unions are not the sites of gender and racial exclusion they are frequently believed to be. As the Bureau of Labor Statistics reported in 2021, Black workers have the highest rate of union membership, with 12.3 percent (3). Unions are also, notably, becoming *more* diverse—union membership among Black workers is up 1.1 percent from 2019, while for white workers the number is only up 0.4 percent (3). Men remain slightly more represented in unions, with 11 percent membership, but women are not far behind, with 10.5 percent membership (2). The gender gap is likewise narrowing (6).

As I attempt to argue in this section, the field's turn toward antiracism has marginalized political-economic criticism, a critique of enormous significance and utility with respect to racial inequality. To utilize McGee's (2021) assertion, combatting racism and critiquing capitalism are not zero-sum propositions. Scholars and activists can, and have, addressed both simultaneously. But many, particularly in composition, have neglected the latter. If the field is to move toward greater equity and inclusion, it needs anticapitalism.

HOW SHOULD COMPOSITION ADDRESS CAPITALISM?

The following chapters attempt to delineate an approach to anticapitalist composition and, more broadly, to indicate both what is valuable in such a stance and what is risked. While, as I previously noted, this work is not indebted to a single anticapitalist tradition but, rather, is more expansively focused to include the broadest number of orientations and perspectives, it is nevertheless guided by a powerful anticapitalist concept: *the common*.[11] As I employ the term, the common is an attitude of solidarity that opposes the divisive and destructive project of capitalist accumulation. It is useful for composition insofar as it informs writing, specifically collaborative writing, as a collective, anticapitalist practice. As philosopher Pierre Dardot and sociologist Christian Laval (2019a) theorize it, the common is not "so much a matter of isolating and protecting some natural 'good' or 'resource' . . . as it is a matter of profoundly transforming the economy and society *by overthrowing the system of* norms that now directly threatens nature and humanity itself" (2). While this abstraction does not deny the consequence of physical spaces and material labor, it suggests a vastly more dynamic and expansive praxis is necessary beyond mere reclamation of privatized sites. Rather, Dardot and Laval frame the common as an insurgent, anticapitalist political theory centered on the notion of "collective work" (336). The concept, in their construction, names "the political principal of *co-obligation* for all those engaged in the same *activity*" (10). As I contend, this intervention is an invaluable resource for the anticapitalist composition classroom insofar as it responds to capitalist hegemony through imagining anticapitalism as a broadly inclusive articulation of solidarity and collective work. Cumulatively, the common presents composition with a deeply needed model of anticapitalist thought applicable to contexts of capitalism's exclusionary and hierarchical function, its instantiation of immense inequality and division, and its appropriation and destruction of natural spaces.[12] However, the common also offers the field something beyond mere functionality. Conceptualizing political engagement through the common emphasizes anticapitalist action as a site of vital togetherness. The common, in other words, can also be a place of encounter, sociality, even laughter. In viewing this as an essential part of progressive political work, I follow Alexandria Ocasio-Cortez's (2021) comments regarding the need for vibrant organizing: "But who's gonna join your book club if it sucks? Who's gonna join your reading group if they feel judged? So the important thing we need to do is to really create something . . . excuse my language . . . but that's fucking fun." The common is such a mechanism of collaboration, critique, and exhilaration that gathers subjects in communities as much social as they are political. This social brio is both what animates activist communities and what allows them to challenge capitalism's forces of division and hierarchy. As a means of orienting composition classes critical of capitalism's expansion, the common weaves through the structure of this book and is the mechanism I utilize to situate composition in the anticapitalist conversation.

In chapter 1, "Gathering," I examine the threat to democratic culture expressed by twenty-first-century political nativism and argue composition might resist this process by teaching collaborative writing as a political, solidaristic, and anticapitalist endeavor. Acknowledging that composition holds a robust history of collaboration and collaborative writing, I contend that scholars, with some notable exceptions (Holt 2018; Trimbur 1989), have yet to substantively explore collaboration's extensive political and anticapitalist potential. Building upon Jodi Dean's (2019) concept of the comrade, the chapter reframes collaborative writing as both a *common* anticapitalist praxis and a democratic endeavor capable of opposing the divisive tendencies of global capitalism. As the chapter ultimately argues, collaborative writing can be a site of cultivating political comrades across lines of difference in defiance of capitalist logics of disunity.

Chapter 2, "Debt," offers an anticapitalist approach to teaching the issue of student debt, focusing on its devastation of graduates' financial lives and social agency, its assault on American families, and its perpetuation of the myth of US meritocracy. As the chapter argues, if it is to confront one of the most pernicious capitalist threats, anticapitalist composition must address debt's rhetorical and material influence and prepare students to do the same. Drawing upon an essay by Jean-Luc Nancy (2017), the chapter contends the rhetoric of debt operates by submitting the breadth of social interaction to the calculus of the financial insofar as the "uses of debt disregard every recognition other than that of the debt itself." The chapter develops pedagogical methods to center these conditions in the classroom and to prepare students to critically negotiate them.

In chapter 3, "Work," I address how writing instruction can support students' resistance to some of the most harmful aspects of the contemporary working world: exploitation, casualization, overwork, and the blurring of the professional and the personal. I exhort composition instructors to examine how declining working conditions exist within a rhetorical context that privileges burnout and absolute fidelity to one's employer. Drawing upon leading scholars of neoliberal labor and philosopher Isabelle Stengers's (2015) analysis of institutional "stupidity" (119), discourses and logics that annihilate "the capacity for thinking and imagining of those who envisioned ways of doing things differently" (119), the chapter argues the twenty-first-century working world has become increasingly dominated by regimes of thought that thwart employee resistance and repurpose collectivity to support capitalist ends. Against these misuses of collaborative potential, this chapter theorizes the teaching of collaborative practice as a mode of resistance against the neoliberal workplace. More specifically, it advocates engaging students in collaborative criticism of the contemporary discourses of work to enhance students' capacity to parse work's narratives and resist its conditions.

Chapter 4, "Data," explores anticapitalist approaches to digital writing and multimedia composition. Contending the field of composition has largely neglected the significance of what Shoshana Zuboff (2019) terms "surveillance capitalism" (9), the transformation of internet users' "data exhaust" (68) into capital, I argue the field has missed an opportunity to position students to parse the political economy of the digital world and resist its influence. Drawing from Bernard Stiegler's (2019) theory of "disruption" (7), the chapter elaborates on how digital capitalism threatens the health of communities. I propose a digital pedagogy based in Stieglerian "dreaming" (199) that orients students to the work of collaboration, invention, and anticapitalist resistance in digital contexts. Regarding composition courses, the chapter advocates teaching students to interrogate the political economy of the data industry and social media discourse to more effectively read and resist Silicon Valley's techno-utopian narratives and the exploitation of the data industry.

The final chapter, "Action," moves to the site of the university and considers anticapitalist writing pedagogy's vulnerable place within contemporary higher education. Specifically reflecting on the decline of academic freedom (Reichman 2019) and the precarity of contingent faculty, the chapter outlines how anticapitalist composition stands in conflict with the conservative, capitalist orientation of the contemporary university, how contingent faculty who practice it risk censure, and how institutional changes must be made to make anticapitalist pedagogy more secure. The chapter draws upon Dardot and Laval's (2019a) analysis of the common and their concept of "instituent praxis" (298) to define three sites of struggle to better safeguard anticapitalist pedagogy and progressive faculty at the financialized university: (1) resistance to the university's capitalist entanglements, (2) the democratization of the university, particularly regarding institutional bodies and boards, and (3) the reduction of faculty hierarchies. The chapter concludes with a defense of faculty unions, which I contend are the sites where institutional change can and must begin.

I wish to close this introduction by acknowledging my positionality relative to these arguments. I am a contingent faculty member. In 2017, I moved across the country to take my current position as a non-tenure-track lecturer (now teaching professor) at the University of Washington–Seattle, a job that offers reasonable pay and security in an expensive city. My position is not an undesirable one. I have the respect of my colleagues, the confidence of my chair, and some opportunities for advancement. I live in a city many people would consider desirable. I am not commuting across state lines to eke out a living as I used to. I have an office to myself. And I have time, just a little, to write. And while I am contingent, I have been assured my position will be renewed. Nevertheless, this life is precarious and uncertain. And yet I am far more secure than most who teach composition.

These circumstances, and those of my contingent friends and colleagues, inspired me to write this book. Prior to taking contingent work, I naïvely did not yet understand the extent to which capitalism has unmade the university and proletarianized most academics. Nor did I comprehend the amount of debt most students take on or the exploitative and unforgiving economic conditions they face when they graduate (if, indeed, they do).[13] Understanding these conditions, however, has moved me to defend centering anticapitalism in our disciplinary work. I argue we must take this on if we wish to deal with the most substantial force disempowering students, faculty, and (really) everyone else. In large part, we are not having this conversation in composition. And things are deteriorating. Economic inequality is deepening, climate change marches along, and students are sinking further into debt. Anticapitalist interventions are needed to address these crises. Composition, of course, represents just a small part of the academic scene—and a neglected and maligned one at that—but prioritizing capitalism's harms and attending to them in our classrooms, research, and labor struggles is, nevertheless, a hugely important task. And it is one we can take on now.

1
GATHERING

Down the narrow side streets of Budapest's District V, just blocks from St. Stephen's Basilica, sit the remnants of the Central European University (CEU) (see fig. 1.1). Founded in 1991 by George Soros "in the spirit of 'open societies' of Karl Popper" (Mudde, *Guardian*, December 4, 2018), the university long stood as the country's leading research institution. In the 1990s, it became known as a progressive haven, building a strong gender studies program and offering extensive access to Roma students (Koltai 2017). Michael Ignatieff, a renowned scholar of nationalism and human rights who once ran for prime minister of Canada (Foer 2019), was hired on as rector in 2016, lending his prestige to the university's increasingly global ambitions. However, the university's good fortune foundered in 2017 when it came under attack by Hungarian President Viktor Orbán, cofounder of Fidesz, Hungary's nativist political party.

Orbán's authoritarianism was already on full display prior to his assault on the CEU. In a speech in 2014, he praised the governments of Russia, Turkey, and China, stating his intention create a similar "illiberal state" (Lendvai 2018, 141) in Hungary. Corruption and nepotism remain rampant under his presidency (153) and, not unlike Donald Trump, Orbán has characterized refugees as "overrunning us and threatening our civilization" (192) and "the Trojan horse of terrorism" (205). Prior to his final act of aggression against the university, Orbán first picked away at its progressive faculty, unilaterally banning the teaching of gender studies[1] in the country in 2018 (Redden 2018b). Later that year, Orbán's government passed legislation that would cast the university out of Hungary: international universities operating in Hungary that offered both international and Hungarian degrees were required to establish campuses in their home countries (Santora, *New York Times*, December 3, 2018). The aggression against the university triggered international expressions of support, extensive local protests, and a robust movement to keep the CEU in Budapest (Koltai 2017). Nevertheless, on December 3, 2018, after failing to reach an agreement, Ignatieff announced the CEU would be relocating to Vienna in the fall of 2019. As Koltai argues, for Hungarians, the campaign against the university represented an epochal escalation of dictatorial rule in the country: "direct state intervention in higher education to wipe out undesirable institutions based on political criteria."

I begin this chapter with the ouster of the CEU to dramatize an instructive example of the illiberal, antidemocratic energies represented by contemporary sites of authoritarian capitalism that render an anticapitalist composition, specifically centered on political collaboration, increasingly necessary. To be sure, this issue is not solely economic—the expulsion of the CEU indexes the racist, nativist, and nationalist position increasingly shared by world leaders (Connolly 2017; Denvir 2020). Nor, for that matter, is this issue entirely new. Karl Polanyi (2001) uncovered capitalism's antidemocratic turn during the nineteenth century in his pivotal work *The Great Transformation: The Political and Economic Origins of Our Time*. As Polanyi contends, the rise of the market economy was a "utopian endeavor" (31) that sought to pose the market system as self-regulating, thus establishing a stark division between economic and political life. However, as he notes, the two are ultimately indivisible, and dividing them violently abstracted the economic order from the social (74). The effects of this abstraction, as Polanyi contends, were nothing short of catastrophic, "annihilating the human and natural substance of society" (3) and creating the conditions for the emergence of fascism in the twentieth century. As he argues, "The victory of fascism was made practically unavoidable by the liberal obstruction of any reform involving planning, regulation, or control" (265). Robert Kuttner's (2018) recent work *Can Democracy Survive Global Capitalism?* returns to Polanyi's central assertion, contending contemporary global conditions, including deregulation and the proliferation of free trade, similarly threaten democratic culture. In an analogous argument, Wendy Brown (2019) asserts the crucial risk of twenty-first-century capitalism is a pincer movement toward a more active and purposeful eradication of solidarity: "The neoliberal attack on the social . . . is key to generating an *antidemocratic culture from below* while building and legitimating *antidemocratic forms of state power from above*" (28). As she argues, capitalism removes the material underpinnings of democratic culture while rhetorically undermining it in the social world.

While the case of the CEU might very well be read as an issue of ideology, a tension between a liberal intellectual elite and a regressive and insular ruling party, reading Orbán's treatment of the university through Polanyi, Kuttner, and Brown exposes an additional

Figure 1.1. Building of the Central European University. (Photograph by Dezidor. Licensed under the Creative Commons Attribution 3.0 Unported license. https://creativecommons.org/licenses/by/3.0/deed.en.)

political-economic tension operative within late capitalism directly relevant to the composition classroom, namely the conflict between the globally oriented, neoliberal model of capitalism ascendant for many decades and an emergent, nativist authoritarian capitalism—what Nancy Fraser (2019) terms a "right-wing 'fundamentalist' version of neoliberalism" (12) and what Dardot and Laval (2019b) characterize as "the new neoliberalism" (xx). Critics observe such an insular and antagonistic turn in Hungary, where Orbán has instituted what Adam Fabry (2019) terms an "authoritarian-ethnicist neoliberalism" (1). From the standpoint of rhetoric, if not policy,[2] this *new* neoliberalism runs counter to the ostensibly benevolent neoliberal discourse of global democracy, shared prosperity, and human rights, ends touted, for instance, by executive chairman of the World Economic Forum Klaus Schwab (2019) and exemplified in his Davos Manifesto calling for corporations to "improve the state of the world." While *old* neoliberalism harms the environment, workers, minority populations, and the global underclass (Chomsky 2011)—and is still very much around—in Orbán's and similar capitalist models, interest in promoting democracy and human rights, even superficially, has been replaced with an insular ethic nakedly antagonistic to egalitarianism.[3]

It is important to note that, in terms of policy rather than discourse, the new neoliberalism is not so profoundly different from prior neoliberal models. As economist Thomas Piketty (2020) argues, Trump's policies, despite his "market-nativist ideology" (886), remain largely neoliberal in practice, with some nominal nativist tweaks. As Piketty notes, despite Trump frequently presenting himself as an ally of working people and an enemy of neoliberal globalism (888), his policies "have combined more or less standard nativist measures . . . with tax cuts for the rich and multinational corporations" (888). Piketty points out that Trump's policies, rather than being an antiglobalist redistribution of opportunity, if not wealth, are effectively in line with the "hypercapitalist" (887) aversion to progressive taxation espoused by other less politically xenophobic world leaders. Piketty, for instance, observes a striking similarity between Trump's tax policy, which included cutting the federal corporate tax rate from 35 percent to 21 percent in 2018, and that of French President Emmanuel Macron, who abolished the wealth tax and reduced corporate tax from 33 percent to 25 percent, in addition to other reforms: "The fact that a purportedly nativist government like Trump's adopted a tax policy similar to that of a supposedly more internationalist government like Macron's shows that political ideologies and practices have converged to a considerable degree" (889). Hence, for Piketty, the current "antiglobalist" shift among Trump and similar leaders should not be seen as a contraction of global capitalism but rather a rhetorical gloss on its expansion. Relatedly, the expulsion of the CEU, while indicative of a rejection of a form of globalist neoliberalism, is not evidence of an anticapitalist populism in Hungary. Rather, it simply represents a kind of rhetorical nativism that, in practice, nevertheless toes a more or less predictable capitalist line—exchanging one vision of capitalism for what critics have termed Orbán's "soft autocracy, combining crony capitalism and far-right rhetoric with a single-party political culture" (Kingsley, *New York Times*, February 10, 2018).

In light of these conditions, this chapter argues composition studies is compelled to respond to twenty-first-century global capitalism's reactionary turn, the *new* neoliberalism, in which diversity, difference, transnationalism, and democracy, once tolerated by neoliberals,[4] are now actively opposed. I contend that, because of the targeting of sites of community and solidarity such as the CEU, one of the most vital avenues for this work must be the development of *common*, collaborative, and critical practices to safeguard sites of community and democratic culture in an age increasingly antagonistic to solidarity. While the neoliberal model is far from gone and, indeed, represents a crisis of its own—Phyllis Mentzel Ryder (2017) contends that "advocates for neoliberalism erase the entry points for public debate about the relationship of democracy and capitalism" (253)—reactionary neoliberalism poses an additional, though generally undertheorized, threat to the social on an enormous scale. As antidemocratic sentiments rise globally, events paralleling Orbán's attacks on the CEU are likely to become increasingly common. Even though Trump has left office, Trumpism remains strong with the GOP and in governments and reactionary groups across the world. One need look no further than to the GOP's Marjorie Taylor Greene, a member of the US House of Representatives who called George Soros the "enemy of the people" and who filmed a campaign ad shooting a sign reading "socialism" (Rogers and Skelley 2021). Composition, as I argue throughout this book, is capable of offering a response to these conditions through pedagogy, research, and an emphasis on labor.

As this chapter argues, assigning collaborative writing as an activist and anticapitalist enterprise is one means of resisting the new neoliberalism insofar as the fundamental processes of social engagement and grassroots activism can be taught in the writing classroom and orient students towards the importance of ongoing, coalitional, anticapitalist work. Students, moreover, can be presented with an understanding of how critique can function as a means of strengthening and sustaining political communities. While the remainder of this book is devoted to identifying an array of specific sites in which capitalism threatens students and workers (and, concomitantly, where the pedagogical critique of capitalism is most valuably articulated), this chapter more broadly addresses the political potential of collaborative writing instruction. Composition has extensively theorized collaborative writing and learning as mechanisms to enhance education and to prepare students for the necessarily collaborative work of public and professional life, yet the political possibilities of this work, particularly the capacity of collaboration to function as a bulwark against capitalism's divisive tendencies, remain largely unaddressed. There is, notably, a robust disciplinary critique of Trumpism and rising authoritarianism in the field (Carter et al. 2019a; McComiskey 2017; Roberts-Miller 2017; Skinnell 2018), yet only a small body of composition scholars, most notably John Trimbur (1989) and Mara Holt (2018), have acknowledged collaborative writing and learning as politically charged or capable of resisting antidemocratic forces. In this chapter, I employ political theorist Jodi Dean's (2019) notion of the comrade to support a model of common, collaborative writing rooted in equity, community, and shared political subjectivity. As I detail, a model of collaborative writing of and among comrades is valuable for anticapitalist pedagogy in three crucial respects: (1) it militates against the divisive interpersonal effects of the new neoliberalism insofar as students are positioned as equal political partners engaged in common struggle, (2) it allows students to work across various sites of division and difference the new neoliberalism deepens, allowing for the gathering of various identities, orientations, and perspectives, and (3) it supports the development of novel models of political connection, engagement, and opposition in an era when solidarity and democracy are at risk.

THE ARC OF COLLABORATIVE WRITING

The lineage of composition's approach to collaborative writing, while expansive, is nevertheless unusually uneven and discontinuous. As Holt (2018) observes, "Collaborative writing in the past ninety years has been 'discovered' at least six times" (126). Holt maintains that a review of these discoveries reveals moments of flourishing interest in the novel potential of collaboration to serve a variety of discursive or political ends marked by extended periods of disinterest and neglect. Curiously, most attempts to parse this history have distinguished between those scholars privileging the capacity of collaboration to be a site of consensus making, namely Kenneth Bruffee, and, alternately, those who view collaboration as effective in supporting productive dissensus, John Trimbur in particular. While such a dichotomy is apparent in much of the field's study of the subject, I regard collaborative writing as marked by an alternate, though no less significant, distinction between those who esteem collaborative writing mainly for its social and professional benefits and those who view it as holding a progressive, political, even anticapitalist valence. To be sure, this tension is not necessarily divisive or even sharply defined. Insofar as nearly all defenses of collaborative writing mark a reaction to "individualistic definitions of authorship that have prevailed since the European Enlightenment" (Heller 2003, 301), writing scholars who study the subject, at least in some capacity, affirm collaborative writing's relevance to communal, social, or civic concerns. Nevertheless, much of the field demonstrates some degree of reticence to connect collaborative writing in the classroom to anticapitalism or radical political action. As I discuss, collaborative writing can support the common in orienting students to the practices and sociopolitical values of solidarity and commonality in contexts where global capitalism has maligned community and collective resistance.

In much of the field's discussions of collaborative writing, the extensive value researchers have placed on collaboration has often excluded political concerns in favor of promoting specific intellectual goods, namely the notion of language as inherently social and dialogic. According to Bruffee (1981), collaborative learning and writing are valuable because they offer to enhance students' encounter with language. "The primary aim of collaborative writing," he writes, "is to help students test the quality and value of what they know by trying to make sense of it to other people like themselves—their peers" (745). He subsequently elaborates that collaborative learning "personalizes language by socializing it, providing students with a social context of learning peers with whom they are engaged on conceptual issues" (745). For Bruffee, the goals of the writing classroom are the enhancement of individual capacities and, as such, he views greater engagement in the social as supportive of this end. Elsewhere, Bruffee (1984) argues that because thinking is effectively "internalized conversation" (1984, 640), a dialogic approach to writing and learning is inherently supportive of the individual's intellectual capacities: "To think well as individuals we must learn to think well collectively" (640). Bruffee likewise argues such work gives students crucial insight into communal meaning making: "[Collaborative learning] is one way of introducing students to the process by which communities of knowledgeable peers create referential connections between symbolic structures and 'reality'" (650). In these path-breaking theorizations of collaboration, he defends an intensely social view of language, though one with little to no overt connection to activism.

An avowed skeptic of the claims of collaborative writing's value, Peter Elbow, while he breaks from Bruffee's assertion of the individual's internalization of the social, nevertheless regards the potential of collaborative writing to ultimately be an asset to individual writing practices. Collaborative writing, Elbow (1999) contends "is difficult and often unpleasant" (7–8), "often pretty bad" (8), and "often silences weaker, minority, or marginal voices" (8). Indeed, rather than viewing the potential of collaborative writing to instill practices of equity and of listening to often suppressed voices, Elbow views these practices as tantamount to empowering the mob mentality often seen in the broader political scene. Nevertheless, Elbow sees some benefit in collaborative writing insofar as writers must test out their choices and assumptions on an audience and are thereby forced "to become more conscious and articulate about rhetorical decision making" (7). For Elbow, such work ultimately improves student writing by allowing the individual to better conceptualize writing's dialogic nature and to more effectively "have thoughtful dialogues with oneself" (13).

Another branch of scholars contend collaborative writing offers a more extensive set of instrumental benefits. Karen Burke LeFevre (1986) advocates teaching collaborative invention in the writing classroom to better support students' understanding of the inherently social nature of invention (129). Ann Ruggles Gere (1987) similarly maintains collaborative writing in the context of writing groups facilitates entry into "literate communities" (121) and helps guarantee "participants will begin to develop the cognitive abilities essential to literacy in the broad sense" (121). While in her collaborations with Lisa Ede, Andrea Lunsford has promoted collaborative writing as supportive of the articulation of feminist rhetorical subjectivity and, indeed, modest anticapitalist ends (Ede and Lunsford 2011), she previously cautioned against linking collaboration to emancipatory politics. As she remarks in an article from two decades earlier, "As the latest pedagogical bandwagon, collaboration often masquerades as democracy when it in fact practices the same authoritarian control" (Lunsford 1991, 4). Lunsford instead encourages collaboration for its scholastic rather than political benefits. Collaborative writing, she claims, holds extensive value in the areas of problem solving, abstract thinking, transfer, academic achievement, and "excellence" (6) more broadly.

More recently, scholars have extended this instrumental view of collaborative writing to digital and new materialist frameworks, frequently arguing collaborative writing upends solitary models of subjectivity and authorship. Stephanie Vie and Jennifer deWinter (2008) have argued for collaborative approaches to web-based writing, contending hypertext web environments like wikis "can be seen to encourage, and possibly even demand, collaborative modes of authorship" (110) that contest common notions of intellectual property. Laura R. Micciche (2014) has defended the relevance of collaborative writing to the recent object-oriented turn, arguing collaborative writing should be understood as "coexistence" (498) rather than the deliberate collaboration of two human interlocutors. "To think of writing as a practice of coexistence," she writes, "is to imagine a merging of various forms of matter . . . in an activity not solely dependent on one's control but made possible by elements that codetermine writing's possibility" (498). In other words, acknowledgment of our material entanglements entails recognizing all writing as collaborative insofar as the objects, places, and agents in our orbit collaborate with us on our texts. For Micciche, this acknowledgment necessitates a revised view of writing as a reflection of these entanglements: "Writing is defined, ultimately, by its radical *withness*" (502). Similarly, William Duffy (2014), critical of the ways collaborative writing has long functioned as a "floating signifier" (420) within the field, considers how object-oriented and interactionist theory promotes the notion that objects of discourse "resist our interactions" (425) and that the process of collaboration is a complex "triangulation" (430) that can be encouraged but not planned or controlled.

As these diverse inquiries indicate, despite that many contemporary approaches to collaborative writing are extending the boundaries of the subject and of writing, much of this work refrains from linking collaboration directly to politics. However, a relatively small branch of composition scholarship has indeed approached collaboration as inherently associated with social change. In a 1987 article Trimbur coauthored with Harvey Kail, the authors contend collaborative writing in a peer-tutoring setting prepares students for the crucial work of resisting classroom authority and developing their own intrinsic sense of agency: "Collaborative learning precipitates a crisis of authority. It asks students to rely on themselves, to learn on their own in the absence of faculty authority figures or their surrogates" (Kail and Trimbur 1987, 10). In his canonical article from a few years later, "Consensus and Difference in Collaborative Learning," Trimbur (1989) breaks with Bruffee's privileging of consensus, arguing that collaboration need not be the site of authoritarianism critics allege but that the building of consensus can be "a powerful instrument for students to generate differences, to identify the systems of authority that organize these differences, and to transform the relations of power that determine who may speak and what counts as a meaningful statement" (603). For Trimbur, the application of such a method entails employing consensus to produce a vibrant ecology of difference: "Consensus offers a way to orchestrate dissensus and to turn the conversation in the collaborative classroom into a heterotopia of voices—a heterogeneity without hierarchy" (615).

Carrie Shively Leverenz (1996), like Trimbur, views collaborative writing as a politically relevant means of interrogating difference in the writing classroom. Collaboration, as she argues, can be a means of "providing students with the opportunity to initiate conversations about cultural difference" (298). However, Leverenz acknowledges the significant limitations of this approach, including the substantial risk of student resistance to the aims of such pedagogical exercises (299), the tendency of students to collaboratively reproduce exclusionary norms (299), and, ultimately, the limited utility of recognizing difference alone: "If the goal of multicultural education is to raise critical consciousness and equip students to work for social change, then more than mere exposure to differing perspectives is needed" (311). Rather, Leverenz argues that interrogating and negotiating difference is only the beginning of meaningful social change whose necessity is clear but whose path is not (311).

An alternate argument among scholars who share the view of collaboration as intimately tied to politics is that collaborative writing and learning support students' subsequent civic engagement. W. Michele Simmons and Jeffrey T. Grabill (2007) argue participation in contemporary civic contexts requires collaborative skills. As they contend, to prepare students for effective participation in the civic world, the teaching of collaboration is needed in addition to the teaching of coordination, writing done in concert while not necessarily done collaboratively (441). As they argue, "No document is singly authored, no speech a solo performance, no organization outside a complex institutional infrastructure" (442). Ede and Lunsford (2011) take such an argument a step further, suggesting that in the capitalist context of graduate education, subverting the single-author model of writing, either through collaborative writing or other means, is necessary if scholars wish to oppose "late capitalist tendencies of commodification" (359).

Most recently, Holt's history of collaborative writing continues this line of reasoning, reading the political currents of collaborative writing's disjointed history through John Dewey's American pragmatism, noting collaborative writing supports critical thinking and democracy in contexts beyond the classroom. As Holt (2018) argues, the latter serves as "a measuring rod by which we can evaluate collaborative pedagogy in support of democracy" (11). As she frames this history, collaborative writing, while not inherently supportive of democratic ends, is faithful to Deweyian values, specifically in feminist approaches to collaborative writing by scholars such as Betty Sasaki (93). Holt contends collaborative writing's history bifurcated between 1940 and 1961, a period in which one strain represented "an attempt to wed pragmatist and positivist beliefs" (26) and another emphasized "teacher authority, on the individual's place in a hierarchy of knowledge, on clarity of thought and expression, and on a self-conscious appraisal of collaborative pedagogy as administratively functional" (6). She notably groups Bruffee with the former branch insofar as "he strove to make students dependent on one another and thus capable of gaining authority through group interaction" (27). She later details how Bruffee's model supports the development of students' collective authority in notably political ways: "Students gain a sense of collective authority if given the right tasks. [Bruffee] didn't *give* us authority.... We *took* it" (34). Holt also elaborates how this transfer of authority facilitates students' development of a "community of knowledgeable peers" (34) capable of functioning independently from the managerial authority represented by the instructor.

Within this political strain of collaborative writing scholarship, another body of scholars has explored the practice's feminist aspects, many locating an inherent political valence in collaborative work. In their article "Rhetoric in a New Key: Women and Collaboration," Lunsford and Ede (1990) distinguish between two forms of collaborative writing, a "hierarchical mode" (235) that is "linearly structured, driven by highly specific goals, and carried out by people who play clearly assigned roles" (235) and "the dialogic mode" (235), a model of collaborative writing "loosely structured" (235) with fluid roles and in which "multivoiced and multivalent ventures" (236) are esteemed. As they assert, while the former describes a typically masculine model of collaboration, the latter captures feminine collaborative patterns and offers "the possibility of subverting traditional phallogocentric, subject-centered discourse" (238). Janice Doane and Devon Hodges (1995) hold a similar view, positing that collaboration offers the potential for "a feminist subversion of patriarchal norms for writing" (53). Lorraine York (2002), however, is more cautious in her theorizing of the subject, noting the potential for essentializing when characterizing feminine collaborative practices. She regards women's collaborative writing as holding a variety of ideological possibilities, "some more hierarchical, some more liberatory and subversive" (4). While she also refrains from making essentialist claims about women's writing and collaboration, Karyn L. Hollis's (2004) *Liberating Voices: Writing at the Bryn Mawr Summer School for Women Workers* details how "interdisciplinary, democratic, working-class, largely collaborative, and female" (1) modes of writing have supported women's labor organizing. Lindal Buchanan (2003) likewise refrains from broad generalizations about women's writing, instead contending that collaboration is "one of the greatest resources available to silenced and marginalized groups" (59) and that it has particularly served women in their socially and politically subordinated roles.

Cumulatively, the political orientation of collaborative writing scholarship suggests there is a tradition of understanding collaborative writing as supporting solidaristic or even anticapitalist ends. In addition to Trimbur, Ede and Lunsford (2011) offer one of the most explicit arguments on collaborative writing's capacity to oppose capitalism, namely insofar as it, in their assessment, resists the logics of commodification through transforming the model of authorship (359). Nevertheless, these arguments remain largely circumscribed and politically modest. While proponents of the political view of collaborative writing suggest collaboration supports the vital, coalitional work of political activism—Buchanan (2003) notably defends this view of collaborative writing as a means of transforming work environments (1)—composition scholars have largely refrained from theorizing collaboration's confrontational capacities or, indeed, its potential to offer a public challenge to contemporary capitalism, particularly capitalism's nativist turn. Building on these assertions, this chapter contends collaborative writing bears a radical potential to confront the logics of the new neoliberalism and to support anticapitalist change. Regarding the threats to democratic culture extended by the new neoliberalism, I contend collaborative writing can challenge the divisive and antidemocratic effects of capitalist dominance and enact a site of anticapitalist collaborative subjectivity. Dean's theorization of the comrade, her term to describe a form of intimate, political collective subjectivity, offers a valuable means of guiding this work.

THE COMRADE

In *Comrade: An Essay on Political Belonging*, Dean (2019) theorizes a deeply cooperative and inclusive model of political action that militates against the contemporary capitalist forces of division, competition, and exploitation. In her construction, such a formation is particularly necessary under the conditions of the emergent, antidemocratic capitalist order Brown (2019) and others have critiqued. "Breaking from capitalism's 24–7 injunctions to produce and consume," Dean (2019) writes, "the discipline of common struggle expands possibilities for action and intensifies the sense of its necessity" (8). The comrade, as she argues, counters the neoliberal fantasies antagonistic to community, ideologies "of self-sufficiency, hierarchy, and individual uniqueness" (53). "Capitalism," according to Dean, aims to disaggregate individuals, making them "competitive, self-interested, and afraid" (62), while the comrade seeks both the liberation and interconnectedness of political subjects. As she contends, a site of common struggle against capitalism, the comrade is a communally oriented subject position based in the collective struggle toward a common purpose: "As we fight together for a world free of exploitation, oppression, and bigotry, we have to be able to trust and count on each other. Comrade names this relation" (7).

For Dean, a crucial, and arguably controversial, component of the comrade is its capacity to gather and orient disparate individuals towards common political ends without eliding difference. Identity, privilege, and positionality are not ignored in this model, yet they are ultimately subordinated insofar as being a comrade entails radical equality. As Dean (2019) writes, "Comrade insists on the equalizing sameness that comes from fighting on the same side of a political struggle" (34). While this concept might easily come in for critique for promoting colorblind racism or other forms of ignorance, Dean is careful to note the comrade "does not eliminate difference" (35) but, instead, "provides a container indifferent to its contents" (35). Effectively, the comrade allows a vast array of intensities to collaborate and overcome the antagonisms of identity through "a new form of relation among equals on the same side of a struggle" (53). In Dean's controversial formulation, one's relation to another comrade takes precedence over alternative aspects of relation or difference.

In adopting the concept of the comrade, I am not advocating for the deferral of promoting racial equity, the neglect of racism as an issue of acute concern, or the abandonment of other areas of social justice. Rather, in promoting radical solidarity across multiple axes of difference, I am advocating what I believe is a necessarily coalitional model of social, political, racial, and economic change that should be adopted in the writing classroom. Interrogation of racism, ableism, sexism, and genderism must continue, but this interrogation, quite crucially, should not mean solidarity must wait or the fight against capitalism must be postponed. Rather, comrades can fight racism while also joining forces to combat the effects of global capitalism. Indeed, as Angela Y. Davis (2020) argues, it is precisely through creating solidarity across lines of difference that racism and capitalism can be fought.

> I learned how to express solidarity with the Algerian Revolution while still a teenager. And, of course, my own trial on charges that initially carried the death penalty ended in victory largely due to the vast international campaign that touched people in Africa, Asia, Europe and Latin America. The Black Panther Party and many of the other organizations promoting Black liberation in the 1960s and 70s were inspired by and created links with revolutionary struggles in the Third World. During the 1980s in the United States, the call for solidarity with the anti-apartheid struggle in South Africa was heeded by virtually every progressive organization in the country. This solidarity not only helped to raise the international profile of the anti-apartheid campaign, but also greatly strengthened our anti-racist movements at home.

In her construction of solidarity, Dean (2019) invokes the work of philosopher Alain Badiou (2005), whose notion of the generic truth procedure posits subjects are produced by epochal shifts in the areas of politics, science, love, and art, what he terms *events*, and are tasked with affirming the truth of the events that bore them (201–239). Similarly, Dean contends the comrade is united by political truth "and the fidelity with which they work to realize this truth in the world" (82). However, Dean amends Badiou's thesis, noting that "the comrade is not a faithful subject but a political relation faithful to the divided people as the subject of emancipatory egalitarian politics" (84). In this revision, Dean breaks with the notion of the subject defended in Badiou's *Being and Event* (2005) and returns to the Alain Badiou of *Theory of the Subject* (2009)—for Dean, the subject is a collective and communal response to the crisis of political disenfranchisement. In her formulation, individuals step into the politically positioned role of the comrade and are, hence, poised to enact "new values, intensities, and possibilities" (96) capacitated through political intimacy. While Dean notes such a model is hardly "the magical solution to all the problems facing the left, much less the world" (135), she maintains it is nevertheless the means through which activists might evade the contemporary political crisis (135). Dean's application of Badiou to current events notably follows the most recent course of the philosopher's own political theorizing. In *Trump*, Badiou (2019) refers to the election of the US president as "this counter-event, this disaster" (2) and cites the need for an intellectual and collective alternative to the notion that "capitalism is the only possible path" (19). As Badiou writes, "This Idea could also make possible an action gathering together very different subjectivities under the clear power of a shared idea" (19). This is precisely the notion of crossing, not annihilating, difference this chapter defends—in this case, with an idea that counters the capitalist nihilism of Trump, Orbán, and others.

In this respect, Dean's comrade resonates with Krista Ratcliffe's (2005) conception of "rhetorical listening" (1), which she defines as "a stance of openness that a person may choose to assume in relation to any person, text, or culture" (1). For Ratcliffe, rhetorical listening can be employed to parse people's "intersecting identifications with gender and race" (17) and to manage what she terms "troubled identifications" (17) such as racism and genderism. More significantly, Ratcliffe suggests rhetorical listening can facilitate different kinds of identifications than those operative within standard discursive conventions. While, as Ratcliffe notes, we frequently identify with others "in places of commonalities" (32), through rhetorical listening "we are invited to consciously locate our differences in commonalities *and* differences" (32). In other words, rhetorical listening permits identification with a vast array of potential interlocutors, not merely those with whom we hold something *in common*. Distinct in terms of focus, both perspectives center on the potential of solidarity to operate on a higher intellectual order and in defiance of exclusionary norms. For Ratcliffe, listening permits identification and solidarity across racial lines, while for Dean this boundary crossing emerges from anticapitalist aspiration.

In several respects, Dean's model echoes many of the most political approaches to collaborative writing across the past several decades. Her work particularly relates to Trimbur's (1989) notion of the writing classroom as "a heterogeneity without hierarchy" (615) insofar as it promotes political intimacy without discounting difference. However, Dean presents a means of advancing disciplinary approaches insofar as her model understands the comrade not merely as instilling the knowledge or values of democratic practice, as Holt (2018) views collaboration, but as a uniquely forceful entity capable of challenging capitalist hegemony precisely because it enacts what capitalism denies—solidarity across difference. For composition, the model of the comrade presents a view of collaborative writing and learning not merely as an enterprise for an enhanced encounter with language's social valence (Elbow 1999; LeFevre 1986), or even a mechanism of civic participation (Simmons and Grabill 2007), but as a site of social change and radical political invention. It likewise provides support to the unconventional position that conflict and community are not opposed but rather mutually sustaining.

More concretely, I regard Dean's (2019) model as informing disciplinary approaches to collaborative writing in three meaningful ways. First, as Dean frames the collaboration of the comrade as an anticapitalist praxis insofar as it counters the narratives and ideologies of the new neoliberalism, she offers the discipline a means of framing collaboration as irreducibly antagonistic to the capitalist demands of "self-sufficiency, hierarchy, and individual uniqueness" (53). Teaching in these terms, writing instructors can better communicate the value and anticapitalist potential of collaborative writing to students, not to mention the necessity of engaging in anticapitalist critique through presenting the close political collaboration of equals as opposing capitalist division. This pedagogical model attempts to build upon Trimbur's (2000) suggestion that collective and communal engagement with writing, specifically "the circulation of writing" (215), necessarily participates in expanding "public forums and popular participation in public life" (191). As I conceptualize its value, this form of collaborative writing offers an intrinsic affront to capitalist division. Second, Dean presents a vision of working across individual difference in the interest of political change, thereby providing a means with which to address prejudice, exclusion, and the marginalization of minority groups while also gathering a body of comrades for anticapitalist work. In the context of writing, this vision offers a way of addressing the extensive axes of individual difference present in diverse classrooms and writing contexts while promoting collaborative writing practices that aim to empower these groups to convene in seeking pragmatic change. This, effectively, offers an alternative to both Bruffee's (1981, 1984) emphasis on consensus and Trimbur's (1989) "heterotopia of voices" (615). Rather, such a model recognizes the heterogeneity of subject positions but seeks to organize these in a formation oriented toward a political end. This model, crucially, is not consensus as Bruffee defines it but the collective fidelity of comrades to the power of political collaboration. Third, Dean's conception of the comrade presents critical collaboration as a model of inventive political praxis that produces novel actions, discourses, ideas, pathways, and discoveries. For Dean, comrades are not only political militants but also de facto political theorists who develop novel modes of enacting their subjectivity (96) that, in turn, support solidarity. For contemporary conditions in which the norms of democracy are in retreat, subordinated to waves of conservative populism and hypercapitalist policy, Dean offers composition a means of theorizing political action and civic engagement as the formation of new connections and possibilities for those working in concert.

"THE BRILLIANCE AND COLOR THERE": WRITING AMONG COMRADES

As my discussion of the field's approach to collaborative writing seeks to illuminate, the extensive research by composition scholars in collaborative writing and learning, civic engagement, and service learning provides ways of gathering students in productive intellectual communities. Dean's comrade, however, presents the potential of something further, namely of forging deep political connections between students. As I contend, the concept offers composition the potential of teaching the process, the utility, the potentiality, the thrill, and maybe even the joy[5] of solidarity in ways that prepare students to understand the potential of using collaboration to enact meaningful social, political, and economic change.

In employing Dean's model, I approach collaborative writing as a means of supporting and strengthening the common. While I don't use the term in my teaching, I carefully articulate the costs of inaction in the current political moment—climate change, precarity, economic inequality, monopoly capitalism, racism, sexism, homophobia, transphobia—and illustrate for students the utility of community, working across difference, and grassroots activism. In writing-across-the-curriculum (WAC) courses actualizing this approach, I prepared students for this work by placing them into small groups and asking them to collectively discuss their respective identities, political preferences, and backgrounds, highlighting both commonalities and fault lines between their various positions and isolating potential points of agreement, tension, or disagreement. Following Trimbur's (1989) framing of collaboration as a place of productive difference (614) and Dean's (2019) evocation of solidarity as a means of overcoming, though not eliding, difference (35), my interest here was to establish existing differences as starting points for subsequent collaboration. Once students vocalized these differences in conversation, I then moved them toward assignments that asked them to collaboratively identify potential issues, movements, sites, and events that would allow them to intervene in a political, social, or economic issue *as comrades*.

One assignment was modeled chiefly after the manifestos and statements of the 1960s, what I regard as one of the most effective genres for communicating the political utility of collaborative writing while also engaging students in public-facing rhetorical work. While students may have become largely inured to the position paper, as shabby a genre as any in higher education, assigning a political statement, specifically one requiring collaboration, forces many students out of some of the ruts of college writing and, when done effectively, into an engaged political dialogue. This is of course not to suggest the assignment is immune to indifference but to note that students, when nudged toward political discussion and negotiation with their peers, may be hard pressed to find ways of *not* engaging when they are asked to defend a position. Naturally, the apathy of students is, as Kellie Sharp-Hoskins and Amy E. Robillard (2012) contend, a perennial problem. While Sharp-Hoskins and Robillard advocate the use of narrative (330–331) to negotiate student indifference, I advocate a collaborative, political approach that places students in contexts that require negotiation. When the assignment succeeds and students are actively engaged with a political problem, they learn to cooperate in the creation of a text that collects the diverse voices of group members and intervenes in the public world.

One obvious obstruction teachers assigning such explicitly political writing may face is student resistance to assignments bearing little apparent relevance to the professional transition. As filmmaker and activist Astra Taylor (2019) recounts of her interviews with college students on education and the decline of democratic culture, "Most students I spoke to made clear that they weren't attending college to become better democratic participants. They were there to be able to get a good job after graduation" (207). She further notes all but the most privileged students were preoccupied with the prospect of repaying their student loans (207). My own experience at the University of Washington is similar, with many students oriented, often passionately so, toward lucrative future careers they hope will help them pay off their student loans and live comfortable lives. While many students, particularly those from progressive cities, are attuned to social issues, especially race and gender, and are gravely concerned with climate change, their most immediate concerns tend to rest with their own economic well-being. Hence, part of the task of engaging students in any form of social justice work, let alone the radical project of anticapitalism, is based in compromise and negotiation. Students must see the connections between the work of the writing classroom and their professional lives even if a specific assignment is not mainly concerned with professional development. In part, this can be achieved by adopting some of the strategies of Ira Shor's (1997) conception of power sharing (29), namely democratizing the classroom, minimizing "teacherly discourse" (41), and permitting students a degree of control over the content of the course and topic of assignments (42). By sharing power and framing this work as complementary to broader forms of writing, collaboration, and leadership, an instructor can help students see profitable links between the assignment and life after the university.

In preparing students for writing a political statement, I provided them with a variety of models to familiarize them with the genre and the breadth of possibilities. Cinzia Arruzza, Tithi Bhattacharya, and Nancy Fraser's (2019) *Feminism for the 99%: A Manifesto* is a progressive and deeply compelling collaboratively written political statement that not only presents students with an effective and persuasive model of the genre but also reflects the potentials of Dean's (2019) comrade by modeling intimate political solidarity insofar as it is it a collaborative, feminist work seeking to make common cause between feminists and anticapitalists. Teaching the text, I noted how students were quickly able to grasp the rhetorical power of the collaborative statement and, concomitantly, to understand its collaborative valence is both an essential aspect of its egalitarian, democratic project and the source of its authority. I've also assigned political statements from 1960s counterculture to express the possibilities of a more expansive and radical, albeit dated, form of political writing. "The Port Huron Statement" (Students for a Democratic

Society) written in 1962 by Tom Hayden and Students for a Democratic Society is one such text that articulates an expansive yet approachable set of political positions on disarmament, antiracism, freedom from social mandates, and the university as a site of social action. Students identified with the document's critique of racism and aspirational language regarding social transformation and the transition to a new era of social liberation and communality. I also taught Valerie Solanas's (2016) *SCUM Manifesto* as an example of uncompromisingly polemical, antipatriarchal, and anticapitalist rhetoric. As negative as "The Port Huron Statement" is utopian, *SCUM Manifesto* unfurls a caustic assassination of men. While most of my students notably viewed Solanas's lack of a positive political program and the absence of an uplifting or unifying view of women as ultimately disqualifying, a surprising number of students respond positively to the text's anger, if not its specific exhortations. Some praised Solanas's vibrant energy and palpable sense of rage at gender and economic inequality, noting how the text's characterization of male domination, cruelty, and uselessness effectively appeals to female rage. Some students responded that her passionate political energy is something desperately needed in a political climate marked by risible calls for "civility." One student, Lanya, whose work I subsequently address, argued that what we need is young activists and politicians like Solanas who are willing to "say and do what it friggin' takes" to go against those mired in outdated ideologies.

The collaborative political statement I assigned follows these documents in asking students to jointly articulate and defend a political position in a series of short, tightly argued paragraphs. In many respects, the essential learning outcomes of the assignment follow not from the writing—though this paper indeed aims to teach students to articulate and defend a political argument—but rather from learning to negotiate a political position that fairly represents the various stances of group members and from considering both the political value of and the hindrances to collective negotiation. In addition to Dean's (2019) comrade, the assignment is also indebted to Shor's (1997) model of power sharing (29) and Trimbur's (1989) revised concept of consensus "not as the goal of the conversation but as a critical measure to help students identify the formations of power that inhibit communication among readers" (614). As students began their work, I outlined a structured brainstorming process for each group to follow, with the understanding that they should develop and follow their own collaborative methods whenever necessary. In this approach, the assignment sought to actualize both the goods of collaborative writing and the notion that writing, as a social phenomenon, benefits from connection to a community of writers, from "brainstorming ideas, seeing other points of view, eliminating jargon, explaining that thing you think is clear but isn't" (Smith 2019, 106). First, I prompted students to free write on the most pressing social, political, and economic issues influencing the world today, specifically those with an impact on their lives. Subsequently, after placing them in groups, I asked them to discuss their ideas in round-robin-style sessions with a notetaker. In these sessions, I followed Bruffee's (1984) lead and maintained my distance, repositioning my authority and allowing students agency in directing their own learning (649). My one intervention at this early stage was to push students to see this process as something different from the standard position paper, something both more personal and more demanding, an actualization of their political beliefs and an opportunity to connect with others around a mutually important political goal. In attempting to enact Dean's (2019) model of quasi-Badiouian fidelity to comradeship (82), I exhorted students to interrogate how their own lives and subjectivities had been shaped by political issues, to consider what they feel passionately about, to consider how collectives might respond to problems, and to discuss these positions at length with their groups. Again, following Trimbur (1989), I also asked that students not gloss over or ignore the political disagreements that arose but dwell in them and find ways of articulating a political position that was not consensus but, rather, a synthesis of the group's various political positions.

Once students settled on a topic, I then extensively walked them through various models of collaboration, suggesting methods for refining arguments, outlining their statement, conducting research, and dividing labor. For these processes, I was careful to provide multiple possibilities and avenues for their collaborative work rather than handing students a script. This approach, I believe, provided them with a significant amount of autonomy without leaving them utterly adrift as they learned to cooperate and to navigate an unfamiliar genre. I also offered students multiple options for the division of labor. For example, I presented them with the option of operating, following Michael Hardt and Antonio Negri (2017, 3), as leaderless, an option all groups chose. I also presented students with a method in which group members are each responsible for a different portion of the text. Notably, Lunsford and Ede (2011) caution this method can permit a largely solitary form of authorship that only becomes collaborative in the final phase, "People can co-author articles without ever being together or doing any writing together" (28), but my interest was not merely in helping students to produce coauthored texts but in moving students toward understanding and forging political collaborations. I built upon the work of Lunsford and Ede by suggesting extensive brainstorming activities and a lengthy editing process in which each portion of the text would be read and commented on by every group member so as to cultivate a more collaborative process. I also offered another more cooperative model in which students were each responsible for a section of text but any group member could make changes to any part of the written document. I presented yet another model that involved a notetaker (a role that could periodically shift from student to student) who recorded and synthesized elements of a freewheeling group conversation to be drafted by members later. Throughout offering these suggestions, I continually presented students with choices regarding these possibilities but rarely made suggestions as to which were more appropriate.

As with all major writing I assign, I also met with groups outside class for a peer-review session to discuss the assignment and to gauge the success of their collaboration. In the case of the statement and other collaborative assignments, these sessions were mainly devoted to a discussion of the various successes and challenges of the collaboration process. In leading the session, I asked students about their collaboration to date, the methods they had chosen, and their effectiveness. If there appeared to have been problems in collaboration, I strived to help the students identify what these were and to formulate alternative arrangements. I also provided feedback on the draft itself, discussing my comments with students and working with them to develop a plan for revision and submission.

Texts produced under such conditions were inevitably varied. Students focused on such issues as economic inequality, poverty, the cost of college, and climate change. While, per the previous discussion, I allowed students free rein over their chosen topic, I strongly encouraged them to consider the ways their topic related to economic conditions. This approach ultimately represented a compromise between my desire, on the one hand, to introduce students to the enormity of capitalism's effects and, on the other, to share power. The results, while all politically engaged, predictably demonstrated varying degrees of engagement with capitalism. A group of students in one of my WAC courses in the fall of 2019[6] offered an explicit critique of neoliberalism's destructive effects in a statement titled "Scrutinizing the System: A Look at Neoliberalism," specifically analyzing neoliberal reason and proposing an extensive set of policies to combat it. The text, most significantly, isolated neoliberal ideology's meritocratic logic: "The neoliberal mindset puts blame on the lower class individuals for not working hard enough and not attaining the fullest stature of which they are capable. The reality is that our institutional system creates many hindrances for those at the bottom of the social hierarchy." I was thrilled with how the statement offered an extraordinarily sophisticated assessment of neoliberalism, linking material effects with ideological conditions. However, another group focusing on the crisis of climate change chose to center effects rather than the causes and entirely elided the subject of political economy. As they argued, "We as humans are killing the Earth and indirectly slaughtering animal species through pollution. By coming up with solutions to avert pollution, we can find a way to create a greener planet and a healthier future." They continued by detailing the various kinds of pollution affecting the planet, ending with a call for greater attention and action to combat the problem. While I certainly wish the latter group had been more ambitious with their critique and had mentioned, for instance, the wholesale slaughter of animals capitalism directly undertakes to meet market demand or the way the United States has undermined clean energy in the past (Wolff 2018), my approach to collaborative writing, per Dean (2019), maintains that a group need not necessarily take up political economy to offer a challenge to the capitalist status quo. While anticapitalist critique can profitably gather and sustain communities, comradeship is inherently antagonistic to capitalism insofar as the work of political collaboration stands in open opposition to the divisive and antidemocratic nature of twenty-first-century economic life. I believe, in learning to draft a collaborative political statement and in practicing some of the fundamentals of dialogue, cooperation, and grassroots activism, students are encountering writing in ways that push against capitalist division even if the subject matter of students' work fails to address capitalism explicitly.

A second, far more ambitious assignment I frequently assign in collaborative writing contexts extends many of the anticapitalist practices involved in the statement and situates them publicly within ongoing social, political, and cultural movements. Building upon Nancy Welch's (2008) utilization of working-class rhetorical action (108), Deborah Mutnick's (2019a) defense of "straddling the worlds of the classroom and other social locations" (101) in the interest of connecting students with radical progressive movements, and Dean's (2019) conception of comradeship more broadly, the assignment seeks to move students out of the classroom and into a variety of public engagements with activists. For a class I taught in the fall of 2019, I divided students into groups and provided them with a calendar of social and economic justice events in the Seattle area such as protests, talks, readings, exhibitions, and workshops; options that fall included a punk show raising funds for RAICES (the Refugee and Immigrant Center for Education and Legal Services), a talk by Gloria Steinem, and rallies against Trump and Amazon, among numerous other events. The assignment required students to attend, participate in, and, subsequently, collaboratively analyze the political rhetoric of several of these events in a multimodal text—a podcast, a zine, a video, a series of blog posts, or any additional format students proposed. As with the previous assignment, emphasis was placed on the formation of a political community and the collaborative process necessary to produce an artifact. This assignment bore an explicit political and activist element in that students were encouraged, among other options, to identify political events that they supported, or, at least, that they were interested in learning about and to take part not merely as observers but as participants. Specifically informed by Dean's comrade, this assignment also attempted to build a political community by engaging students in immediate, real-world political struggles, events, and concerns meaningful to them and, optimistically, to create an intimate political community transcending social and identity-based forms of difference.

An important point must be made here regarding the suitability of the city of Seattle to these kinds of assignments. As many readers well know, Seattle is a largely progressive city with a rich labor and protest history. Home to the General Strike of 1919, an important site of the 1934 West Coast Waterfront Strike, and, briefly, the epicenter of the antiglobalization movement with the WTO protests of 1999, Seattle has long been known as a crucible of progressive activism. In 2020, activists established the Capital Hill Autonomous Zone, an occupied, police-free camp, in response to police violence (Kaste 2020). The past decade has also seen the rise of numerous progressive politicians, most notably Kshama Sawant, a city council member and avowed socialist who has staunchly defended workers' rights (Rosenblum 2021). It is also the home of Amazon and Microsoft and accordingly boasts enormous income inequality that falls starkly along racial lines—as Gene Balk reported in the *Seattle Times* on October 23, 2019, while Seattle claims the third-highest median income in the United States ($93,500 in 2018), Black families' median income is just $42,500. James N. Gregory (2015) explains this contradiction in *Dissent*, noting that West Coast cities like Seattle and San Francisco "share what we might call 'the left coast formula,' a historically developed set of institutions and expectations that keep radicalism alive while allowing political elites identified as liberal or progressive to stay in power pretty consistently." While, as Gregory notes, such conditions often serve to cultivate the kinds of progressivism that fail to challenge dominant capitalist conditions,[7] they nevertheless offer extensive opportunities for engaging students in social movements and progressive actions. Likewise, the ostensible progressivism of the University of Washington means students tend to offer little to no resistance if asked to observe or participate in Leftist political action.

Many compositionists wishing to implement similar methods may, of course, find themselves in quite different contexts, that is, in rural areas or conservative states where participation in civic action may be limited and viewed unfavorably. While the assignment as I detail it here may not necessarily translate to all contexts, I nevertheless believe similar assignments, albeit with some modifications, can be implemented almost anywhere. First, it must be noted that protests and labor actions are not confined to coastal urban centers. Suburban Bessemer, Alabama, for instance, was the site of a massive unionization campaign for Amazon employees (Oliver, *Guardian*, March 11, 2020). Following the killing of George Floyd in May of 2020, there were protests in over 350 US cities (Bustillo 2020). Protests, social movements, and labor actions are often accessible even in rural areas and can potentially serve as sites of student engagement. Second, in cases where expressions of progressivism are limited by state, local, and university politics, students can engage in similar work virtually. Relevant speakers can video conference with classes—a practice that seems more realistic in the era of COVID-19—and students can research the online spaces and social media communication of progressive groups. Students can likewise conduct interviews over Zoom or take part in online meetings of labor or protest organizations in ways that allow for ethnographic research to be conducted.

A more significant issue is that this work is not without some risk to the instructor, a concern I address more substantively in chapter 5. In more conservative areas and institutions, instructors wanting to engage students in progressive politics may be met with resistance from administrators, parents, or students themselves. Notably, having taught at several institutions in southern states, I am not unfamiliar with such attitudes. One gambit, which I have utilized on a few occasions, is framing this work in terms of a necessary openness to differing views. Rhetorician Mark Garrett Longaker (2015) articulates such a position, noting, "Today we are still obliged to listen to those with whom we disagree, not just to make our argument stronger but also to preserve the collegial ethos that permeates a healthy conversation" (135). Instructors can ask students to attend a rally or talk in this spirit and the concerns of avowedly conservative students, parents, and administrators may be allayed by such an argument, though it potentially inoculates students against actually engaging with what they encounter. A preferable though certainly riskier option is to frame such struggles not simply as articulations of Leftist politics but as legitimate and necessary demands for rights. Actor and activist Danny Glover, in a 2021 interview with *Jacobin*, said as much: "The point is that human beings sell their bodies, sell themselves, for a price, in order to survive. You have to place some sort of context or place some sort of structure around it to make sure that the benefits of what they produce are shared in some way." While many may wish to reframe such struggles as mere politics, connecting these issues, as Glover does, to the fundamental matters of survival, equity, and justice may be persuasive.

In my class, there were many successful collaborations that expressed the potential of the comrade. In one notable instance, three men of different backgrounds recorded a podcast that detailed their discovery of the University of Washington's reliance on prison labor. Previously unaware of the practice, the men recorded a process of fact-finding in which they debated the issue and concluded the university benefits from a system of "elaborate slavery in disguise." As Arthur, one member of the group, observed, "Everyone has their own rights and using these people to build [for] little to no pay is just not right." One peer group, however, uniquely exemplified what is possible in collaborative writing assignments oriented toward issues of consequence. Evident in the group's work was the potential for collaboration to support political engagement and, moreover, to gather an integrated intellectual community uniquely focused on political work.

Bobby, Roger, and Lanya were among the most vocal and engaged students in my classes in the fall of 2019. Per the assignment, they chose to record a podcast, selecting four social justice events from the roster of preapproved options: an exhibit on redlining at the Wing Luke Museum in Seattle's International District (see fig. 1.2); a talk on transgender issues by Azure Savage, a local high school student, at Elliot Bay Book Company; a reading and discussion on climate change by political theorist Alyssa Battistoni at the University of Washington Bookstore; and an exhibit on youth activism at the Bill and Melinda Gates Foundation Discovery Center. Organized as a series of short, oral essays followed by lengthier group discussions, the podcast focused predominantly on issues of rights, both those held by US citizens and those denied to them, and the necessity of radical intervention in the areas of social justice and economic inequality. Lanya framed the podcast in her opening statement: "We are living in a time when activism is what's required to shift the status quo."

While the scripted portions of the podcast bring keen critical insights to the various events and exhibits, it is in the moments of largely unscripted dialogue in which group members unpack and analyze what they've witnessed that the capacity of collaboration to promote discovery, develop solidarity, identify new ideas and discourses, and more deeply engage students in political work becomes apparent. In a moment after the redlining exhibit, the group reflected on the continued existence of the American Dream and what that term means for them personally. It is evident from this exchange that while the exhibit pushed the group to consider how prejudices impact them personally—and, indeed, unequally—as gender, racial, and sexual minorities,[8] the group is also discovering the importance of working across difference:

> BOBBY: So for me, not to pull out a picture of a bald eagle and be like *freedom*, but as a trans person my American Dream is the freedom to medically transition as much or as little as I want to.
>
> ROGER: And for me. . . . I just want to have a nice stable place to live and just spend time with my partner. And just like kinda live . . . a normal life . . . I guess . . .
>
> LANYA: Right, just to be accepted as I am, and be free to live my life the way that I see fit, is primarily what that means for me.

In this exchange, Bobby, Roger, and Lanya effectively reinterpret the American Dream, often understood as a raced, classed, and heteronormative concept (Bukowczyk 2016), considering what political and social belonging means to each of them. While their reading widely differs from the term's typical interpretation, I read their exchange as an attempt to negotiate their individual positionality within a profoundly shifting American political scene. The moment is also a telling one insofar as it speaks directly to Dean's (2019) defense of a collaborative political subjectivity that recognizes difference but works across this difference to gather comrades in collective struggle. While Bobby, Roger, and Lanya are positioned differently as minorities and hence have different needs and desires regarding equity and inclusion, they recognize the need for a collaborative political praxis that gathers individuals and protects the belonging of minorities.

In a later moment following Battistoni's talk, the group further reflects on the importance of solidarity and working across difference in the context of social justice activism:

Figure 1.2. Seattle's Wing Luke Museum. (Photograph by Kbh3rd. Licensed under the Creative Commons Attribution 3.0 Unported license. https://creativecommons.org/licenses/by/3.0/deed.en.)

> ROGER: And everyone needs to come together—that's been like a common theme in all of these things . . . everyone needs to come together.
>
> LANYA: Unity . . . they've been driving home that fact at every single event that we've been to. And literally in this one she says that we need . . . to combine socioeconomic and ecological points—that's critical for us to find that unity.

Responding to calls for unity reflected in Battistoni's talk but repeated across the various social justice events they visited, Roger and Lanya ponder the need for unity both among different kinds of individuals and, crucially, between differing groups and ideologies. As Lanya reflects on the talk, she stresses the need for political unity between anticapitalists and climate-change activists in order to develop effective political coalitions. This observation, once again, indexes Dean's (2019) focus on working across difference in addition to the prioritization of political and economic goals. This sentiment is also reiterated in Lanya's final statement of the podcast: "We're so much more powerful when we work together. . . . We must all learn to communicate in a manner that acknowledges the struggles of others if we wish to bridge the gap between social movements and unite."

Through their project, Bobby, Roger, and Lanya forged a community based in political comradeship and in defiance of dominant capitalist logics of division and insularity, actualizing the three essential benefits to composition I see in Dean's conception of the solidarity of comrades (2019), namely the intrinsically anticapitalist valence of collaboration, working across difference, and the support of novel political action. The final benefit of Dean's comrade, the discovery of novel ideas and approaches, was particularly borne out by the group's work. Their collaboration, I believe, allowed the group to discover the vast potential, creativity, and utility of protest. While Bobby, Roger, and Lanya were not involved in a specific or prolonged political struggle, they nevertheless expressed a sense of discovery at the diversity and plurality of potential political action. Following the group's visit to the Bill and Melinda Gates Foundation Discovery Center,[9] Bobby observed, "It really gave me that sense of involvement, that sense that this is not something distant from me. This is a world I am part of and need to be working in. It was turning, being inside that, the brilliance and color there." Lanya similarly responded,

> And what was so beautiful was that it was shown that there was not one kind of person that could be an activist. There wasn't just one strategy or tactic used to achieve universal liberation, and it really really made clear that we have to discuss everything. We have to be outspoken about the way we feel in our realities and use whatever tools we have, and perspective we have, as our superpower to impact change.

In both comments, Lanya and Bobby appear to discover the vast potential shape of activism and, critically, observe its essentially communal form. Bobby alludes to feeling called to participate in the collective struggle of transgender activism and the vibrant world, "the brilliance and color," that collective struggle offers access to. Lanya, likewise, expresses her discovery of the multiplicity of possibilities for activists and the understanding that these forms, whatever shape they take, must be collective.

These findings were expressed in writer's memos on the collaborative process, in which members reported viewing their work not only as a success but also as an occasion where a group project became something more meaningful and substantive than is typical, namely an opportunity for a higher order of social engagement, learning, and solidarity. In her writer's memo, Lanya describes a rigorous and productive collaboration in which equity and shared labor were prioritized: "Throughout this process, my group and I all bounced ideas off of each other, we analyzed things together and each member of the group was able to voice elements of the events we attended. . . . I feel like I derived so much more value from this project *because* of my group, than I would have alone." Lanya additionally speaks to the extensive benefits of collaborative writing as a mode of instruction. She notes, "Through this project, I have learned so much about activism, social justice and communication. Truly. But more than that, I've learned how beneficial it can be to work with a group of peers who actually want to learn, who actually want to participate." Layna also celebrates the interpersonal value of the assignment insofar as collaborative work can, in some cases, foster friendship and understanding among peers: "I feel so incredibly blessed to have been in this group. It has been a pleasure to do this project . . . [it] combined that opportunity with an experiential immersion in Seattle life *and* social justice issues." In many respects, Lanya revels in a sense of communal accomplishment akin to what Dean (2019) terms "joy" (88). Roger echoes many of Lanya's sentiments, noting, "This final project was potentially one of the most interesting and most pleasant final projects that I have had at the UW." In his reflection, Roger similarly reports feeling collaborative writing offered opportunities for intellectual discovery and propelled the project in fruitful ways. Like Lanya, he also reports feeling he gained useful knowledge from the collaborative process and that he will be "well-equipped and able" to approach future collaborative work.

Despite my postulation that solidaristic anticapitalism should allow comrades to work across difference for political ends, I certainly do not believe the writing classroom should neglect the difficult work of investigating and addressing prejudice. While the project I've just described was certainly a success, allowing students to explore various movements, ideas, and spaces and to engage in incisive, collaborative analysis, compositionists must remain attuned to the potential of collaboration to deepen difference. Elbow's (1999) assertion that collaborative writing "often silences weaker, minority, or marginal voices" (8) and Leverenz's (1996) contention that collaboration can reproduce dominant forms of exclusion (299) are reservations that must be taken into consideration when assigning collaborative writing. It must be further noted that compositionists cannot assume students' progressive political engagement will necessarily translate to equitable comportment within groups. As Keeanga-Yamahtta Taylor (2017) argues, the contemporary feminist movement is divided by class differences and racial exclusion—"shattering glass ceilings that impede their ascent into corporate boardrooms, electoral politics, and other destinations in white and wealthy America" is, in her view, the ultimate goal of many contemporary white feminists. Regarding collaborative work, while I believe Dean is not wrong to aspire to radical solidarity operated by shared political commitments, I believe, in pedagogical practice, that her approach neglects how prejudice can fester even among supposed comrades. Dean (2019), to be sure, is not unrealistic about collaboration, noting it is not "a magical solution to all problems facing the left" (135), yet I nevertheless believe comrades may need more preparation than she concedes. More specifically, I believe that, in addition to being trained to collaborate and engage in the critique of capitalism, students must also be taught strategies with which to practice equity so as not to reproduce oppressive norms. For this work, I draw upon writer Ijeoma Oluo's (2018) *So You Want to Talk about Race* and her treatment of microaggressions to prepare students to be respectful, inclusive, and reflective concerning their own biases as they engage in their collaborative work. Microaggressions, as Oluo defines them, "are small daily insults perpetrated against marginalized or oppressed people because of their affiliation with that marginalized or oppressed group" (169). She recommends a protocol for both the recipient and the speaker of a microaggression. For the recipient, Oluo recommends clarifying the microaggression, asking "uncomfortable questions" (174) regarding the prejudiced nature of the statement, and reminding the speaker that intentionality is irrelevant. For the speaker, Oluo advises pausing, self-assessing, asking "Would I have said this to somebody of my race?," contextualizing the remark in the lineage of microaggressions, using the occasion to become more informed, and, finally, apologizing (178). I teach this method to students, expanded to account for differences beyond race, to protect minority students and to quell the expressions of prejudice that can arise in otherwise progressive contexts. I believe these methods, along with training in respectful language and comportment, allow students to better actualize the progressive benefits of the comrade in ways that resist capitalist dominance, particularly the effects of the new neoliberalism (Dardot and Laval 2019b) that reside in hypercapitalism twinned with nativist hate.

CONCLUSION

As I have claimed in this chapter, one of the most vital means of developing an anticapitalist pedagogy is creating opportunities for productive collaboration among student writers insofar as this work counteracts one of the most pernicious effects of global capitalism, the undermining of community and democratic culture. Collaborative writing potentiates the kinds of radical, solidaristic critiques that are both at risk and also the most capable of challenging the escalating power of contemporary global capitalism. In bringing this chapter to a close, I wish to respond to those who will undoubtedly question whether the emphasis I've placed on collaborative writing mythologizes community or ignores the tendency of collaboration and collaborative movements to be reactionary rather than emancipatory. It is, of course, the case that coalitions—whether they be small groups, social movements, or entire societies—can be both politically conservative and economically capitalist. Hungary's Fidesz, with which I began this chapter, is but one example of a body of collaborators who have worked together to secure a more exclusionary, hierarchical, and antidemocratic society. Acknowledging the reactionary aspects of such arguments, Miranda Joseph (2002) articulates one of the most incisive Leftist critiques of community in *Against the Romance of Community*, alleging communities necessarily serve politically regressive ends: "Capitalism and, more generally, modernity depend on and generate the discourse of community to legitimate social hierarchies" (viii). Articulating an argument that resonates with Geraldine McNenny and Duane Roen's (1992) charge of the "fallibility of the community of collaborators" (1), Joseph (2002) contends that both the discourse of community and the relationships it potentiates are "imbricated in capitalism" (ix) and tend to define communities in opposition to an Other. Communities, she argues, constitute themselves based upon an original practice of exclusion (xix) while minimizing important differences of identity within their ranks.

My response to these claims is to concede that some iterations of collaboration and community are indeed imbedded in and complicit with the new neoliberalism. Orbán's "illiberal state" (Lendvai 2018, 141) and Trump's enthusiastic body of supporters[10] demonstrate how communities can be both conservative and capitalist. Where I break with Joseph (2002), however, is in the suggestion that community is inherently conservative either in its articulation or in its production of relations and that the most effective means of opposing capitalism lies in direct critique (xxxi) rather than in solidarity. I, rather, follow Dean's (2019) argument that radically egalitarian communities can be generated when members are committed to the notion of equity and solidarity. I further suggest critique itself can be complementary to community not simply for its capacity to oppose a site of power but also for the ways it can contribute to the formation of political collectives based in solidarity. In other words, community and critique are ultimately intertwined, at least insofar as the anticapitalist project is concerned. Of course, individual critics are often remarkably effective actors—consider the contributions of Chelsea Manning or Edward Snowden—but critique, I argue, is communal. Communities are essential for lasting progressive change. As previously noted, unions are an instructive example of a community presenting an anticapitalist challenge—the success of the 2019 Chicago teacher's strike, in which three hundred thousand teachers walked off the job to demand salary increases and reduced class sizes, is but one example (Smith and Davey, *New York Times*, October 13, 2019).

Additionally, while she effectively speaks to many of the troubling uses of community under the neoliberal model of capitalism, elements of Joseph's (2002) critique are now out of step with the blatantly exclusionary orientation of the new neoliberalism. With respect to the pervasive ethic of meritocracy[11] and the seemingly unbridled celebration of wealth, the valorization of self-reliance has largely supplanted the various calls for community in contemporary culture. In the current context, defenses of collaboration and equity run largely counter to the reactionary individualism that pervades much of the economic scene. While nationalist discourses remain strong in many countries, the United States for one, our deeply individualistic moment is one in which virtually any call for solidarity or community represents something of a counterstatement to the new neoliberalism. This is, of course, also Dean's (2019) assertion, namely that the comrade "can provide us with a view of political relation necessary for the present" (66). In her view, being a comrade is itself an instructive transformation of identity capable of communicating what is both necessary and possible in the current political environment. In the contemporary political context of hypercapitalism, the building of networks of solidarity across the lines of race, gender, sexuality, nationality, class, and other markers of difference is a radically progressive act. As I further defend in subsequent chapters, engaging in radical critique is also a means of building and advancing communities of solidarity. Effectively, the work of coalition building, whether in the formation of unions and social movements or in classrooms, resists the pervasive forces of division present in the current moment and, when taught in the writing classroom, offers students the opportunity to extend the mutual relation of community and critique into their future lives. In the following three chapters, I elaborate the three sites where I believe the work of communal critique is most necessary: student debt (ch. 2), the world of work and the rhetoric of productivity (ch. 3), and the scene of digital technology (ch. 4).

2
DEBT

In 2019, the *Cut* ran a story about college graduates deep in student debt. Alex, a working-class, first-generation student, admittedly knew nothing about college loans before taking them on, only that a degree was supposed to be the gateway to a middle-class life: "There was an assumption that if you go to college, you will get a great job and make tons of money" (Arnold 2019). Alex is $62,000 in debt and now pays about $650 a month on a $50,000 salary. Feeling enormously constrained by her financial entanglements, she is unable to "take a trip, take that freelance job, not be scared of getting fired or not having a job." Casey took on $50,000 in loans paying out-of-state tuition at a public university and now is similarly unable to make major life choices: "I can't imagine saving enough to put a down payment on a house. I feel like a lot of things we want to do eventually will be delayed because we'll be getting a late start to truly saving." Kate, who struggles with health problems in addition to student loans, describes debt constraining every life decision and career choice: *"Would this job prolong my debt? Should I take a higher-paying job I'm not passionate about?"*

Stories like these are pervasive. Student debt now tops $1.5 trillion, distributed among forty-three million debtors (Federal Student Aid). The class of 2018 averaged $29,200 per person, up 2 percent from the year before (Friedman 2020). For the average borrower, financial immobility and reduced choice, as described by Alex, Casey, and Kate, are typical consequences of the current student debt system. The 66 percent of students whose parents are unable to pay for college entirely out of pocket are effectively indentured and bound to a system that manages their personal and financial lives and profoundly constrains their choices (Friedman 2019). For many, however, the effects of debt are far worse. Currently, there are approximately 3.9 million college dropouts who carry student debt but no degree (Nadworny and Lombardo 2019). As Elissa Nadworny and Claire Lombardo report, for these students, the enormous burden of debt comes with negligible advantage over those with no college experience whatsoever. The impact of student debt is also, critically, not limited to students themselves. Caitlin Zaloom (2019) details how paying for college is forcing middle-class families into increasingly leveraged and insecure positions in their efforts to provide opportunity and a middle-class life for their children. As she argues, the higher education payment model forces many families to engage in "*social speculation*" (6), a process by which parents and students must gamble on higher education, both facing enormous financial risk if a child's college education doesn't "pay off" (6). As she details, many of the necessary investment vehicles for paying for college, such as 529 plans and prepaid tuition, attract families through exploiting parents' sense of moral duty while leveraging harsh penalties if certain conditions are not met (31–32). In other cases, there are those whose loans have doubled, tripled, or even quadrupled due to nonpayment (Nova 2018). In the most extreme cases, there are some whose unpaid college loans have resulted in court summonses and, in some cases, arrest warrants (Lieberman 2019). In a February 16, 2021, *New York Times* article, Gene B. Sperling observed the irony that the United States was one of the first nations to eliminate debtors' prisons in the early eighteenth century but has effectively reverted to them today.[1]

This chapter argues that these conditions are of paramount concern for students attending the university and, moreover, are a critical site of potential intervention for the anticapitalist composition classroom. As these conditions lay bare, debt, far from the neutral mechanism lenders and universities claim it to be, informs where, how, and how much we work, our social capital, our ability to envision and plan our lives, our sense of self, and, most crucially, our relations with others. Student debt, in particular, is far from an innocuous financial agreement that enables prosperity and economic freedom. Instead, it is a class fiction and a mechanism of punishment and control, forcing debtors into states of financial subordination in exchange for the promise of dignity and security. Insofar as debt becomes an all-consuming aspect of one's life, it can remove debtors from engagement in the public world, forcing them into isolation, ceaseless menial labor, and states of depression and disconnection. While the previous chapter explored the formation of intimate political communities of comrades (Dean 2019) capable of resisting, albeit modestly, capitalist dominance through the ethic of the common, this chapter takes up student debt as both a challenge to these communities and a site of needed intervention. In this chapter, I pose debt as one of the most significant and destructive sites of capitalist power, a rhetorical and material formation whose primary function is one of erasure, a mechanism that flattens human agency, undermines community, denies its own ideological and moral function, and occludes all forms of life that fail to fall under an economic calculus.

In response to debt's monumental sway, I detail a politically responsive, anticapitalist pedagogical approach that entails both teaching debt's coercive function and presenting students with opportunities for collaborative resistance and critique. Regarding the core assertion of this book, that capitalism must be opposed through collective praxis, this chapter draws from philosopher Jean-Luc Nancy's critique of debt in his 2017 essay "Gratuitousness and Recognition." The text, complementary to the philosopher's broader theorization of collective subjectivity and community (2010, 2016), frames debt as a financial relationship that intervenes and destabilizes what is essential in human community, namely the capacity of humans to recognize one another, to form bonds, and to engage in ways that lie beyond the financial calculus. For Nancy, a debt imposes a financial worldview that excludes the political and the social, prioritizing the logics of extraction in their stead. In short, per Nancy, debt represents the impossibility of community. In the classroom, I employ Nancy's critique to inform my practice of asking students to analyze debt in ways that expose its oppressive and anticommunal nature and its status as both a material burden and an ideological apparatus. In teaching students to recognize this valence of debt—as a mechanism of control and social separation stifling the possibility for alternative forms of relation rather than a gateway to a middle-class life—I cultivate critical, public, and collective writing practices aimed at opposing debt's power.

Regarding this intervention, some might naturally question the timing of teaching student debt in the college writing classroom as students will have already taken on debt by the time they attend college, thus potentially obviating the need for a critical intervention. Admittedly, students' decisions regarding what school to attend and how to pay their tuition will indeed have been made before stepping into the composition classroom. Studying debt will effectively arrive too late to inform this decision and could potentially serve to offer students an unsettling perspective on choices they've already made. In a recent composition class, for example, when confronted with the extent of debt's effects, one student became understandably exasperated, asking what he was supposed to do with this information. While I certainly identify with the student's emotion, I contend there is much to be gained by understanding as much as possible about the material, ideological, and rhetorical function of the student loan industry. I believe this study might not only help students as they negotiate the conditions of their own debt throughout their college years and into the long years of repayment but could also be applicable to the broader ideology of debt that informs global society.

Others might suggest composition is simply methodologically ill-equipped to address the issue. However, having now taught the subject to composition students in a variety of different contexts, my contention is that debt, while an uncomfortable topic for many, is nevertheless available to the methods of rhetoric and composition. As Bruce Horner, Brice Nordquist, and Susan Ryan (2017) point out, "Rhetoric, stylistics, language, cognition, and teaching methods" (8) are "always and inevitably participants in, shaping and shaped by, political economies in their concern with forms of valuation, production, and circulation of knowledge; with labor; and with capital" (8). In accordance with this perspective, composition scholars have extensively attended to various economic concerns, including educational value (Bollig 2015; Bousquet 2008), social class (Bloom 1996; Carter and Thelin 2017; Harris 2000; Lindquist 1999, 2004; Parks 1999; Peckham 2010; Scott 2009; Zebroski 2007), austerity (Bernstein 2016; Larson 2016; Welch and Scott 2016), neoliberal logic (Ryder 2017; Welch 2008), language and capitalism (Lu 2005), and political economy (Abraham 2016; Cox et al. 2016; Scott 2009, 2016; Kalbfleisch and Abraham 2016; Sano-Franchini 2016; Zebroski 2017). Nevertheless, to date, only a modest number of scholars working in the field have explicitly explored the problem of debt (Bollig 2015; Bousquet 2008). This reticence is somewhat surprising given that many in the professoriate carry student loan debt well into their teaching years (Kelsky 2014). One explanation may be that the student debt crisis is simply too recent to have become a major interest of the field. Academics may also have avoided addressing the subject pedagogically out of a sense of shame regarding their own debt, what philosopher Elettra Stimilli (2016) calls a "state of lacking" (12). However, other professors, as Leontina Hormel and Lynn M. McAlister report (2017), often simply fail to connect their own outstanding student debt to the mounting debt obligations of their students (16).

Notably, there are several crucial reasons student debt specifically, and not debt broadly conceived, should be taken up in the anticapitalist writing classroom. For the roughly three-fourths of college students who graduate with debt, the net economic value of education is the framework through which higher education will inevitably be viewed. While a purely financial assessment of the value of academic departments has long been the prerogative of university administrations,[2] the growth of student debt also entails that composition, along with all other disciplines, will increasingly be understood by students through an economic lens. As I contend, this trend necessitates a pedagogical response to the pervasive logics of valuation. Additionally, while all forms of debt operate persuasively, situating debtors as powerless and deficient, the student-loan industry is particularly pernicious for the ways it leverages security and middle-class membership to attract young customers it will pursue antagonistically.[3] Last, and perhaps most obviously, as student debt is the form of indebtedness our work as compositionists touches most vitally, it is the form of debt upon which our field can have the most impact.

In this chapter, I first provide a brief timeline of the college loan industry[4] to demonstrate the extent of the contemporary debt crisis and to illuminate how it emerged from the privatization of higher education and the attendant transition from grant programs to debt. I then discuss how composition scholars have glossed over the consequence of student debt, missing opportunities to engage students in a crucial aspect of contemporary capitalism that uniquely disempowers them. I subsequently discuss how disciplinary approaches to debt, in overestimating composition's ability to prepare students for capitalist conditions, have failed to offer a sufficiently realistic assessment of economic conditions or of the profound impact of student debt upon individuals' agency and capacity for commoning. Addressing the discipline's restricted view of debt's operation, I turn to several leading theorists of debt from beyond the discipline, Nancy in particular, to illustrate debt's complex material and ideological function and to support a pedagogical program devoted to its analysis.

STUDENT DEBT: A TOUR

As Sara Goldrick-Rab (2016) details, the federal government was not always in the business of giving concessions lenders. The Higher Education Act of 1965 and the creation of Pell Grants in 1972, along with such previous initiatives as the GI Bill in 1944 and the National Defense of Education Act of 1958, were indeed designed to support access to affordable higher education (13–14). As Goldrick-Rab explains, in their heyday, a Pell Grant could pay for over 80 percent of four-year-college tuition and the entire cost of community college (17). However, beginning in the 1970s, conservative resistance to federal support of higher education emerged, as did the rise of what scholars term "academic capitalism" (Cantwell and Kauppinen 2014), the increasing privatization and financialization of higher education. These shifts set in motion the processes that would allow the college loan industry to become the $1.5 trillion hegemon it is today.

Beginning in the 1970s, tuition at US colleges and universities dramatically increased, driven by a complex set of shifts, including increased privatization and the explosive growth of university administration (Busch 2017, 22–23; Newfield 2016, 25).[5] At the same time, government grants, Pell Grants most notably, were reduced by half between 1979 and 2011 (Newfield 2016, 198). Pell Grants now cover under one-third of four-year college tuition and only 60 percent of community college costs (Goldrick-Rab 2016, 17). Students who were previously able to rely on grants to fund their tuition turned to loans. Christopher Newfield (2016) details how an additional long-term shift from federal to private loans began with the Nixon administration's creation of Sallie Mae, initially a government-run lender (199). The corporation, as Newfield reports, would gradually come to act as a "commercial lender" (199) over the coming decades and eventually cease to function as a broker of affordable higher education.

A variety of similar policies have contributed to increases in student debt since Nixon. Consistent with his administration's larger push to starve the undeserving poor, Ronald Reagan cut higher education spending by a quarter and tightened the eligibility for more favorable federal loans (Fergus, *Washington Post*, September 2, 2014). In the early 1990s, unsubsidized Stafford Loans and private loans were implemented and borrowing limits were increased, leading to a significant increase in the volume of loans (Hershbein and Hollenbeck 2015, 86). Unsubsidized loans, of course, are significantly less favorable to borrowers than their subsidized counterparts, most notably because interest accrues immediately (86). In 1992–1993, these loans made up only 1.9 percent of the loan market (87), yet they soon became ubiquitous, growing to 32.5 percent in 1999 (87). In 1997, Bill Clinton implemented a tax-credit program that, while billed as subsidizing higher education, funded the private-loan industry, allowing these loans to further expand (Newfield 2016, 200). In 2011–2012, unsubsidized loans increased fivefold, totaling almost $50 billion (Goldrick-Rab 2016, 89). While, as Newfield details, Barack Obama expressed concern over the problem, his various interventions, including increasing the Pell Grant ceiling and allowing loan consolidation, did little to curb it (203).

Due to these various shifts, the loan industry has seen a 1,300 percent increase over the past four decades. To put this into perspective, in 1970–1971, students borrowed $7.6 billion,[6] averaging just over $1,000 per student per year (Baum 2015, 15). By 1985–1986, these numbers had tripled, with borrowing just over $21 billion. This number would more than double by the end of the century, with $52 billion borrowed at the turn of the millennium, and then again by a decade later, with $1.1 trillion borrowed in 2012–2013 (16). Between 1999 and 2011, student loans grew over 500 percent (Newfield 2016, 195). The individual burden of student loans has also grown significantly. In 1992–1993, only 51 percent of graduates left college with outstanding loans and, on average, owed just $10,200, while among students who did not attend graduate school, 75 percent paid off their debt within ten years (Lederman 2006). By contrast, a recent study by the Institute for College Access & Success (2014) found that 71 percent of graduates from four-year colleges now hold some form of student debt and owe an average of $29,400. The study also found college graduates expect to take an average of 19.7 years to repay their debt (Hess 2017). Regarding these almost unbelievable expansions, Goldrick-Rab (2016) is unambiguous about the significance of federal resistance to subsidized loans and other forms of support for affordable education. As she writes, "The attack on loans is fundamentally an attack on the accessibility of today's system and must be understood as such" (241).

Two additional factors have contributed to the enormous growth of student loans. The first is an explosion in the attainment of higher education. As Thomas Piketty (2020) observes, in the 1960s, only about 10 percent of the population of wealthy nations attended college (535). This number has since risen to between 30 and 40 percent (535). An enormous expansion in college attendance, of course, means more students are paying for college. This rise, however, has been coupled with an attendant disinvestment in public education in the United States (535), further contributing to heavier reliance on loans. As F. King Alexander (2019) reports, public funding for higher education has declined by about half since 1981. A complicating factor here, as Piketty explains, is that the United States' funding apparatus for primary and secondary education is state-based, meaning the system is "extremely decentralized" (535) and "depends essentially on local property taxes" (535). This decentralization can lead to enormous differences in state policy concerning university funding and need-based aid. The University of Alaska is one of the most extreme examples. In 2019, the state's Republican governor Mike Dunleavy reduced the system's budget by $70 million, and to accommodate the cuts, the university's Board of Regents has since voted to shrink or cut 40 programs (Redden 2020). However, despite the cuts, in 2020, the Board of Regents voted to raise tuition by 5 percent (Clark 2020). Such conditions have effectively transferred the burden of paying for college to students themselves, who inevitably turn to the student loan industry.

COMPOSITION AND DEBT

Composition scholars have long explored political-economic issues, yet relatively few have investigated debt, let alone its rhetorical, emotional, or psychological dimensions. In glossing over these elements, writing scholars have often neglected the ways debt troubles composition's capacity to adequately prepare students to participate discursively in the contemporary world and, furthermore, to understand the processes by which debt destabilizes many graduates just as they are preparing to begin their careers. The modest disciplinary work that takes it up has been extensively influenced by cultural theorist and literary critic Jeffrey Williams's (2015) framing of debt as a didactic, affective enterprise that situates debtors within the frame of global capitalism. Williams contends that, in a localized sense, loans encourage students to view education as a "*consumer service*" (129) rather than as a site of intellectual development. He suggests more broadly that debt encourages students to see the world in purely financial terms (130–131). Williams additionally argues that the very act of paying off student debt produces an affective state of "stress, worry, and pressure, reinforced with each monthly payment" (131). Bousquet (2008) adopts Williams's metaphor of indentured servitude, suggesting debt transforms students' agency by removing financial independence and miring them within neoliberal paradigms. For Bousquet, the economics of debt create "a regime of indebtedness, producing docile financialized subjectivities" (53) that hold far-reaching sociopolitical consequences. Echoing Williams, he observes that students are encouraged to approach problems of indebtedness as consumers rather than as students or citizens (153) and hence are compelled to view education as a purchased commodity rather than as a process. Chase Bollig (2015) likewise responds to several of Williams's critiques in his investigation of college "worth-it" debates. With Bousquet, Bollig acknowledges student debt reduces the agency of workers and causes "stratification within higher education as lower-income students opt for less selective and less costly institutions" (158). He additionally contends student debt constructs a veritable underclass that "cannot afford to challenge their employer on working conditions or whose employment choices will be tailored around their debt" (158). Regarding these conditions, Bollig argues the writing classroom can and should strive to teach students to "resist and thrive" (166) in the capitalist workplace.

Pegeen Reichert Powell (2014) additionally considers how the interests of universities and students problematically diverge, particularly on financial matters such as debt. Discussing the problem of students who leave the university, she argues institutions work to improve student retention while often remaining oblivious to the exclusionary conditions that drive them away. In her estimation, universities reduce the work of education to the basic calculus of "butts in seats" (5). A crucial outcome of this oversimplified approach, she suggests, is the neglect of affective conditions at play when students leave the university. "Financial failings," she argues, "are conflated with moral failings" (88). This sense of failure, she contends, has migrated to students who leave the university with debt but no degree (88). She further speculates it is precisely because of the association of debt with moral failure that institutions have avoided the important work of self-examination concerning their own role in students leaving the university and continue with retention efforts that have little to do with supporting students (92).

While many of these approaches laudably acknowledge debt as an ideological construct, all but Bousquet generally gloss over its enduring effects while overstating composition's capacity to prepare students to navigate it. Even Reichert Powell (2014) only briefly addresses the subject of debt, yet her notion of immediately actionable pedagogy contends students who leave the university in debt but with no degree may recuperate some marginal value from their writing courses once teachers "invite the student to *participate now* as a reader and writer of the world" (118). Bollig (2015) paints a similar picture of composition's value in the context of neoliberalism and debt, arguing that by framing the writer as a "citizen-worker" (163), composition may help "students to enter the workforce conscious of how power relations . . . bear on their understanding of themselves in rhetorical workplaces" (168). Bollig is acutely conscious of how literacy myths and contemporary economic conditions intervene in questions of educational value, yet, like Reichert Powell, he defends the value of composition: "We should seek out ways to demonstrate that our work in the composition classroom is both culturally and economically valuable to students and the public at large" (Reichert Powell 2014, 168).

While I agree with Bollig and Reichert Powell that composition can confer powerful critical and collaborative skills that may help students negotiate capitalist conditions, as I defend throughout this book, I am also dubious about many of the claims of compositionists and educators regarding the value of our work. In my view, economic inequality, precarity, and student debt, in addition to the many other indignities of fast capitalism, are not merely challenges college writing, or any course, can help students simply prepare for. Certainly, we may position students to read and challenge capitalist conditions, but this work cannot hope to allow students to entirely negotiate capitalism's devastating consequences, debt specifically. Moreover, the composition classroom, due to its relationship to the university, is necessarily entwined with the problem of student debt such that any value we can hope to confer will invariably be tempered by the debt most students acquire to attend college.

I argue that, rather than believing we can confidently "prepare students for not only academic writing but also for the realities of the workforce" (Bollig 2015, 166), we must situate debt within a more expansive anticapitalist project. In the short term, compositionists should strive to communicate to students the material and persuasive power of debt and encourage them to engage in collaborative forms of critique and resistance. At the same time, we must explicitly acknowledge, to our students and to ourselves, that while our pedagogical efforts may prove useful, the composition classroom cannot entirely prepare students for the conditions they are likely to encounter. Because of the tenuous nature of twenty-first-century employment coupled with the burden of debt and countless other financial challenges, many of our students may never find lucrative work and may be utterly immobilized by debt. To be clear, these are not conditions students can handle on their own. There is no pedagogical intervention that can properly prepare a student, as an isolated individual, to navigate these conditions. It is my contention, rather, that when it comes to capitalism's influence, debt specifically, our task is to present students with the value of collective solutions so they can cooperatively seek economic justice in the years ahead. In the following section, I discuss several leading critics whose work can support teaching student debt in the composition classroom, most notably Nancy's (2017) analysis of debt as a threat to the common.

ALTERED STATES: DEBT, THE SELF, AND OTHERS

As economic inequality and financial injustices have deepened in the years of the early twenty-first century, scholars in the areas of anthropology (Graeber 2012), media studies (Berardi 2009; Dyer-Witheford 2005), sociology (Lazzarato 2012, 2015; Ross 2013), philosophy (Stimilli 2016), literary and cultural studies (McClanahan 2016), and numerous other fields have turned to the study of debt. While extremely varied, these critiques have focused on debt as a unique persuasive apparatus and a site of coercive power disguised as a banal financial mechanism. For David Graeber (2012), the late anthropologist and activist, debt is a false promise that controls by way of its seeming innocuousness. In *Debt: The First 5,000 Years*, Graeber charts how debt has managed to gain unprecedented sway in human society. As he argues, "A debt is the obligation to pay a certain sum of money. As a result, a debt, unlike any other form of obligation, can be precisely quantified" (13). Effectively, in the linking of human senses of obligation to quantifiable repayment, debt takes on a moral valence, holding the capacity "to turn morality into personal arithmetic" (14). What is, at its core, a financial transaction becomes a method of controlling (and quantifying) human behavior and human relations. This quantification, in turn, permits "things that would otherwise seem outrageous or obscene" (14) insofar as our interactions with others are often dictated by the demands of the market. In addition to creating a quantifiable sense of obligation, a debt also functions by creating an asymmetry between the debtor and the creditor. As Graeber argues, as long as a debt remains unpaid, "the logic of hierarchy takes hold" (121). This hierarchy, in turn, places the debtor in a position of culpability: "If the debtor cannot do what it takes to restore herself to equality, there is something wrong with her; it must be her fault" (121). This sense of deficiency, and of our desire to redeem ourselves, is, again, where debt obtains its power. For Graeber, the wielding of this power is broadly observable across human history. One particularly potent site is in uses of "primordial debt" (71) that provide the basis for nationalist rhetoric. As Graeber writes, "Once we owed our lives to the gods that created us. . . . Now we owe it to the Nation that formed us, pay interest in the form of taxes, and when it moves to defend the nation against its enemies, offer to pay it with our lives" (71). Another essential site of debt's power is the way it organizes human lives in the hypercapitalist era in which currency has become virtual: "Most of those working for wages or even salaries feel that they are doing so primarily to pay off interest-bearing loans" (368). On a global scale, Graeber observes a similar mechanism in which the UN, the World Bank, and the WTO employ debt peonage to enforce an imperialist system where "one has to pay one's debts" (368).

Theorist Maurizio Lazzarato, in a similar vein, constructs debt as a moralized institution with extensive coercive capacities. Beyond Graeber, Lazzarato sees debt as responsible for producing a new, deeply denatured human subject. In *The Making of an Indebted Man* (2012), he poses two central arguments: that the "paradigm of the social" (11) lies in credit and that "debt represents an economic relationship inseparable from the production of the debtor subject and his 'morality' " (11). Lazzarato contends that our contemporary social world is thoroughly and comprehensively financialized, specifically running on the mechanism of debt, and that this debt places the debtor in a position of moral obligation that is not merely a social phenomenon, as it is for Graeber, but a profound transformation of agency. Under such a system, "the debtor is 'free,' but his actions, his behavior, are confined to the limits of the debt" (31). Among its extensive consequences, for Lazzarato, debt denatures social relations and delimits the subject's behavior: "The logic of debt is stifling our possibilities for action" (71). This, of course, has extensive societal implications. As Lazzarato writes, debt effectuates "the neutralization of collective attitudes (mutualization, solidarity, cooperation, rights for all, etc.) and the memory of the collective struggles, action, and the organization of 'wage earners' and the 'proletariat' " (114). Debt, so deployed, produces an attenuated subject unable to engage ethically with the Other and thereby precludes such political goods as class consciousness or collective action. In *Governing by Debt* (2015), Lazzarato addresses the issue of student debt in the United States, a "factory of indebted students" (67). As he notes, contemporary US students who take on enormous debts to pay for their education suffer the effects of neoliberalism's long game: "the substitution of social rights . . . for access to credit. . . . No more pooling of pensions, instead individual investment in pension funds; no pay raises, instead consumer credit; no universal insurance, individual insurance" (66). Effectively, for Lazzarato, US students have taken on the burden of educational cost to free up money for "the true welfare recipients" (67), that is, "corporations and the rich" (67), what Bernie Sanders has critiqued as socialism for the 1 percent (Levitz 2019).

In a similar critique, Annie McClanahan (2016) investigates debt's function as a bad faith argument that exhorts compliance through the false promise of wealth and freedom. To be in debt, she writes, "is to be caught in an endless cycle of discredit and dispossession" (185). She frames this discussion around an evocative protest sign at UC Berkeley: " 'Thanks to Berkeley,' one protester scribbled onto the sign, 'I'm in debt forever' " (191). McClanahan interprets this and other critiques of debt's enormity as framing debt as a "shared condition" (192) and combating its rhetoric of entrepreneurship (192). She additionally argues that students acknowledging debt's permanence assert an alternative relation to the institution and "possess a demystified, canny, and radical kind of knowledge. They do not believe in a future 'good life' of financial security and middle-class mobility" (195). What follows from such acknowledgment, McClanahan asserts, should not be despair concerning the immutability of our financial burdens but rather a collective consciousness antagonistic to late capitalism. "To be in debt forever," McClanahan writes, "is to refuse to be in debt at all" (197). As she concludes, to accept debt's permanence is, paradoxically, to oppose its transactional logic and to "throw a wrench into the very machinery of social production" (197).

These approaches offer a much-needed level of depth to composition's existing investigation of debt. In particular, they present a view of debt as a living, rhetorical enterprise that exerts various forms of control, precisely the opposite of the way lenders strive to present it. They likewise frame debt as a form of bad faith, what Graeber (2012) terms "the perversion of a promise" (392), an enterprise that presents prospective debtors with a rigged bargain in which prosperity is promised but moral judgement and enduring debt are delivered. These perspectives are invaluable for conceptualizing a pedagogical approach to debt's social role and persuasive power. However, my own teaching of the subject has been most significantly informed by Nancy's (2017) essay "Gratuitousness and Recognition," a work that extends the philosopher's critique of capitalism articulated in other texts, most significantly *The Truth of Democracy* (2010), which critiques capitalism for imposing a regime of "equivalence" (23) upon the world. Like Lazzarato (2012), Nancy (2017) argues debt profoundly transforms subjects. However, in Nancy's construction, non-unity, that is, difference, is the mechanism from which the work of politics emerges and, consequently, what is threatened by the imposition of financial logics of equivalence. This argument, I contend, suggests a pedagogical approach of staging an essential conflict between debt and the common.

In "Gratuitousness and Recognition," Nancy (2017) argues monetary debt and its mechanisms of extraction and exploitation represent an affront to the essential capacity of humans to be together, to share a life *in common*. Financial forms of debt, he suggests, "disregard every recognition other than that of the debt itself." At the core of human relations, as Nancy contends, is the act of recognition, the event through which the individual registers and is registered by another. For Nancy, it is through this event of mutual recognition that one indeed becomes a subject. He further argues recognition constitutes the essence, the brick and mortar, of the social. "Sociality, community, or collectivity," he writes, "represents nothing else than the imbrication of language, of recognition, and of mutual engagement . . . togetherness is not added to being but constitutes it." Financial debts, he asserts, intervene in the essential processes of human relations by imposing a financial order, a deficit, upon interpersonal relations and occluding the crucial site of politics. Like Graeber (2012) in his equating debt to a form of financialized operation, Nancy (2017) posits that an "economy of recognition," a system of debt and credit, are always operative in interpersonal relations, albeit with several significant differences from the financial world. "Debt and credit," he writes, "circulate originally between all. Debt first, when one considers the expectation or the demand for recognition; and credit first, if we imagine a recognition that precedes the demand." In these contexts, debt and credit constitute the natural, even necessary, essence of relation. For Nancy, subjects are continually giving and receiving recognition, paying abstract debts, and collecting abstract credits in ways supportive of social life. While these forms of debtor-creditor relation run the risk of going unreciprocated—"The condition of recognition implies the possibility of refusal to be recognized. The condition of debt implies the possibility that it will not be honored"—the lack of reciprocation, as Nancy contends, is not catastrophic. In his formulation, to be willing to give recognition without receiving is an act of kindness, what he calls being "gracious." This is a crucial component of building a life with others. Nancy juxtaposes these conditions with the intrusion of the debtor-creditor relation in the contemporary financial world. As he argues, "Interest-bearing loans, borrowing, and other financial operations" adulterate the economy of recognition. Nancy contends that, by forcing subjects into financial relations that ignore alternative, noneconomic forms of recognition, financial debt threatens the potential of being-with and community more broadly. In interacting with others as mechanisms of the financial, as subjects, we no longer recognize others in a social sense and are no longer willing to comport with them, to be gracious. Unlike in social contexts in which one acts without the expectation of reciprocation, asymmetries in the financial relation are destructive and exploitative; they are gratuitous rather than gracious. These changed mechanisms of the social relation capitalism imposes, Nancy argues, threaten the substance of community.

Beyond composition's as yet tepid critique of debt's role, Nancy and similarly oriented critics provide a framework for understanding debt in far more expansive and attentive ways than the discipline has previously done. Across these varied and nuanced critiques, debt is not simply an apparatus of late capitalism's material expansion but rather an extension of capitalist logic that imposes a debilitating set of ideological constrictions upon the political subject. For Graeber (2010) and McClanahan (2016), debt represents the false promise of business as usual, moral standing, and impermanence, claims that unwittingly draw individuals into conditions of enormous exploitation. For Lazzarato (2012), the consequences are even more dire insofar as the contemporary conditions of financial capitalism create an indebted (and ultimately powerless) political subject that only ever exists within the context of the financial world. Similarly, and most significantly, Nancy (2017) understands debt as an acute risk to the social, a form of homogenization that flattens and attenuates the potential of human connection, submitting it to a financial calculus of equivalence. In his view, the potential of the subject to relate and engage with the Other has been fundamentally displaced by the logics of debt such that the formation of the common, through "gracious" acts, is imperiled.

In pedagogical terms, these approaches, Nancy's in particular, suggest a variety of applications. Three are particularly evident: (1) working with students through critical examinations of debt as a persuasive actor, specifically a mechanism of erasure that dissuades consideration of debt's own persuasive and moral function and deters social and communal participation, (2) helping students to see debt as specifically detrimental to the common insofar as it imposes a financial calculus upon social relations, and (3) encouraging students' exploration of solutions to debt's power that reassert human connection over financial relations. In the following discussion of my own pedagogical practice, I suggest how these principles might guide the teaching of debt in the writing classroom.

"WITHOUT YOU THERE—THERE YOU ARE": TEACHING DEBT'S PEDAGOGY

Approaching debt with students, it must be said, is difficult going. In my own experience, I would be hard pressed to name a topic that, at least initially, stifles conversation more or makes students as uncomfortable. One, cannot, however, oversimplify these responses. Some students I've encountered, a surprising number, in fact, seem to have no opinion whatsoever on debt and resist being drawn into discussions on the subject. Typically, these are students who hold no debt themselves and who, consequently, resist seeing the subject as relevant to their lives or education. Despite the fact that these students have peers many thousands of dollars in debt, they are often unaware and seemingly unconcerned with how the student-loan industry functions. In a recent advanced writing class, a nontraditional student several years older than the rest of my sophomore class raised such an objection, announcing debt didn't concern him as he was paying for his education entirely out of pocket. In another course, a debt-free student remained staunchly undisturbed by the operation of the debt industry, even after having read an affecting portrayal of wage garnishment. Many of these students hold a surprisingly inflexible view that debt is not their problem and are defiant when asked to view debt critically. As I understand it, this position is not simply born of general ignorance but rather reflects that debt, re Graeber (2012, 14), occupies a deeply moralized, even taboo, position for many students.

I've encountered another subset of students, more informed than the first, who nevertheless resist seeing the conditions of student debt as problematic or the college loan industry as exploitative. Even when presented with evidence of the disreputable actions of lenders, these students contend that because students enter willingly into debt agreements, blame cannot be placed upon lenders. For students articulating this argument, if there is a problem, it is the rising cost of tuition, not debt. One student offered this argument in a recent course when the subject arose, contending that debt is simply a transaction, something not really worth thinking about, and that tuition is the real culprit. Of course, the student was not wrong to point to the rising cost of education—Goldrick-Rab (2016) notably views tuition, not debt, as the central issue in college's lack of affordability (241). Nevertheless, debt holds and deploys a unique set of persuasive powers that, as I contend, are worthy of specific attention. I attempted to explain this to the student, noting that the rising cost of college and the exploitative nature of the debt industry are, in fact, associated insofar as they reflect the effects of neoliberal educational policy over the past several decades. In this defense of my focus, I mentioned Andrew Ross's (2013) argument that the United States government has long been in the process of transferring responsibility for the funding of education to individuals (and, by extension, to the loan industry) but has accelerated this effort in recent years by dramatically cutting its funding of higher education (25). The student, however, remained resistant to the notion that the debt industry, or debt itself, could be either rhetorical or, for that matter, problematic.

A third type of student is already aware of debt's power and its connections to neoliberalism's ascendency. These students, in the minority to be sure, often speak passionately and articulately about student debt and strive to inform others about the problematic state of the college loan industry. In general, they are active in social justice organizations on campus, participate in community service, and are generally informed about politics. In other words, the students who are already progressive are often able to speak on the issue and need little persuading that debt represents a unique source of capitalist power worthy of critique. Naturally, such students are rare.

To build on my previous assertions, the reasons most students are reticent to approach debt are, to my reading, largely a reflection of debt's material crisis and ideological power. With every passing year, college students take on increasingly burdensome debt loads as they work to obtain a credential with diminishing value (Vedder and Strehle, *Wall Street Journal*, June 4, 2017) and prepare to encounter a working world that, in many respects, is more unequal and precarious than it has ever been. Students, variously, face the prospect of wage garnishment and default if they are unable to pay their monthly premiums. They are additionally facing down a retention crisis, which debt compounds. As David Kirp (2019) reports, 34 million Americans over the age of twenty-five, over 10 percent of the population, are college dropouts (3). These students overwhelmingly carry significant amounts of college debt but are twice as likely as graduates to be unemployed and four times as likely to default (3). Students are additionally positioned by debt's ideological effects such that discussing their debt load, let alone critiquing it, is affectively charged. Re Graeber (2012) and Lazzarato (2012, 2015), for many students, even if they claim to hold no opinion on the subject, to be in debt is to be deficient, to have erred, to be wanting. For college students, being in debt implies an intrinsic imperfection, to come from a family too poor to afford to pay for college outright or to not be meritorious enough to have been awarded scholarships. For these reasons, even simply generating a discussion on debt can be nearly impossible. However, I maintain our students' reticence to address the subject reveals the necessity of doing so, particularly for students who are aware of the enormity of student debt and the power of financial institutions. Because these students invariably bear the burden of debt but don't have the perspective to understand how they have been positioned and disempowered by it, presenting them with debt's power and preparing them to critique it is a crucial task. The pedagogical interventions I now turn to attempt to help students map the enormity of the student debt problem, to understand how the debt industry and debt itself have obtained and maintained financial and affective power, and to consider responsive action. Regarding Nancy's (2017) assertion that the order of debt imposes a regime of equivalence, I believe what is fundamental to this task is guiding students toward an understanding that debt imposes economic ways of thinking that displace other forms of relation and, indeed, the political work that emerges from the recognition of others as potential collaborators. However, as previously noted, this pedagogical approach can only hope to push students toward collective critique. To solve the problem of student debt, students, along with graduates, instructors, and other members of the public, must be prepared to construct a massive anticapitalist coalition. This pedagogical approach prepares students to envision it.

For students to approach debt with the level of sophistication necessary to understand both its material and ideological operations as sites of profound exploitation and potential resistance, they must at least have a passing sense of how capitalism has expanded and accelerated across the past four decades, with particular attention to the student-loan industry. Readings and short writing assignments on topics such as social class, economic inequality, and consumer debt can productively set the scene for later analysis. While a variety of texts could be effectively used to support such an introduction, and indeed could be scaled up or down in difficulty depending on students' level of preparation, works by Noam Chomsky, Naomi Klein, Henry Giroux, and Yanis Varoufakis are accessible for college students with no economic background. In particular, Varoufakis's (2018) *Talking to My Daughter about the Economy, or How Capitalism Works—And How It Fails* is valuable in this regard. Varoufakis, economist, former Greek finance minister, and cofounder (with theorist and activist Srećko Horvat) of the Democracy in Europe Movement 2025 (DiEM25), provides a nontechnical introduction to various concepts relevant to contemporary global capitalism. On debt, for example, Varoufakis employs the story of Doctor Faustus to illustrate how debt and profit have long been entangled in capitalist societies, fueling both enormous gains in wealth and economic inequality. Varoufakis writes, "Debt, as Doctor Faustus shows us, is to market societies what hell is to Christianity: unpleasant yet indispensable" (59).

To offer such an introduction, I've asked students to rhetorically analyze portions of *The Debt Resisters' Operations Manual* (Strike Debt 2012), a document that allows students to study public activism critical of the neoliberal rhetoric of class membership and debt's impermanence. Deeply resonant with Nancy's (2017) construction of "gratuitousness," the document's chapter on student debt illuminates how fear appeals are employed to thrust students into compromised financial positions: "Fear of an uncertain financial future drives many of us toward higher education.... Lenders are making profits off of that fear, and so education has become one of the biggest debt traps in our society" (30). The assignment also allows students to learn actionable information regarding debt's precise function, details that could significantly inform their agency. The text, for example, explains delinquency, default, deferral, consolidation, and forgiveness programs (33), providing debtors with information about how their debt will be assessed and tactics for negotiating it. Additionally, the text offers advice about contesting debt and defaulting (33–34), suggesting, echoing Graeber's (2012) claims regarding debt's moralization (4), that the repayment of debt is not an obligation but rather a transaction that can be negotiated or even refused. In analyzing the document's expository function and its call for collective action, students are exposed to models of resistance against an economic institution that demonstrate the utility of public critique and offer reproducible examples of resistance. *The Debt Resisters' Operations Manual*, for example, details the work of Student Loan Justice, Forgive Student Debt to Stimulate the Economy, and the Occupy Student Debt Campaign (35–36), groups that organize in opposition to the debilitating operation of the student-loan industry, and clarifies how people can become involved.

While such a document effectively introduces both the material and persuasive conditions of student debt, discussions and written analyses have yielded mixed responses. Some students, those who already are versed in the material conditions of student debt, have said little is surprising about the conditions *The Debt Resisters' Operations Manual* describes. Others, however, have described surprise and anger at being confronted with the ways paying for college have been subject to rising levels of exploitation. Others have responded with sadness and dismay that the United States, despite its wealth, allows students to be penalized with extreme debt. Others still have been struck by the nature of the privatization of student debt, namely that debt has become an industry rather than a service. In their discussion of the issue, students with this point of view have noted the dissonance between public claims to debt's benevolence and its operation as an industry. Taking a different tactic, other students have remarked how the public discourse on college education, along with student debt, typically occludes the financial operation of debt. These omissions, students have noted, allow universities and lenders to promote success and a middle-class life while often entirely obscuring what students are getting themselves into. An additional, deeply illuminating perspective has been that of international students, who often have limited experience with debt and approach it from the perspective of outside observers. Students of mine from China and Germany, for example, have described vastly dissimilar conditions of higher education funding in their home countries. To these students, the concept of college debt is often alien and, frequently, dismaying. Some of the most adamant critiques of debt have come from these students, many of whom have been socialized to view higher education as a right.

An alternative approach to the introduction of debt is to present students with literary expressions of debt's current economic function. An unorthodox strategy that risks occluding the material aspects of debt in favor of the persuasive, the affective, and the cognitive, selectively employing literature nevertheless offers to introduce debt in ways relatable to students. I've assigned Timothy Donnelly's (2010) poem "To His Debt" from his collection *The Cloud Corporation*, a humorous work that explores debt's mercurial positionality, its permanence, and its agency. Ostensibly a poison pen to debt, the poem positions debt as a beloved adversary the author cannot distance himself from. Donnelly presents debt's protean nature through a variety of shifting metaphors: "my massive shadow / dressed in numbers" (7), "my history, my backdrop" (7), and "My phantom, my crevasse, my emphatically unfunny hippopotamus" (7). McClanahan (2016), notably, provides an erudite reading of the text, analyzing the poem through the framework of Paul de Man's concept of prosopopoeia, a literary device in which the author speaks as another person or object. Quoting de Man's definition, McClanahan notes that prosopopoeia "posits the possibility of [an absent, deceased, or voiceless entity's] reply and confers upon it the power of speech" (91). Donnelly's poem, McClanahan argues, "gives debt voice" (92) by addressing it directly. "Debt," she elaborates, "is given body, face, feeling, will" (93). She further contends the poem "stages transformation of quality into quantity" (93) and dramatizes both Friedrich Engels's second law, "the interpenetration of opposites" (93), by juxtaposing debt's immensity with its lack, and his third law, "negation of negation, since debt appears to flicker in and out of personhood . . . and becomes a kind of suspended, ephemeral, and thus ultimately dissolvable subject or annihilable subject" (93). She additionally argues that the final lines of the poem, which depict the speaker as being fed upon by a bat and, paradoxically, as the bat itself, "both starved and predatory" (93), illustrate debt's capacity for "self-reproduction" (93).

When faced with this poem and with the task of combing through the various metaphors in order to link the evocation of debt to its real-world valence, students were able to make an analysis approaching McClanahan's level of sophistication. In presenting this poem in class and asking groups of students to study passages, I was largely pleased with the incisive discussions, analyses, and questions that arose. Though, upon an initial reading, Li announced the poem "kind of sucks," she and others eventually moved past its somewhat silly metaphors toward effective exegeses of what ultimately amounts to a provocative critique. Looking to the poem's contradictions, depictions of debt as both presence and absence, students discussed the contradictory phenomenological aspects of twenty-first-century debt. They discussed, for instance, the poem in relation to student debt as a staggeringly high figure, a "weight," and as a negative or an absence in the form of diminished options and life opportunities. Students were particularly struck by the final lines of the poem, which many interpreted as depicting the consumer's forced complicity in their own exploitation. As many read it, the poem depicts the ways debtors are effectively pressed into debt through societal expectations and the promise of a middle-class life only to find their own decisions have been self-annihilating. Insofar as debtors agree to lenders' conditions, debtors are exploiting themselves.

With the poem, debt can be presented to students as a limitation of subjectivity, a view resonant with Nancy's (2017) critique of capitalist blinkering. In the context of the poem, debt submits all relations to the calculus of indebtedness, diminishing all other possible forms of relation to that of the financial. Debt, for the poet, is "my history, my backdrop" (Donnelly 2010, 7). It is ubiquitous and hegemonic, seemingly preventing other forms and valences of experience. Debt, moreover, constructs the poet's life as one of privation: "you who put the kibosh / on fine dining and home theater, dentistry" (7). In these lines, debt is not only preventing access to care, experiences, and material goods, but it has organized the poet's life as one of absence. Other forms of desire or valences of experience are extirpated and replaced with debt's calculus. Debt anxieties, likewise, occupy the poet's unconscious—the poet dreams of being buried in a potter's field: "even when I dream / I awaken in an unmarked pocket of earth / without you there—there you are" (8). Here, debt controls the poet's experience so extensively it has populated the life of the mind with economic fears. An acid love letter to the author's debt, the poem notably acknowledges no other human subject or social relation. Debt, rather, seems to have subsumed them all. This, according to Nancy (2017), is precisely how debt functions, by assimilating all forms of relation into the financial relation. Debt, in his construction, "sublates recognition and confidence." In reading the poem in this way, students can be positioned to consider debt not simply as something to be paid or endured but rather as an institution in need of critical opposition.

Moving beyond introductions to contemporary policy and the role of debt, it is advisable to engage students in more direct readings of debt's material and persuasive function and, likewise, to assign them forms of analysis that seek to understand how debt functions in contemporary society as a persuasive apparatus. While, as I've suggested, students benefit greatly when provided with the appropriate context with which to understand debt's general operation, it is valuable to assign critiques that synthesize debt's persuasive aspects with its concrete, material ones. To this end, I've asked students to analyze and respond to anthropologist Hadas Weiss's (2019) *We Have Never Been Middle Class*, an epigrammatic work contending the middle class is less a viable class category than an ideological mechanism exhorting greater participation in global capitalism. In framing the work, Weiss argues capitalist dominance "projects an image of every human being as a self-determining investor of money, time or effort, if not at this very moment then in potential aspiration" (11). In such a context, individuals are persuaded to adopt a variety of beliefs concerning independence and self-sufficiency, as well as to engage in risky financial activities in order to acquire middle-class respectability. Debt, for Weiss, is one aspect of this ideological system that requires that we continually invest in ourselves, amassing cultural capital for the prospect of a better future and taking on debt that will be paid once our lives improve. While Weiss is ultimately less critical of debt as an institution than Nancy or others mentioned in this chapter, she nevertheless contends that debt amounts to a false, bad faith exchange and that it is this discovery that promotes critical subjectivity. As she writes, "The real turning point in our potential awareness comes when the value of our indebted property becomes too unpredictable to make the promised prefigured by investment in it plausible" (49–50). Whether this property is a house with an underwater mortgage or a degree devalued by the contemporary job market, for Weiss, this diminished value is both inevitable and instructive. Among numerous benefits, the text presents students with a model for interrogating debt's rhetorical function by asking them to consider the ways education and housing are sold as necessary and stable investments—necessary, in particular, for participating in the middle class—despite the fact that going into debt to acquire these things is precarious and often harmful.

In a writing class I taught that focused on the subject of debt and the cultures of work, I asked students to consider Weiss's argument about the ideological valence of the middle class and to respond to her argument that debt, along with education, housing, and consumerism more broadly, is a mechanism of control. In many of their papers, students demonstrated a heightened understanding of the complex financial entanglements contemporary students are enmeshed in when they enter the university system. In analyzing the text, one student, Samra, expounded on the senseless process of "getting a university degree, buying a house by taking out a mortgage, and getting credit cards to build credit, when all it does is just accumulate debt." As she noted, the rhetorical conditions of this exchange secure the buy-in of the aspirational middle class while delivering far less than promised. "People," she argues, are habitually "failed by a system that they have trusted in . . . that was supposed to help them succeed and prosper in society but it has only left them with incredible debt and situations where the promises, that middle class has been all about, became a burden to carry." In her analysis, Samra recognized the bad-faith arrangement debt represents. As she contends, debt functions rhetorically to secure trust, with promises of financial success, but this promise amounts to a false exchange in which the consumer invests for greater security only to become more precarious. Another student, Rhiannon, mirroring Caitlin Zaloom's (2019) critique, noted how these conditions do not simply harm students but injure families as well: "Families fall victim to this cycle for innocent reasons, to hopefully create a better life for themselves, and an even better life for their children and family members." Li offered an even more incisive perspective, isolating debt as a specifically US problem in which the dominant forms of financial power have successfully persuaded the public to accept a model of prosperity that leads them into debt. "America," she writes, "has sold us this image that the middle class is 'good' despite the fact that the middle class must take on investments in education, assets, etc. which lead to financial debt." She further elaborates that "debt is something that we almost celebrate in America, and we allow for these institutions to tell us that in order to have 'good' standing in society, we must follow rugged individualism and pool money into these assets that may not even become useful to us in the future." Similarly, in class discussions of the text, students agreed with Weiss's critique and expressed similarly critical perspectives on debt as an aggressively sold commodity that entails enormous risk. However, in both writing assignments and in class discussion, students were often left without a clear sense of the utility of their critiques. Some expressed a sense of resignation, a feeling that student debt is harmful but that, at least under the current system, it is an unavoidable feature of attaining a college education. This, critically, is why any treatment of debt in the composition classroom, however brief, must include discussion of potential solutions to the contemporary student debt crisis.

Following my overarching commitment to common anticapitalist solutions, and, more specifically, to Nancy's (2017) conceptualization of debt as the annihilation of collective politics, I suggest students must be presented with collaborative models of debt resistance to communicate the potential and utility of popular activism. *The Debt Resisters' Operations*

Manual (Strike Debt 2012), a text I previously mentioned teaching as an introduction to the persuasive and exploitative conditions of contemporary debt, also potentially serves as a primer on resistance and a template for collaborative writing. Students could be asked, for instance, to emulate its model and produce public writing on the rhetoric of the contemporary financial world. Inviting students to create a manual, a podcast, a video, a website, a petition, or a series of blog posts, such an assignment could allow students to actualize their coursework by communicating it to a broader audience, thereby underscoring the utility of public communication to challenge dominant discourses and schemes. Such public engagement is, of course, supported by composition scholars of the social turn (Deluca 2013; Farmer 2013, Mathieu 2005). Frank Farmer (2013), for example, offers an impassioned defense of such forms of public, politically engaged writing by way of the zine. "The zinester bricoleur," Farmer writes, "crafts the latest installment of her homemade zine, and in so doing, crafts an identity, a politics, an ethic, a culture, and a way of being in the world" (53). Similar forms of nonstandard public writing on debt could effectively provide students with a means of circulating their study of the financial world in ways that would work toward crafting oppositional discourse communities while illuminating the power of public rhetoric to confront neoliberal institutions. Concerning Nancy's (2017) assertion that debt refigures the Other as a purely financial entity—"I exist and I recognize them as the existents who carry this (con)fidence or this fiduciary quality, which I dispense back to them"—collective labor organized as the critique of capitalism, rather than its fulfillment, offers to challenge dominant financial logics by gathering people as partners, collaborators, and comrades (Dean 2019) rather than those entering into a financial exchange.

Insofar as the current debt movement, while rhetorically successful, has few policy victories to claim, presenting students with recent historical examples of more materially successful debt resistance movements offers to provide valuable insight into what can be achieved through activism. One case study that could serve as a model for productive debt resistance for students is Mexico's El Barzón movement of the 1990s, which began in Jalisco in 1993 and grew to five hundred thousand members (Caffentzis 2013, 826–827). As George Caffentzis (2013) details in his analysis, El Barzón began to grow dramatically in 1994 when it confronted the Mexican government over the effects of the peso's devaluation on loans and interest rates (826). Employing a variety of strategies such as civil protest and the filing of legal briefs, the movement successfully forced government intervention (827). For Caffentzis, El Barzón is pedagogically useful because it offers a model of successful collective action on the issue of debt and because it models a movement comprised of "interclass alliances" (828). This model, likewise, offers the promise of nonfinancial forms of unity, "sociality, community, or collectivity" (Nancy 2017) that rest in "recognition" rather than exploitation. Studying this movement through Nancy's framework allows students to approach an alternative modality of social relations, one managed by the debt relation but oriented through solidarity. These alliances, as Caffentzis (2013) notes, demonstrate both the strengths and weaknesses of large social movements. While they are illustrative of the creation of a common movement comprised of enormous diversity, "small farmers, middle-class urban homeowners, and capitalists in 'declining' industries" (828), this diversity was also a source of political tension. For Caffentzis, studying this tension can be illustrative for contemporary debt resistance movements looking to create diverse coalitions. From the perspective of the composition classroom, understanding debt resistance is both possible and, moreover, effective when comprised of diverse groups can help suggest to students the utility of common solutions and the necessity of rhetorical approaches that seek to gather large and diverse bodies of interlocutors.

CONCLUSION

In 2018, Natural Light, the budget, low-calorie beer brand, released a Super Bowl ad announcing a $1 million giveaway in support of student debt relief (Hess 2018). Featuring college students sliding down a dorm hallway converted into a Slip N' Slide, the ad exhorted viewers to "keep your college stories epic, not epic college debts." The following year, the brand expanded the giveaway to $10,000,000 over a decade—as Daniel Blake, senior director of Value Brands at Anheuser-Busch, said, "Natty Light is committed to our loyal drinkers, and we recognize that student loan debt is something that has a particularly big impact on many of their lives" (Hess 2019b). In 2021, the company unveiled the *Da Vinci of Debt*, an art installation in New York City's Grand Central Terminal featuring twenty-six hundred college diplomas spiraling up to the ceiling as if caught in a cyclone (Zhang 2021). As Madeline Luckel (2021) observed in *Architectural Digest*, "If each degree represented was priced at $180,000—the average cost of a four-year college education in the U.S.—the sculpture would be valued at $470 million."

The repositioning of a beer brand once known only as a budget option for college binge drinkers—in 2018, the brand introduced a seventy-seven pack, "77 Natties in a box" (Nelson 2019)—as an ostensive critic of college debt is indicative of the extent to which anxieties about college debt have become fully integrated into the college experience. Debt anxieties are now apparently ubiquitous enough to be the main ploy through which a popular consumer product is sold, even one supposedly about cutting loose. Such branding suggests students, even when working through a case of cheap beer with friends, are never not thinking about debt. While some scholars in composition have begun to address these conditions, as I argue in this chapter, direct attention to student debt remains nominal in the field. Given the enormity of the student debt crisis and its obvious relevance to composition, it is time to begin having critical conversations on the issue of debt in the writing classroom.

While I have previously advocated an entire course on student debt (Daniel 2018), subsequent experience has shown this to be risky. I continue to support McClanahan's (2016) assertion that debt is "the defining feature of economic life today" (1) and is hence worthy of sustained attention, but I have come to believe the difficulty and emotionally charged nature of the subject matter necessitates a more cautious and less sustained approach. A unit, assignment, or even a conversation on debt will likely be illuminating for students, most of whom will not have considered debt's persuasive capacities or viewed lenders as anything more than neutral entities. A discussion of debt, I believe, is ideal if integrated into courses grounded in work (Reichert Powell 2014, 120; Scott 2009, 139) and positioned, as Reichert Powell puts it, to be "relevant to real problems and questions that circulate in the students' lives" (119). While such work will certainly do little to forgive the enormous debt students acquire, it may better prepare students to parse debt and, perhaps, to become engaged in coalitional movements to do away with the student debt crisis for good.

Some might notably be perturbed that the anticapitalist approach I am adopting is drifting further and further from what, for many, constitutes best practices in composition. In the introduction, I address my reasoning for this somewhat untraditional approach as a necessary direction for the writing classroom given the enormity of capitalist crises. In chapter 1, I present collaborative writing assignments that are more devoted to transforming students into political collaborators, albeit ones deeply engaged in writing and learning, than with simply improving students' writing facility. In this chapter, I likewise suggest that what is most important is that students come to understand debt as a rhetorical mechanism that, per Lazzarato (2012), "stifl[es] our possibilities for action" (71). Writing, while it lies at the center of this chapter, is nevertheless posed as less significant than the intellectual and social encounter with and against debt. Consequently, it might be alleged that teaching debt, particularly in the way I propose, is not the most effective means of providing students with the kinds of writing competency they require or, indeed, demand. To return to an issue I raise in the introduction, Irving Peckham (2010) argues that writing instruction's central aim, particularly regarding the needs of working-class learners, should be to build students' writing skills. Critical interventions, in his estimation, only serve "to blur our focus on problems with style, grammar, and conventions" (142). He further asserts students may resent attempts to alter their thinking (142). However, Patricia Bizzell, one of several scholars to have countered this argument, compellingly suggests taking up social issues and viewing them rhetorically is entirely consistent with building critically engaged writers insofar as it contributes to students' critical abilities and their future success: "We help students develop abilities that will help them succeed in and beyond college. . . . [W]hile we are doing this teaching and to aid us in doing it, we can assign materials that raise issues of social justice and foster reflection on rhetorical methods of engaging such issues" (Bizzell and Fish 2009, 98). With Bizzell, I suggest that studying how debt intervenes in students' lives and how activists have opposed it offers to grow students as writers while immersing them in the work of social and public engagement. I additionally contend that studying social and political issues, particularly the mechanics of economic inequality, austerity, and debt, enhances students' practical knowledge in ways that may serve them as they confront the immense challenges of capitalist life.

3
WORK

In her 2018 novel *Severance*, Ling Ma satirizes the twenty-first-century iteration of Max Weber's Protestant work ethic, depicting the lives of precarious young workers toiling throughout a global pandemic. The novel tells the story of Candace Chen, a Fujian-born New Yorker who puts in long hours at an unfulfilling job in publishing. Underemployed and underpaid, Candace's tenuous financial life is a constant source of anxiety: "My salary was enough to keep my head above water month to month. Given my rent and lack of financial savvy, I had very little in savings, let alone retirement funds. . . . I'd be priced out of every borough in another decade" (13). For much of the novel, Candace toggles between feverish productivity—"I sat down at my desk. Once I started, I was good at losing myself. I popped some Tylenol and the morning passed in a blur" (23)—and various forms of housebound entertainment available to those without disposable income. Someone with a corporate position who nevertheless feels herself to be financially doomed, she typifies the unstable position of many millennials, underpaid but consummately industrious. When the apocalypse comes in the form of a low-key zombie plague, Candace continues to show up to work, furiously multitasking as the city empties out. "In the end," she writes, "there was the empty office. It was dark inside, smaller and more sparse. . . . We, the remaining employees, circled around in our smaller confines, bumping against locked rooms we weren't allowed to enter" (232). In a dark irony, Candace's eventual destination after the fall of society is "the Facility," an abandoned mall in Illinois where the occupational rhythms of the prior world continue unabated: "In the end, we have come to the Facility to work. We work on the weekdays, rest on the weekends. Adhering to the typical work week schedule, however ridiculous, feels strangely comforting" (221).

Many have since noted how Ma's novel anticipated the way the coronavirus outbreak of 2020 would further expose the profound inequalities within late capitalism. Jane Hu (2020), writing on this connection, observes that, like in the novel, COVID-19 "links the world not only through a circulation of a shared virus, but in how it has brought out our overwhelming reliance on capitalist accumulation and its vicious supply chains." This reliance has been painfully laid bare in the ways workers in the global supply chain, most of whom are precarious and lacking in paid leave, have been compelled to work regardless of the dangers. Many have noted the irony of these workers being termed "essential"—as sociologist Ruha Benjamin (2020) comments, essential workers are "essential to exploit, essential to sacrifice, essential to expose, essential to gaslight, essential to coerce, essential to romanticize." Studies now show that those most exposed to the disease were low-income workers (Jin and McGill 2020), effectively deemed disposable by the global financial apparatus.

Looking to orient students to the capitalist valence of occupational logics, this chapter moves to the subject of the working world, specifically the question of how the composition classroom can productively approach the increasingly unequal, precarious, demanding, and exploitative conditions of contemporary work and position students to parse and resist them. As this chapter contends, contemporary forms of work, what Horner (2016) defines as the formalization of labor practices, often localized in sites or organizations, "which have . . . been ongoing throughout human history" (97), have become a critical site of late-capitalist dominance and exploitation rivalling some of the most egregious conditions of the industrial revolution. Workers today suffer the consequences of antiunion policy and rhetoric, casualization, the exponential growth of productivity expectations, and the expectation of ideological buy-in, conditions profoundly harmful to both individuals and collectives. However, despite these circumstances, composition's criticism of capitalist exploitation remains scant. Some critics, of course, have addressed these issues over the past several decades, though mostly on the subject of the working conditions of precarious academics (Abraham 2016; Bousquet 2002; Horner and Lu 2010; Welch and Scott 2016). However, compositionists often neglect what literary critic Anna Katharina Schaffner (2016) regards as a crucial shift from prior paradigms, namely that the "boundaries between public and private selves, between work and leisure, and profession and calling, are becoming ever more blurred" (13).

This chapter argues the anticapitalist classroom must attend to the metastasis of work Schaffner (2016) names, specifically the exploitation, the control, and the disposability of workers, as well as the dominance of the logics of "peak performance"[1] that typify the contemporary scene of work. These rhetorical and material conditions, I suggest, pose acute risks to both individual workers and to the common more extensively, exposing the individual to physical and mental harm and attenuating the capacities for recognition, organizing, and solidarity among workers in contexts of contemporary labor. Throughout its varied iterations and formations—in gig and contingent labor framed as "flexible" (213) by employers; in superfluous professions that demand the appearance of industriousness, what Graeber (2018) terms "bullshit jobs"; or in professions like those in the tech world that demand identification with the company ethos—the contemporary working world represents a site of capitalism's profound attenuation of critical potential and collective spirit. Because of this, I believe it ought to occupy a more central position in the anticapitalist writing classroom insofar as the workplace represents a unique threat to collectivity and, at the same time, a site for a radically reimagined common ethic.

These concerns are particularly relevant to students in the composition classroom, who, as Tony Scott notes (2009), often work while they attend college and do so under increasingly exploitative conditions (153). In 2018, 70 percent of full-time college students worked, though what these workers experience is dramatically different from those of several generations ago. Students can no longer pay for college with part-time jobs due to the staggering rise in the cost of higher education coupled with the stagnation of wages (Carnevale and Smith 2018, 6). Rather than working their way through college, "working learners" (4) can merely hope to offset the cost of tuition (4). Of course, the conditions of this work vary widely according to demographic, with low-income working learners experiencing comparatively poorer conditions than middle- or upper-middle-class students. While the number of students working full-time has decreased, low-income workers are more likely than their peers to be working full-time (4). Additionally, low-income college workers tend to be "Black and Latino, women, first-generation college-goers, and new citizens and residents of the United States" (4). Grimly, low-income working learners are less likely than their peers to graduate regardless of academic performance. As most of our students are already working, often in scenarios that compound racial and economic inequality, my pedagogical focus on work is not about preparing students for a prospective future but about dealing with the immediate realities of their working lives.

In what follows, I begin by briefly sketching the conditions of the contemporary working world to isolate the dominance of precarity and productivity culture. I then demonstrate how composition has glossed over many of the most concerning conditions of contemporary work, namely the increase in productivity mandates, the rise in precarity, exploitation, and the shift toward the ideological identification with one's job. I subsequently demonstrate how numerous theoretical approaches beyond the discipline of composition offer a powerful means of understanding and responding to these conditions. In particular, philosopher Isabelle Stengers's (2015) analysis of "stupidity" (119), the capacity of capitalist logics to catastrophically upend thinking, provides a compelling means of organizing critical composition courses on the subject of work and pushing students to approach their work more critically.

BETTER WORK

In *Work: The Last 1,000 Years*, economist and social historian Andrea Komlosy (2018) characterizes how precarity and a new productivity culture have developed in the wake of the neoliberal escalations of the 1970s. As she contends, in the West, increased economic competition brought on by "cost-cutting and rationalization" (200) transformed the scene of work from one with relative stability to one in which cost saving and productivity mandates are now pervasive. As Komlosy explains, this wave of changes has profoundly affected the conditions of workers across the globe and at nearly all levels of economic security, comprised of both the outsourcing of mass production (200) and "a new flexibility in labour relations" (200) in Western nations. The most profoundly harmful conditions of the new economy, she argues, are visible in nations to which jobs have been outsourced and in which "huge factory complexes, often located in special economic zones" (201) exploit nations' natural resources while maintaining poor labor standards including "hard and precarious working conditions, low wages, extreme exploitation and bans of trade union activity" (201). These conditions are mirrored in Western countries where job security has all but vanished and where "working conditions and employment biographies are now highly fragmentary" (203). Part-time, seasonal, and contract work is now ubiquitous, offering employers "additional ways to reduce wage costs and other expenses" (204). As Komlosy observes, the paradigmatic site of this shift is online platforms like Uber and TaskRabbit, where "the employment contract disappears into an uncontrolled grey zone outside state regulation or legal certainty" (205).

Analyzing this shift toward precarity, economic historian Louis Hyman (2018) details how, following the growth of precarity in the 1970s, the 1990s saw a particularly pernicious escalation of these tendencies in the rise of temping and gig labor. As he recounts, in 1991, formerly full-time office workers who had been laid off in the recession of the early 1990s were increasingly pushing into temping and contract work (256). In 1991 alone, 3.5 million Americans were employed on a temporary basis (256). In the subsequent jobless recovery, the GDP rose while the number of jobs did not, and many of the ousted workers remained in contingent positions (257). Consultancies like McKinsey grew enormously during this period, allowing companies to outsource crucial functions rather than retain full-time employees (259). Despite the diminishing of labor security during the 1990s, a college education, unlike today, still offered relative economic security—only 15 percent of temps in the 1990s were college educated (268). However, continued austerity and the two significant economic disruptions of the twenty-first century, the 2008 recession and COVID-19, have led to increasing numbers of precarious and part-time workers. While most of these workers work seasonal or part-time jobs, many have been drawn into the gig economy, a system in which digital platforms have undermined various business models by allowing users to collect fees for performing services traditionally the province of more highly paid employees (Kim, *New York Times*, January 10, 2020). As Hyman (2018) notes, these platforms have further contributed to economic inequality, creating "instant wealth" (299) for a small cadre of Silicon Valley developers while the rest can "only look forward to spending their adult lives delivering pizza (and sushi), standing in line for building permits, or creating graphs and spreadsheets for consultants on the other side of the world" (299).

One of the starkest portrayals of precarious, twenty-first-century labor is Jessica Bruder's (2017) *Nomadland: Surviving America in the Twenty-First Century*, a chronicle of the iterant, seasonal labor now undertaken by "downwardly mobile older Americans" (62) unable to retire in the current economy. As Bruder notes, retirement is essentially a recent construct, largely made possible with the advent of Social Security in 1935 (65) along with pensions, savings, and investments (66). However, since the late 1970s, shocks and neoliberal austerity measures have chipped away at these support structures. 401(k) plans replaced pensions while the 2008 recession decimated Americans' wealth (66). Consequently, Americans are retiring older—nine million Americans over sixty-five were employed in 2016, a 60 percent rise from 2006 (62–63). However, rather than working in full-time positions with salary and benefits, many are part time. Increasing numbers are also hitting the road as seasonal employees in a variety of emerging schemes designed to exploit the poverty of older Americans. Amazon, perhaps unsurprisingly, is home to one such program, CamperForce, "a labor unit made up of nomads who work as seasonal employees at several of its warehouses" (45). Amazon, Bruder details, strives to frame the nonmonetary benefits of these positions with exhortations like "Work hard. Have fun. Make history" (53) and "You'll be surrounded by fellow CamperForce associates who get together to make new friends and reacquaint with old ones, share good food, good stories, and good times around the campfire" (53). However, as Bruder reports, senior employees face unforgiving conditions in these positions: "The workers' shifts last ten hours or longer, during which some walk more than fifteen miles on concrete floors, stooping, squatting, reaching, and climbing stairs as they scan, sort, and box merchandise" (45). As Linda, a CamperForce worker Bruder profiles, contends, "There's nothing to describe the misery, physically" (99). On her days off, Linda tries not to leave her bed (99). Amazon, notably, has its own on-site medical facility—AmCare—to treat the abundant injuries employees sustain (58). While these facilities are presented as in the service of employees' health, H. Claire Brown (2019) explains that numerous OSHA investigations of AmCare have revealed Amazon's employees have been "pressured to sweep injuries and medical issues under the rug at the expense of employee health."[2]

Unsurprisingly, those who have avoided sinking into precarity are subject to increasing productivity mandates. As Komlosy (2018) argues, these "new social climbers" (204) are "kept on their toes by the drive towards constant self-promotion and availability" (204). She further contends that the "standardization and modularization" (204) of work has introduced "a new form of Taylorism from which not even the new knowledge workers are immune" (204). In *Bullshit Jobs*, Graeber (2018) describes how uncompromising devotion to productivity has created a class of jobs with no apparent function other than to present the appearance of industriousness. Per his rough estimate, 37 percent of contemporary jobs are "bullshit" (62), often demanding enormous productivity but serving little purpose. In Graeber's analysis, these conditions are the result of work's moral valence, the pervasive belief that labor is an unquestionable good and the solution to modern ills: "Whenever there's a crisis, even an ecological crisis, there are calls for collective sacrifice. These calls always seem to involve everyone working more" (194). Graeber argues these conditions concomitantly demonize idleness and propel a culture of productivity even when they serve little logical purpose: "Anyone who is not slaving away harder than he'd like at something he doesn't especially enjoy is a bad person" (215). Throughout the text, Graber builds his theory on the testimony of numerous workers who express frustration and even anguish over the evident pointlessness of their positions. In an evocative testimonial, Nouri, a software developer, describes the kinds of self-denial necessary to do his work: "I used to have to go literally 'insane' to get into work. Scrub away me and become the thing that can do this work" (141). Nouri further elaborates how various coping mechanisms, frequently rooted in self-denial, were necessary to continue working. He writes, "I'd have to find all sorts of mental technologies to make my work bearable. The most effective motivations were deadlines and rage" (141).

A parallel valence of the working world Graeber (2018) also describes concerns the development of office perks and amenities designed to extract more labor from workers. In her testimony, Irene, who works in investment banking, notes how the culture of the contemporary working world has replaced traditional benefits and protections with a variety of rituals and postures. She describes a series of "New Agey" (172) seminars aimed at demonstrating the magnanimousness of the institution:

> No, you can't work fewer hours. No you can't get paid more. No, you can't choose which bullshit projects to decline. But you can sit through this seminar, where the bank tells you how much it values flexibility. The mindfulness seminars were even worse. They attempted to reduce the unfathomable beauty and stupefying sadness of the human experience into the raw physicality of breathing, eating, and shitting. (172)

Irene's account details an increasingly familiar bait-and-switch in contemporary office culture, the exchange of reasonable working hours and good pay for a host of supposed amenities that palliate the office experience and keep workers at their desks for longer. This trend is now pervasive across the world of work, particularly in the technology sector. Writing for the *Baffler* in 2018, Josh Hall describes a similar office paradigm:

> "We have an amazing office bar," reads the listing for a position at a subsidiary of a New York internet group, "guitars, a drum kit, a bike mechanic workstation, extensive library, and rotating food team who make lunch for everyone." Another, for a position at food-delivery firm Deliveroo in London, offers a "fun office complete with nap room, onsite gym, basketball court, and rooftop overlooking Tower Bridge."

In his characterization, Hall deftly sketches the paradigm of the modern office that increasingly monopolizes workers' lives through initiatives disguised as play: "We no longer go to the pub; instead, we drink in the office. We no longer read for pleasure; instead, we take books from the workplace library to learn more about the field we're employed in."

These logics are notably echoed in the visual aesthetics and casual vibes of WeWork (see fig. 3.1), the notoriously embattled[3] purveyor of collaborative workspaces. On its website, the company is forthright about

Figure 3.1. A WeWork coworking space in Vancouver, BC. (Photograph by GoTo-Van. Licensed under the Creative Commons Attribution 2.0 Generic license. https://creativecommons.org/licenses/by/2.0/deed.en.)

the complementary relationship between work and play: "While an outdoor terrace or a cool café area can't fuel success on their own, office amenities can reinforce employee-first culture, increase engagement, and boost productivity" (Papandrea 2019). In other words, the features of each office are not meant to enhance quality of life or to change the nature of work but rather to extract more of it. WeWork touts these various perks, distributed across its numerous global locations—hammocks in São Paulo, a pool in San Diego, a ping-pong table in Busan (Papandrea 2019). Echoing Schaffner's (2016) critique of the intermingling of work and life, Peter Fleming (*Guardian*, November 2, 2015) historicizes the phenomenon in the multidecade history of "liberation management," a 1960s trend of incorporating elements of play to further cement corporate control. "Staged fun," he argues, "helps blur the boundary between work and non-work. . . . Work becomes a perverted home away from home, and as a result we are hardly ever not on the job."

Fleming's critique is particularly prescient when read against the backdrop of the COVID-19 crisis. While many workers in the sectors most decimated by the pandemic—namely retail, service, hospitality, and tourism—were furloughed or fired and then given inadequate unemployment benefits and nominal stimulus checks (Thier 2020), those who remained employed frequently faced higher productivity mandates. Naturally, contingent employees at Amazon and similar employers faced some of the most inhumane treatment. As Lauren Kaori Gurley (2021) reported for VICE, in early 2021 Amazon warehouses began transitioning their employees to grueling ten-hour, overnight "megacycle" shifts in efforts to improve delivery times. For those working from home, productivity expectations have likewise expanded despite the inherent challenges of remote work. A study found that workers in the United Kingdom, Austria, Canada, and the United States were working, on average, 2.5 hours longer during the pandemic than they were prior to it (Guy 2021). As Josephine Tovey observed in the *Guardian* on August 12, 2020, "We live at work now."

As these diverse examples suggest, while the scene of contemporary work is enormously varied, virtually all spheres have been profoundly transformed by economic acceleration. The most vulnerable workers, by virtue of vanishing unions and disappearing job security, are often no longer employees as such but rather are contractors, seasonal associates, and gig workers forced to compete with one another for appallingly little pay. Office workers, while they remain substantially more secure and well paid, are likewise squeezed for maximal productivity. Moreover, both sets are managed by increasingly sophisticated dispositifs, aesthetic inducements, social media campaigns, and PR machines that reframe their precarious labor as fun and romantic. Amazon's CamperForce ad promising workers "good food, good stories, and good times around the campfire" (Bruder 2017, 53) is as demonstrative an example as any, reframing the punishing and precarious work on the floor of the fulfillment center as an idealized life on the road. I argue that these conditions render an anticapitalist approach, particularly one that foregrounds the economic causes of and collective solutions to declining labor conditions, increasingly necessary in the composition classroom. However, as I argue in the following section, these conditions are neglected in much of contemporary composition scholarship. I maintain, however, that such a neglect can, at least in part, be amended by turning to anticapitalist approaches from parallel fields.

WORK AND OVERWORK: TWO PERSPECTIVES

As I previously suggested, composition, while it has certainly not been uninterested in the conditions of the working world, has glossed over many aspects of its twenty-first-century acceleration. Writing scholars have specifically been responsive to the issues of contingent faculty labor (Kahn, Lalicker, and Lynch-Biniek 2017; McClure, Goldstein, and Pemberton 2017; Welch and Scott 2016) and writing about work in the composition classroom (Bay 2010; Lu and Horner 2009; Scott 2009; Seitz 2004; Welch 2008). However, despite this interest and scholars' attention to the topics of work and production (Horner 2007; Trimbur 2004, 2012), compositionists have only nominally investigated the excessive productivity that defines the contemporary professional world (Brandt 2008; Danberg 2011; Gunner 2012; Jensen 2010; Rouzie 2000; Scott 2009), the consequences of overwork (Bishop 2001; Bizzaro 2001; Deacon 2013), or the question of what can be done to address these conditions.

Of those compositionists who have explicitly taken up issues of productivity and the changing conditions of work over the past several decades, some have expressed varying degrees of support for writerly productivity through direct theorization of efficient writing processes or through the defense of writing as a productive act. Writing for *CCC* in 1985, Robert Boice investigated "blocked writers" (472), noting, "Failure to teach good habits of productivity . . . condemn[s] many students to a future of difficulty in completing written tasks" (479). Several scholars and professionals offered similar pronouncements in a 1987 special issue of *Technical Communication*. Paul D. Doebler praised the electronic revolution for enhancing the productivity of print publications and applauded technologically wrought productivity gains in the publishing world (256). In the same special issue of *Technical Communication*, Robert Krull and Jeanne M. Hurford pose personal computing as a solution to "physical and psychological constraints" that limit writing production (243). It is worth noting these statements are correct in suggesting word processing and the various technologies to come would vastly improve the speed of writing and publication. What these articles did not foresee, however, was that the various productivity gains would go largely unremunerated (as, indeed, all productivity gains have gone since the late 1970s)[4] or how rising expectations of output would change the lives of many writers for the worse. Contemporary journalists, for example, are subject to increasing productivity mandates in the midst of downsizing newsrooms and are being asked to carry the slack left by absent colleagues (Brey 2018).

Such early enthusiasm notwithstanding, composition has largely avoided treating writing as a quantifiable product and the writer as a producer, particularly as the discipline has transitioned away from current-traditional rhetoric (Elbow 1987; Emig 1971; Murray 1968). Until quite recently, much of the discipline's treatment of writing production since the 1990s has framed writers' output in abstract terms. Horner

(2012), for example, has sought to challenge the reductive valuation of writing as a mere product. In the introduction to the "Economies of Writing" special issue of *JAC*, he writes, "The official status and value of given texts and activities of writing are not and never their full or final value, which is realized not in artifacts but in and through specific means of engaging with them" (459).

Despite the field's reticence to support productivity as such, a modest contingent of composition scholars have defended more material senses of production and productivity as goods associated with the work of writing. In their 2009 article, Jim Ridolfo and Dànielle Nicole DeVoss coined the term "rhetorical velocity," an approach to the question of how writers might keep pace with the "rapidity at which information is crafted, delivered, distributed, recomposed, redelivered, redistributed." In an essay similarly concerned with the need to keep pace with the contemporary demands of digital production, Jennifer Bay (2010) asks, "Why, then, aren't Composition Studies and professional writing constituting themselves as part of this *constant production*?" (36; emphasis added). Unlike critics who theorize abstract or labor-based models of writing, these scholars understand writing to be tangible and entangled with various material and embodied processes. While most of these analyses do not defend productivity as such, they nevertheless conceive of writing as an inherently productive enterprise insofar as they esteem the writer's capacity to materially produce text in response to the exigencies of work.[5] Other compositionists have approached productivity critically, though these discussions have often glossed over the structural aspects of exploitation and overwork and refrained from offering pedagogical solutions.

Albert Rouzie's (2000) "Beyond the Dialectic of Work and Play: A Serio-Ludic Rhetoric for Composition Studies," for example, considers how play can revitalize the drudgery of contemporary work. Beginning with a selective reading of Marx's critique of alienated labor as that which "creates an absolute sense of separation between home and work . . . estranges the individual with his or her sense of connection with nature and the human species as a whole" (623), Rouzie calls for reintroducing play into the space of work as a bulwark against professional demands. "Play in the context of work," he argues, "can help to recapture aspects of creative activity that have been denied to labor" (633). Rouzie accordingly supports a "serio-ludic" (633) approach to composition, combining work and play in a way that, he contends, "can open up a place for the ludic impulses we all feel; it allows us the possibility of the creative engagement with writing that is all but lost in composition" (633). While productivity doesn't directly enter his critique, Rouzie's defense of play offers a counterstatement to the broader culture of overwork and exploitation. Twenty years on, what Rouzie defends has darkly come to pass, at least in contemporary office culture, as evidenced by the proliferation of the "New Agey" (Graeber 2018, 172) amenities offered by the tech industry and other employers. Epic Systems, a healthcare service provider in Madison, Wisconsin, is one such office whose carnivalesque facilities could be charitably described as serio-ludic: "Employees can hurtle down an 'Alice in Wonderland' slide into a room with miniature furniture. . . . A conference room named after a Star Wars planet was reached via a rickety swinging bridge" (Kelly, *New York Times*, Dec. 20, 2018). In years past, the company offered employees free milk and juice (Newman, *Wisconsin State Journal*, March 26, 2016). While these and similar features might solve the problem of alienated labor that concerns Rouzie (2000), namely social isolation and disassociation, few would argue it solves the other problem, that is, that the worker is "a personal source of wealth, but deprived of any means of making that wealth a reality for himself" (Marx 1976, 716). Insofar as such amenities remake the office as "a perverted home away from home" (Fleming, *Guardian*, November 2, 2015), they are intended to *increase* alienation by keeping workers toiling longer.

A modest number of composition scholars have traced how burnout impacts both faculty and students. In her CCCC chair's address in 2001, Wendy Bishop (2001) also addressed the topic of burnout, reporting often feeling "*slow, sour,* or *dim*" (329) in her professional duties. While she acknowledges the difficulties of life in academia, she strikes an optimistic tone about the resilience of her peers "because they are teachers in love with writing and teaching" (329). As Deborah Brandt (2014) contends, writing has become progressively commodified and subject to market forces: "Writing itself is the product that is bought and sold as it embodies information, invention, service, social relations, news—that is, the products of the new economy" (16). Brandt likewise details how writing is particularly subject to exploitation: "Writing is a time-intensive form of labor that tends to follow people home" (17). While these critiques register the effects of rising productivity, they refrain from tracing them to political-economic conditions. One exception is Jeanne Gunner (2012), who critiques economic conditions for pushing the discipline toward an efficiency model and predicts these changes will lead to various forms of institutional decline in the service of profit and speed: "cost-cutting measures leading to curricular and pedagogical shifts, through higher class size, required online format with little or no faculty development, accreditation-inspired standardization of learning outcomes" (639).

Compositionists have also discussed the draining effects of productivity demands in the context of writing program administration. Micciche (2002) investigates the "climate of disappointment" (432) surrounding composition studies and writing program administration specifically. She notes WPA scholarship is overwhelmingly preoccupied with questions pertaining to exhaustion: "It reads like a cautionary tale, expounding how not to get discouraged, burnt out, manipulated by faculty and deans." (442). Andrea Deacon (2013) comparably argues that the numerous tasks WPAs are typically asked to fulfill, including motivating instructors, dealing with student problems, responding to administrative requests, and "initiating curricular reform," often lead to "burning the candle at both ends" (3). By way of a solution, Deacon advocates extensive collaboration as a way to stave off isolation and exhaustion: "[WPAs] must entertain and listen to all views of members of the department" (12). To extend Micciche's (2002) point, WPAs are often in the unenviable position of cheerleading a stable of overworked and underpaid contingent teachers while being overworked, underpaid, and contingent or temporary themselves. While greater connection, as Deacon (2013) suggests, can certainly create a sense of community—a deeply valuable thing, as I argue in this book—without collective resistance to capitalist conditions, it can only hope to have limited effect.

An additional area of composition that has attended to these issues is technical and professional communication (TPC), an area of the discipline in the midst of a social justice turn (Jones and Williams 2020; Walton, Moore, and Jones 2019; Walwema and Carmichael 2020). While TPC is increasingly taking up issues of power, exclusion, and social justice, its critiques of working conditions and capitalist entanglements are more muted. Indeed, the subfield's most pointed critiques of exploitation, capitalism, and overwork lie in the past. In an article from 1986, Susan Wells (1986) notes that "the ideology of technical writing explicitly assents to its instrumental subordination to capital" (247). Carolyn R. Miller (1989) similarly critiques technical writing's tendency to accept the influence of nonacademic actors, noting educational value is frequently assessed in terms of the needs of industry rather than those of academia itself. As she argues, "The good that is sought is the good of an existing industry or profession. . . . These are tied to private interests, and to the extent that educational programs are based on existing nonacademic practices, they perpetuate and strengthen those private interests" (21). In keeping with composition's slow retreat from anticapitalist critique, contemporary work in TPC is comparatively far more attuned to alternate issues of injustice. Elizabeth Walton, Kristen

Moore, and Natasha Jones (2019), for example, analyze sites of inequity across numerous areas, notably racial inequality. In a solution that parallels the orientation of this book, they propose coalitions as a mechanism of realizing social justice in the various contexts of professional and technical writing. They write, "We assert that coalitional thinking and inclusive coalitions are necessary for change because they can shift and change quickly and because they engage difference and different goals without rejecting them" (135). Notably, their critique also takes up exploitation, employing Iris Marion Young's definition of the exploited as those "who do not benefit fairly from their own work, which, instead, maintains the authority of those in power" (26). What is missing in such a definition is recognition of the ways contemporary forms of exploitation are not merely a matter of wage theft but, rather, per Wells (1986) and Miller (1989), an issue of the oversized influence of capitalism and its twenty-first-century accelerations.

Overall, writing scholars' attention to these issues indicates modest disciplinary concern with the unreasonable demands being placed upon contemporary workers. However, among those openly critical of neoliberal conditions, few acknowledge that work's accelerations or declining conditions are the result of economic shifts or contend that composition should address this issue. Latent support of writers' productivity has quietly reemerged over the past decade and reflects the not unreasonable desire to help students keep pace with contemporary accelerations (Bay 2010; Ridolfo and DeVoss 2009). Generally, such attempts to cope with neoliberal conditions, whether critical (Rouzie 2000) or more openly laudatory of productivity (Ridolfo and DeVoss 2009), avoid explicitly intervening in the broader issues of exploitation, overwork, and burnout that increasingly attend the professional world.

This aversion runs counter to other disciplines and perspectives that have long sought to attend to the changing dynamics of work, particularly concerning the ways work is (re)framed and extracted. Writing in the early twentieth century, Max Weber (2002) argued that the ideology of ceaseless productivity has increasingly informed the lives of modern workers. Work, for Weber, is no longer "the means to an end of satisfying the material needs of life" (12). Instead, he argues capitalism is "a monstrous cosmos" (13) that "forces on the individual, to the extent that he is caught up in the relationship of the 'market,' the norms of its economic activity" (13). These norms, in Weber's view, mandate "ceaseless, constant, symptomatic labor" (116). Importantly, he suggests that despite the spirit of capitalism's unrelenting accelerations, workers are often complicit in this process. In the United States, "where capitalism is at its most unbridled"

(121), accruing wealth has effectively become "a sporting contest" (121). Regarding the previously discussed distinction between labor and work, in Weber's view, to oppose work is not necessarily to oppose labor as such but rather to critique participation in the institutionalized and marketized forms of work that structure contemporary life.

Following Weber, much of the tradition of critical theory on the subject of work has focused either on refusal or disengagement. Autonomia Operaia, or simply Autonomia, promoted the renunciation of work to disrupt the extensive harms caused by participation in the capitalist economy. Rooted in Italian Marxist labor struggles of the mid-1960s that articulated "the refusal of wage labor" (Lontringer and Marazzi 2007, 9), Autonomia represented a rejection of Marxism's focus on the elevation of workers. As Franco "Bifo" Berardi (2009) contends, unlike prior forms of work that were "a sort of temporary death from which [the worker] could wake up only after the alarm bells rang" (76–77), work in the age of late capitalism now claims the entirety of the subject's life. In the new economy, a meritocracy in which "many are called but few are chosen" (99), the untenable risk of failure, Berardi argues, propels two chief psychological consequences: panic and depression. Panic, according to his analysis, is a feeling of being "overwhelmed" (100) by constant and ubiquitous precarity: "Survival is no longer based on reading a position of sufficient preparation and abilities, but it is constantly questioned: if one does not win, one can be eliminated, in a few days or a few months" (101). On his account, this state of "cognitive and psychic stress" (101) eventually results in the subject's breakdown: "Once the organism gets overtaxed to an unbearable degree, a panic crisis may lead to collapse, or the organism might detach itself from the flow of communication" (102). In practice, Berardi contends, contemporary subjects afflicted with these conditions are particularly prone to acts of hate and violence. "Collective panic," he claims, "generates phenomena such as irrational aggressiveness against immigrants, senseless mass violence in stadiums" (102). Breaking with traditional Marxist critique advocating the proletariat's reclamation of the means of production, Berardi calls for "a massive reduction in work-time, a prodigious liberation of life from the social factory" (213).

Contemporary critical theory has similarly kept pace with the accelerating conditions of the working world. For critic Jonathan Crary (2014), the culture of "24/7," the de facto ethic of the contemporary age, is now encroaching upon workers' biological lives (9). As he puts it, "Within the globalist neoliberal paradigm, sleeping is for losers" (14). In Crary's account, sleep represents a site of nonproductivity, "one of the great human affronts to the voraciousness of contemporary capitalism" (10), while the self, along with its intimate bodily processes, represents the final frontier of capitalist accumulation. As he argues, the persuasive stance of the nonstop world, what he terms "24/7" (9), "is a time of indifference, against which the fragility of human life is increasingly inadequate and within which sleep has no necessity or inevitability" (9). In his framing, late capitalism holds little regard for the human element in its deterritorial project. Philosopher Byung-Chul Han (2015) similarly argues that the neoliberal culture of work has profoundly transformed subjects' lives. Late capitalism, he contends, propagates a myth of ceaseless productivity: "More capital produces more life, which means a greater capacity for living" (51). As Han asserts, the modern subject is unable to do anything but work, "too alive to die, and too dead to live" (51). Theorizing a solution to these conditions, feminist critic Kathi Weeks (2011) argues workers must continually develop creative methods of denying work access to the self: "[Life] must be continually invented in the struggle to mark distinctions between fields of experience that nonetheless remain intertwined" (232). Unlike Crary and Han, Weeks acknowledges the complex gender politics that, by turns, bar women from working and exploit them in the professions. As she notes, being employed, for many women, is both an accomplishment and a necessity that cannot simply be abandoned: "Life is part of work, and work is part of life" (232). Responding to Stanley Aronowitz, Dawn Esposito, William DiFazio, and Margaret Yard (1998), Weeks (2011) calls for workers to develop radical forms of invention to separate us from the domination of the working world and to form alternate political modalities: "The possibility of the provocation to get a life lies in its capacity to pose a political project that [work] does not stipulate and to open a postwork speculative horizon that it cannot fix in advance" (233).

As this brief tour of the attention to work by compositionists and theorists beyond the field indicates, composition has remained largely disengaged from the critiques of capitalist encroachment long explored by critical theorists, political theorists, and philosophers. While numerous compositionists understand the role of the writing classroom largely as a responsive one, to prepare students to meet the changing conditions of the capitalist world, critical theorists have consistently favored the approach of political-economic diagnosis and, in the case of Weeks, resistance. Developments in critical theory, hence, inform my pedagogical approach, which aims to counter composition's silence on capitalism's encroachment on the professionalization of students. While Weeks (2011), Han (2015), Crary (2014), and other contemporary perspectives inform this work, Stengers (2015) provides the most substantive theoretical basis for my approach to the working world in the composition classroom. As I now detail, Stengers's critical assessment of the disempowering valence of organizational logics and the capacity for a *common* form of resistance supports a collaborative critique of work in the anticapitalist classroom.

ISABELLE STENGERS: CAPITALISM, STUPIDITY, AND THE COMMON

Isabelle Stengers, a philosopher most known for her critique of science,[6] offers an approach to collective action in the context of cognitive capitalism and mounting climate change that supports a collaborative critique of work in the writing classroom. According to Stengers (2015), contemporary capitalism represents an enormous material, existential, and intellectual threat to the world and, even more acutely, to the fabric of collaboration as well: "Cognitive capitalism doesn't appropriate the appropriable, but destroys . . . what is required by the very existence of a *community*" (86). Solutions to these problems, for Stengers, must be imagined in the midst of trying times—workers are not only "submitted to intolerable imperatives like productivity, like unemployment, targeted by policies of activation and motivation, called on to prove that they are spending their time looking for work, even forced to accept any type of 'job'" (21), but they face the looming threat of global climate change. Following the work of James Lovelock and Lynn Margulis (and subsequently Bruno Latour), Stengers argues our current age is witness to "the intrusion of Gaia" (43), "the name of an unprecedented or forgotten form of transcendence . . . a ticklish assemblage of forces that are indifferent to our reasons and our projects" (47). Capitalist solutions or compromises to these problems, she argues, are untenable insofar as capitalism can only ever seek profit: "The logic of capitalist functioning cannot do anything other than identify the intrusion of Gaia with the appearance of a new field of opportunity" (54). Rather, for Stengers, solutions must lie in collectively enacted, anticapitalist practices.

Stengers (2015) suggests that responses to global capitalism's ecological impact specifically lie in solutions enacted by bodies of intellectual collaborators that respond to capitalism's cognitive turn (Boutang 2004), namely its attempts to appropriate knowledge (Stengers 2015, 83). Likening the contemporary appropriation of knowledge to Britain's enclosure acts, "the eradication . . . of customary rights that bore on the use of communal land" (79), Stengers argues contemporary responses to capitalism must lie in reclamation. Like other scholars of the common, Stengers suggests this work must take place not in physical sites but in the area of discourse, knowledge, and practice, a common "that cannot be reduced to a good or a resource" (86). She argues the appropriate response lies in the construction of "cooperative networks, which affirm the immediately social value of the immaterial" (83), noting capitalists have appropriated physical commons and, with them, the "concrete, collective intelligence" (85) intimately attached to them. For Stengers, this calls for communal action to resist the modes of capitalist hegemony that currently operate. The groups who organize such collective responses must be those united by "a common concern" (89) that "gathers" (89) a diverse body of collaborators. Those in the sciences, Stengers contends, are "gathered together by a 'common,' that is to say, by a cause" (91). These individuals, moreover, are united by an extensive set of shared disciplinary norms and obligations that assemble a collective of individuals, a body engaging the common through a shared task. However, as Stengers notes, scientists, along with virtually all other collectives under the present system, have not "invented a manner of resisting the enclosures that are their lot too in the knowledge economy" (91). Rather, as with Dean (2019), collectivity is a site of possibility whose potential, at least under the current capitalist conditions, is as yet unmet.

While this perspective offers a generally pertinent theory applicable to the work of the anticapitalist classroom, what makes Stengers (2015) particularly useful to a collective critique of work, even among similar theorists of the common, is her conceptualization of *stupidity*, a way of thinking and acting that "destroys the capacity for thinking and imagining of those who envisioned ways of doing things differently" (119). While she suggests stupidity is a particular hallmark of climate change denial (118), Stengers acknowledges it is a general feature of all capitalist systems. To my reading, stupidity offers an incisive means of parsing occupational discourses in the context of contemporary work insofar as corporations have become increasingly savvy communicators and employ advertising, social media, and a variety of additional means of address to glorify themselves while undercutting the potential of critique or resistance by employees or members of the public. The aesthetic strategies of WeWork (Papandrea 2019) and Amazon's CamperForce ad copy promising "good times around the campfire" (Bruder 2017, 53) both actualize such a form of stupidity, enforcing an increasingly hegemonic and incontrovertible perspective on work.

Regarding the obligation to oppose this force, Stengers (2015) writes, "It is necessary today to dare to name the stupidity that seizes hold of those whom capitalism has made endorse the responsibility for maintaining public order" (120). For Stengers, stupidity is a mode of political control, the negation of critique and free thought in the interest of maintaining the viability of prevailing systems, whether those of governance or free enterprise. Stupidity, she further elaborates, "affect[s] those who view themselves as the inheritors-rentiers of the Enlightenment, those who continue the noble combat against illusions but who—and this makes for a difference that matters—have abandoned its sense of adventure for that of a mission that made them pedagogues" (121). With oblique reference to Adorno and Horkheimer's critique of Enlightenment logic, Stengers suggests stupidity amounts to the warping of reason and thought and their authoritarian transformation. Crucially, she contends recognizing and calling attention to stupidity entails a form of collective thinking re Deleuze: "Thinking *in the sense that matters politically, that is to say, in the collective sense*, with one another" (131). In other words, naming or opposing stupidity as an individual is insufficient. Rather, such work must be a political and broadly collective endeavor that breaks out of the restrictive intellectual mechanisms imposed by the status quo. As she argues, it is in collectives

> that one also deals with those who are engaged in experimenting with what "thinking" means to live or survive, thinking in the sense that matters politically, that is to say, the collective sense, with one another, through one another, around a situation that has become "a common cause" that makes people think. (131)

For Stengers, simply naming the logics of stupidity is only a first step in a more substantive process of liberation. Rather, through collective engagement, interlocutors must learn and develop *another way to be.*

Stengers specifically praises the collective formation of the citizen jury, a body of equals deeply resonant with Dean's comrade (2019) that is poised to engage in this kind of emancipatory thinking. For Stengers (2015), the jury's capacity to do this lies in its emergent egalitarian structure. The jury, she contends, is "*an apparatus that brings about a 'making equal'*" (134). More specifically, it is a body that "must not presuppose a postulated equality but must translate operations for the *production of equality* amongst its participants" (141). Effectively, a jury, a cooperative network gathered by a shared purpose, is precisely so effective because it is a site of the collective invention of equality, an invention that emerges from a body of cooperating interlocutors rather than one imposed by managerial stupidity. Because of these features, the jury, as a site of political encounter akin to Nancy's (2017) theorization of recognition, offers the potential of crucial intervention in the contemporary age. The citizen jury, Stengers (2015) argues, "gathers its participants around a common cause, that is to say, *achieves the transformation of a problematic situation into a cause for collective thinking*" (137).

Akin to prior approaches to the common previously explored in this book, Stengers offers composition a critical, collective approach to conceptualizing and resisting the contemporary working world. As I detail in the following section, her understanding of the function of stupidity and its potential resistance through collective opposition provides a particularly needed foundation for a writing pedagogy attentive to both the coercive discourses of the workplace and their potential opposition. Insofar as modern work is increasingly precarious and managed by corporations employing a revived Taylorist methodology (Komlosy 2018, 204), as well as strategies to undercut resistance,[7] a collective approach to stupidity is desperately needed to attune students to the immensity of contemporary work's power and, concomitantly, the capacity of resisting it.

"ANYONE ALIVE DISRUPTS": WRITING ABOUT WORK

Following Stengers's (2015) approach to the common in the context of institutional logics, I have often adopted a pedagogical strategy in my writing courses that first aims to understand the persuasive conditions of work under late capitalism and to name the "stupidity" (119) of the contemporary working world before moving to collective and collaborative solutions to its logics. Employing Stengers's approach in a WAC course focused on humanities writing in the spring of 2020, I divided the exploration of occupational discourse into two stages: diagnosis and critique. In the diagnosis phase, I positioned students to understand the working environment as one rhetorically charged and motivated by capitalist logics. I moved students toward the analysis of these logics, positioning them to analyze the capacity of capitalist managerialism to constrain, disempower, and divide workers. More precisely, I encouraged them to see these discourses as manifestations of Stengers's concept of stupidity. However, insofar as "learning to recognize and name stupidity . . . is not an end in itself" (131), I also encouraged students to develop collective solutions to work's dominance. This positioning represented the critical aspect of the course, in which students theorized the possibility of employing collaboration to challenge and transform working conditions. These strategies specifically attempted to offer students a productive and empowering vision of opposition to contemporary capitalist conditions that celebrates the capacities of communal and political engagement.

In the initial assignments of the diagnostic phase, I engaged students in the analysis of working conditions and inducements from an autoethnographic perspective. This approach allowed them to engage with the course material by way of their own experiences and to approach the more critical aspects of the course from an experiential rather than an abstract position. While these initial assignments provided students with an intimate introduction to how capitalism is antagonistic to what is "required by the very existence of a *community*" (Stengers 2015, 86), they additionally drew on the scholarship of scholars advocating assigning personal writing on the subject of work (Scott 2009; Seitz 2004; Shor 1977), particularly David Seitz's (2004) advocacy of work memoirs as a means to "elicit writers' multiple orientations toward cultural values of work through reflection on situated moments of their continually evolving work identity and persuasive influences on work issues in their lives" (214).

In these writing assignments, students reported a range of experiences; while many described feeling gratified and enriched by work, many others related distressing narratives of indignity, frustration, injury, exploitation, and overwork. Unsurprisingly, given the unequal nature of working conditions for college students, these experiences often diverged along the lines of class and race. White, middle-income students detailed positive experiences working in government, law, and entertainment and reported that these early career working experiences were supportive of their long-term goals. Common among many less privileged students, however, was a pervasive sense of devaluation. As Li noted, reflecting on her history of monotonous, minimum-wage jobs, managers "see you as a cog in their machine." Mateo, a Latinx student from the Yakima Valley, described working in the freezer of a fruit warehouse. As he recounted, the physically demanding job only paid fifty cents an hour more than working on the floor and often required hours of unplanned overtime, sometimes lasting all night. Others detailed experiences of pervasive sexism and sexual harassment. One student working as a host described her manager often encouraging her to "show off that sorority smile." Another described a manager encouraging her to show off her body. Others told stories of managerial indifference to workplace injuries and the unpredictability of cancelled shifts. In a destressing example from some years ago, a low-income student wrote about suffering a heart attack while in the middle of a long, frantic shift at a fast-food restaurant. These and other student experiences expose the physical, psychological, and subjugating effects of work, though students often refrain from extending an explicit critique of working culture. When asked how she viewed an employer and a position that risked her health, the student who had suffered the heart attack remarked she was determined to take better care of herself in the future. While perhaps dismaying, such a response is typical of students who have internalized society's mandates for higher productivity, entrepreneurialism, and ceaseless hustle, whether in prestigious positions or in multiple part-time jobs. Like Scott in his discussion of a student named Sophia (2009, 176–177), I have often wished for more critical perspectives from students, a fervent rejection of capitalist narratives of self-reliance and success. This critique, however, is often one students are not yet positioned to make as they lack both the perspective and, indeed, the permission to view work, broadly conceived, as a site for critique. Absent from many of these accounts is any sense that worker disposability and the culture of productivity are the products of a capitalist society striving to derive maximal profit from an increasingly contingent and unorganized workforce.

Following these initial autoethnographic accounts, I sought to move students into more explicitly critical assignments to parse the stupidity (Stengers 2015) of institutional discourses that deflect, diminish, or reframe the potential of envisioning alternative models of work. Because it is a Seattle company (and because of the company's abysmal record on working conditions), Amazon has been a frequent site of my classroom critique. Prior to more sustained texts and analyses, I began with short texts that allowed students to understand the substance of the criticism of Amazon as well as the corporation's defensive and misleading rhetorical posture. I asked students to analyze the allegations and rhetorical choices of a letter to Jeff Bezos signed by senators Sherrod Brown, Bernie Sanders, Tammy Baldwin, and others critiquing the company's labor practices. The letter graphically lays out the conditions that have been reported at the company in the extraction of maximal productivity. The authors, for example, critique the rate of injury for Amazon workers, noting that it is three times higher than other private employers and that "pressure to meet their quotas is so great that workers report urinating in plastic bottles on the warehouse floor" (Brown et al. 2020). The letter calls upon Bezos to "reduce workers' quotas and speed requirements," "ensure workers are allowed and encouraged to hydrate and use the bathroom as needed," and "implement a . . . company policy that prohibits supervisors and managers from discrimination or retaliation when workers report injuries or safety concerns," among other requests. While several students were familiar with the conditions inside Amazon fulfillment centers, many were unaware of them and were shocked by the descriptions of the dehumanizing conditions. In analyzing the letter, some students saw the text as a compelling inducement to change and an "effective way to start the conversation," particularly insofar as the letter lays out specific policies its authors wish the company to adopt. Others, however, found the text "a little soft" for not taking a stronger tone. Li opined that because Jeff Bezos "doesn't give a crap," the letter's neutral tone would have little effect on the CEO. Rather, she suggested laws and consequences are the only means of creating change. In some respects, this response mirrors Stengers's (2015) call for structural changes that can only be produced though coalition (134).

I also presented students with Amazon's defense of its policies, an archetypal example of which was released in a manifesto-like statement in late 2019. Titled "Our Positions," the statement defends the company on numerous issues, such as those raised by Brown and others. In particular, Amazon notes that it pays employees $15 per hour, that it "prioritizes equal pay," and that it "stand[s] together with the LGBTQ community." It also publicly supports a variety of progressive political issues, noting that "climate change is real" and that "diversity and inclusion are good for business." Students were enormously critical of the company's "superficial" attempts to defend its record. Regarding the congressional letter, students argued the company failed to respond to the most censorious attacks on its safety record. Others, notably, observed how the company selectively used data to deflect criticism. Simeon raised the point that while the company proudly touted its policy of paying workers $15 an hour, this wage hike had been hard won in 2018 through a protracted battle for fair pay (Matsakis 2018, 208). Most significantly, students noted the dissonance between the company's framing of itself as progressive, with frequent references to "diversity," "sustainability," and "inclusion," and exploiting workers at the same time. A graphic example of Stengers's (2015) concept of stupidity, the document normalizes the state of risk and precarity workers face by framing Amazon as a labor champion and a progressive force. Mentioning its fair labor practices exceed those of other companies, while also touting its political bona fides, Amazon strives to be understood as an ideal organization, a company *doing the right thing*. This strategy, it is worth noting, has been enormously successful. A 2018 survey found that the company was among the most trusted institutions in the United States, along with the military and the FBI (Tiffany 2018). With its capacity to amass enormous public trust given its abysmal labor record, Amazon, in Stengers's (2015) terms, "destroys the capacity for thinking and imagining of those who envisioned ways of doing things differently" (119). By gathering students in a critique parsing these logics, I aim to move them toward a place where *thinking*, and, indeed, collective thinking gathered around "a common cause" (137), can take place.

In pushing students toward more rigorous analysis, I assigned Heike Geissler's *Seasonal Associate* (2018), a timely novel fictionalizing the author's employment at an Amazon fulfillment center in Leipzig, Germany. Actualizing Stengers's (2015) critiques of stupidity as a mechanism that inhibits critique and the ideation of alternatives, I asked students to analyze how the novel dramatizes the impact of institutional rhetoric and coercive working conditions. Throughout the text, Geissler demonstrates how the casualized workplace both degrades workers' agency and vitiates their capacity for resistance. Though she ultimately regards her tenure at Amazon as a failure to resist, she nevertheless conveys her experience as valuable to others struggling against precarity and organizational oppression in the context of the new economy.

A central arc of the text concerns the author's surrender to the dissociative rhetoric of the precarious workplace that strives to subordinate workers. Despite enjoying a literary career outside her seasonal work and knowing her time at Amazon is limited, Geissler (2018) nevertheless finds herself defeated by the experience. Throughout the text, she highlights the effects of company discourses that reframe the experience of labor, exhorting employees to be compliant, enthusiastic, and ardent defenders of the company. At an unpaid training session at the beginning of Geissler's tenure, a trainer explains, "We're all on a first-name-basis from the bottom to the top, that's how it works here" (35). This ersatz collegiality, however, is coupled with an entrepreneurial, bootstrap rhetoric that seems to promise the possibility of success if employees maintain their productivity standards: "We at Amazon think every day is a first day. Remember that. This is a good opportunity to make a note of that and get in on the ground floor and move up" (35). Employees, in other words, are on thin ice. No one can expect to build up a reputation, a history, or a cushion if they fall. Workers, rather, are expected to hustle as if they could be fired at any minute. The only incentive in the equation is a largely implausible, and conveniently vague, promise of promotion. Already, at this early stage, Geissler experiences a sense of personal failure in being unable to counter Amazon's rhetorical posture. "You'd like to contradict him," she writes, but "you're shy; you can't get your mouth open" (39). Geissler, notably, constructs the narrative in the second person. Rather than framing these failures as her own, she positions the reader as the focalizer. Effectively, these failures are not simply hers, but ours as well.

Throughout the text, Geissler (2018) continually finds herself defeated by her work. She reflects, "You've completely forgotten that you have a profession and are only here to alleviate momentary poverty. Something inside you is essentially unsettled and will never calm down again" (29). Working for Amazon drives Geissler not only to lose sight of her outside life but also to continually find her mind inhabited by the mandates of work. Describing the way the company has profoundly impacted her subjectivity, she writes, "You won't talk the way you normally talk, by then. You'll end up talking to yourself in employee language" (27). When she leaves the position, having finally succumbed to burnout, she is unable to feel relief at the prospect of release. Instead, Geissler hears the call of work:

> *And then a choir proclaims:*
> What are you doing?
> You can't just stop!
> You coward!
> You lazy thing!
> Work takes skill!
> Work takes some learning!
> Now you know what it's really like!
> And you just cut and run. (203)

In these and other instances, despite her efforts to compartmentalize her experience, logics of efficiency and productivity invariably trouble Geissler's ability to separate herself from her job and her capacity to even conceptualize the possibility of resistance. This moment could be read as the internalization of Amazon's logics of stupidity (Stengers 2015). Even though Geissler understands her employment as nothing more than a paycheck and perceives her employer as exploiting her, she nevertheless has adopted Amazon's productivity mandates. She likewise finds her work obviates the possibility of resistance. When an employee explains she doesn't have a choice but to accept the position at Amazon, Geissler (2018) thinks, "You could have contradicted her and said: Yes, you do have a choice. But you stood there tired and shocked next to her, like you're standing there tired now; the reflexes you'd need are numbed, so you nodded and now you nod and you think: That's one way to see it" (167).

Despite her purported failure to assert herself or resist the disempowering forces of the contingent working world, Geissler's (2018) novel nevertheless affirms the importance of resistance in ways that are valuable for the anticapitalist composition classroom. Reflecting on how others might approach laboring under similar conditions, she notes, "You ought to have more guts than me and not try to perform your work as well as possible; you should be trying to perform your work badly. Or, as Elfriede Jelinek writes: 'Anyone alive disrupts.' You ought to prove to your employer that you're alive" (169). Such a statement, quoting the Austrian Nobel Prize-winning novelist and playwright, exhorts readers to oppose the professional discourses that mandate workers disappear into their labor. Geissler further speculates one could engage in small acts of resistance like hiding products, writing, "Of course they'd catch you, because everything gets found out in this company, but up to that point you'd have lived a little more in your workplace and you'd have ordered your obedience to retreat" (170). In her construction, the act of resistance is not ultimately about offering a substantive challenge to one's employer but rather about mitigating the employer's attempts to diminish the worker's capacity for resistance. In this sense, the preservation of autonomy is a generative act that looks forward to the future agency and capacities of the worker. As Geissler contends, the worker who has proved to their employer that they are alive also has the potential to act (169).

I asked students to conduct an analysis of the text, situating Geissler's representation of her employment within larger capitalist logics, particularly the ways contemporary forms of work divide and disempower workers while occluding the potential of other formations and possibilities. As Li observed, capitalist conditions isolate workers insofar as "no one really wants to be your friend" because everyone sees you as competition. In his analysis, another student, Osman, offered an extended discussion of the ways contemporary forms of work aim to divide, exhaust, and disempower workers: "Capitalism demands production and efficiency, forcing workers to follow strict requirements. Their leisure time is restricted severely, and they are expected to maximize their productivity."

Other students focused more concretely on the cognitive control the employer holds over the employee. Samra was particularly interested in the elaborate pantomime Geissler was forced to enact when she was sick in order to convince her physician and employer she was *truly* ill. As Samra writes, such an experience portrays the employer as "ever-present in the employee's mind because the employee starts to forget about their own priorities and instead of worrying about their own health they worry about the effect their sickness has on their employer." In her analysis, Samra perceptively observed the extent of the cognitive control that exhorts employees to subordinate the self in favor of productivity and profit. Offering a similar analysis, Juana described how Geissler is dehumanized by her employer and loses the expectation of humane treatment. As she writes of Geissler's experience, "It's become normalized to be treated like garbage at work and clamp down on yourself respect and dignity."

Anticipating the final collaborative project, some students focused on the text's utility for the thinking of resistance. Juana additionally notes Geissler's text allows us to see Amazon in "a different way." As she writes, "We can be more cautious when purchasing from them and be sure we want to support them despite what they make their workers do." This, of course, remains a restrained solution. Donatella struck a more censorious note, contending the text "allows us an opportunity to reflect on the values that are currently held in society and asks us the question of how long we will continue to value economic profit over the wellbeing of the people within our society." Such a critique moves closer to examining Amazon's disempowerment of workers, perceptively framing its capitalist logics as the exchange of people for profit. However, both Juana and Donatella stop short of proposing collective solutions to Amazon's actions. Rather, both conceptualize the task of critique as individual and internal. For Juana specifically, Amazon presents a conundrum *to the consumer* that can be navigated through different or, at least more informed, consumption. To be sure, this response is not uncommon or entirely inappropriate. The educational model in both high schools and colleges seems to favor individualistic thinking, and students, in my experience, appear trained to approach problems solely from the perspective of their own choices and actions without questioning the capitalist status quo. Because of this, I encouraged students to develop robust and communally minded responses to capitalist conditions. The final assignment for the course, while not explicitly activist or confrontational, nevertheless encouraged this mode of thinking.

Following Geissler's novel, I asked students to collaboratively create public, multimodal texts drawing attention to various aspects of contemporary working conditions. Actualizing the common, collective critique of stupidity Stengers affirms, I envisaged these projects as building upon students' prior critical work and bringing it into public contexts. In the winter quarter of 2020, I assigned Natasha Stagg's 2016 novel *Surveys*, a text that explores multiple valences of contemporary labor, including the precarious work of part-time employees and the world of internet celebrities, exalted but thoroughly shaped by the currents of digital capitalism. The novel follows Colleen, a young woman fresh out of college who begins the novel working for a survey company at an Arizona mall.

Colleen and her colleagues spend their days administering surveys to the mall's dazed patrons in the service of Corporate, a vague and distant data-collection agency. The novel, however, takes an unexpected turn as Colleen becomes an influencer and begins traveling the globe with her internet-famous boyfriend, Jim. While at first blush Colleen's second life is a glorious cavalcade of parties and travel, it ultimately proves to be just as constrained by capitalist logics as her dead-end job at the survey company. The life of the internet celebrity, the novel suggests, is one in which the boundaries of work and play have blurred so absolutely as to render one's life entirely constrained by branding, sales, and corporate sponsorship, which is illustrated in her description of the parties she attends: "I couldn't get enough of 'sponsored' events. Sometimes they were dance parties, but we never danced, just stood behind the DJ booth with other celebrities" (80).

The associated project aimed to engage students in a collaborative, public critique of the novel that would actualize collective praxis on the capitalist logics of work. The assignment, like others described throughout this book, aimed to gather students in a political critique. In focusing on the working world specifically, I sought to create engaged collectives in which the critique of institutional logics and "the *production of equality*" (Stengers 2015, 140) could take place. Insofar as it also aimed to instill in students an understanding of how creative collaboration could create social change, it was designed to offer students a sense of what, similarly to Dean (2019), Stengers (2015) calls "the production or discovery of a new degree of freedom . . . the joy of thinking and imagining together, with others, thanks to others" (156). The varied projects actualized many of these aspirations, demonstrating rigorous critique, creative expression, and a unifying focus among group members. A series of blog posts by Juana, Osman, Rhiannon, and Blythe offered a scathing critique of capitalism's carceral logics. Noting the entrapment of both precarious labor and commercialized internet culture, their opening post proclaims, "There is no way out of our societal framework. . . . Everyone is immersed in capitalism, whether they want to be or not." A zine produced by Li and Simeon used artwork, poetry, and analysis to extend a multifaceted attack on contemporary forms of work and the capitalist system in which they are embedded. As Li argues in her contribution, "The nature of capitalism values profit over the human being, not only creating mundane lifestyles of repetitive tasks that we are bound to forever, but it tricks us into thinking that there are those who escape from this system." She continues, "This system of capitalism that exploits our insecurities and reduces us to only what we are monetarily worth will always follow us." For his contribution, Simeon created artwork and images and collected his impressionistic notes. In one description of the automation of contemporary work, he writes, "The perfect business machine. A well-oiled engine. Instead of controlling our machines we become machines ourselves. We describe ourselves as machines. We measure ourselves by the things we create and we see as better than us." In her contribution to a separate project, Samra critiques the cynicism of our relationship to contemporary capitalism, particularly the corporation: "We solely believe that corporations care about our interests and we trust them completely. . . . This whole working scheme that comes with capitalism is all about a business model that puts money before people. So long as the cash is flowing it is business as always." In his section of a blog series, Mateo analyzed the conditions of work that, per Schaffner (2016), blur the boundaries between work and leisure. Work, Mateo argues, "begins to consume an individual's everyday life. To a point where there is no more separation between the two." Focusing on the novel's description of joyless working parties, Mateo writes that Stagg illustrates "how one's life and work are starting to coercively become one. That there is no separation between the two." As he concludes, "You literally cannot enjoy your time at home because all you worry about is that workload. Their whole life becomes consumed by just work."

It must be acknowledged that while these various projects represent the kinds of collective, public criticism I, following Stengers (2015), suggest are necessary in an era of work's oppressive growth, opposition to work nevertheless remains a deeply conflicted project. One aspect of this conflict, indeed one brought up by my own students, is that those most in need of occupational reforms are those who are most at risk in seeking to achieve them. With respect to social class, those of limited economic means, like Geissler, can rarely afford to confront their employers and are likely to find themselves in similarly exploitative contexts if they leave one position for another. In *The ABCs of Socialism*, Wright (2016) raises a similar point, arguing that "a wealthy person can freely decide not to work for wages; a poor person without an independent means of livelihood cannot do so easily" (25). Wright is certainly correct here in that the relative political capital of middle-class workers renders them far more capable of resisting exploitation than those who most desperately need improved conditions. Of course, autonomy and agency are also unevenly distributed along the lines of race, sexuality, gender, ability, nationality, and numerous additional sites of difference. While workers from marginalized or precarious groups have contributed substantially to the tradition of US labor organizing and workplace resistance,[8] workers from these groups are also more thwarted in their activism. As Joe William Trotter Jr. observes (2019), African American workers have historically been met with "mob violence, racial job ceilings, and color lines" (xviii) to foil their attempts to enter and equalize the workplace. Simply put, those who already lack autonomy and agency face greater obstacles and risks when it comes to challenging their working conditions. Nevertheless, labor struggles by vulnerable and contingent employees are a crucial means through which organizations change, rights are won, and capitalism is challenged. While the risks are indeed significant and should not be minimized, I believe teaching the value (and the risks) of such struggles is crucial work in the composition classroom.

An additional question arises from the political economy of composition. As an enterprise embedded in the financial mechanisms of late capitalism, austerity, and the declining support for public universities, composition is deeply informed by the logics of profit and productivity (Brownstein 2018). Departments and writing programs tirelessly chase student credit hours, compete to produce majors, and manufacture their institutional brand (Gunner 2012), a process that, as Robert Samuels (2016) argues, "often pushes composition programs to reproduce the structures that place writing, teachers, form, and practice in a debased position" (A3). Likewise, as Ann Larson (2016) contends, composition, as a field that largely subsists on part-time labor, "is inseparable from low-wage work" (166). Given these conditions, Samuels is right to ask how composition can be critical of capitalism when it is itself so deeply informed by it. It is also likely students who notice the degree to which "the managerial subjectivity dominates in composition studies" (Bousquet 2002, 494) will be left confused and may be persuaded by the neoliberal discourses of the university that promote industriousness, excellence, and tireless productivity. Such challenges are considerable and cannot simply be dismissed if teachers decide to engage in pedagogical practices like those I outline here. However, despite the challenges, I maintain this kind of work is worth attempting. As I argue in this book, composition's intrinsic relation to the language economy (Marazzi 2011) and its positionality as a site of exploited labor render an explicit critique of capitalism necessary. Situating students within the capitalist valence of writing and the financial contradictions of the university, I believe, is a necessary part of teaching writing, specifically its social, material, and institutional conditions and contradictions. The pedagogical orientation I advance, I believe, is valuable to students because it offers to contextualize the suffocating and disempowering occupational rhetoric informing both the university and the world of work. Students taught the value of collective opposition to intolerable conditions of the modern workplace, even if such education is conducted within the neoliberal context of higher education, may better understand the stakes, risks, and potential of striving to "prove to your employer that you're alive" (Geissler 2018, 169).

A final challenge to what I propose concerns the controversial nature of preparing students to see the world of work as often antagonistic to their own interests. Insofar as academic institutions frequently frame the goods of writing education as in the service of professional success, instructors may find themselves at odds with colleagues and administrators. Writing teachers, it must also be acknowledged, additionally have complex relationships to both institutions and students that might trouble this work. While we wish to provide students with the knowledge and skills that will most secure their success and well-being, we also work at the behest of our institutions. To return to the arguments of Bay (2010), Scott (2009), and Samuels (2016), pedagogies more concerned with promoting criticism and resistance than with promoting skills may be profoundly misaligned with the orientation of the university. As I contend in the introduction to this book, while potentially at odds with institutional norms—and, frequently, disciplinary convention—this work remains crucial as it engages students in analyzing the kinds of exploitation that will manage their lives. While the university and many in the field of composition do not, and may never, see capitalist working conditions as a crisis, I believe writing teachers who understand the urgency of this work must practice it. Of course, pedagogy that questions or challenges the discourses of professionalization dominant in higher education may be dangerous to teachers of composition. Most of us are contingent employees striving to remain in the good graces of our employers. These are serious concerns that should be carefully considered when engaging in any form of risky pedagogy (I discuss the risk of anticapitalist pedagogy more extensively in chapter 5). Nevertheless, my purpose in this chapter is to suggest that the professional conditions of exploitation and overwork, including our own, have not only become increasingly harmful but pose unacceptable risks to workers. I believe if instructors hold the requisite security to be direct about the threats posed by contemporary working culture—acknowledging that many of us do not—then we have an obligation to resist the professionalizing orientation of many of our programs, departments, and institutions to better orient students to the capitalist working world.

CONCLUSION

In an entirely predictable and deeply illustrative move, companies during the COVID-19 epidemic enthusiastically embraced wellness initiatives. Tracking the same lines as the "New Agey" (Graeber 2018, 172) perks described earlier in this chapter, these initiatives sought to promote employees' emotional well-being in the context of escalating occupational demands, though crucially without making any substantive changes to the conditions of work. In 2021, Jefferies, an investment bank and financial services company located in Lower Manhattan, offered its 1,129 analysts and associates the choice of "a Peloton bike, a MIRROR home workout system, or an Apple package that includes an Apple Watch, iPad and AirPods" (Benveniste 2021). Pinterest provided its employees with "creative mask-making tutorials" (Wortham, *New York Times*, February 17, 2021). As an employee of the University of Washington, I was offered access to a virtual yoga series in Rome, a watercolor painting class, and a mindfulness workshop. As Catherine Liu (2021) argues, these programs seek to ease the pain of capitalist working conditions without addressing or even acknowledging their causes. "Wellness initiatives," she writes, "are designed to disguise the role that a solid paycheck plays in people's overall wellbeing." She further contends that such programs "infantilize workers while undermining our autonomy as private, suffering subjects."

By not attending as seriously as it might to declining working conditions or the various strategies and initiatives employers use to exploit workers, composition has allowed these developments to pass under its radar largely undetected. Our field, moreover, has frequently glossed over the acute exigence of capitalism's accelerations. Composition, I argue, must not strive to keep pace with the accelerating global conditions by preparing students to respond to whatever occupational demands come their way. While such a tendency might nominally support students in the short term and, of course, is certainly an understandable direction given the precarity of the humanities and higher education in general, it nevertheless does students a disservice to neglect the logics of the increasingly precarious and injurious working world. Because these discourses represent an enormous threat to the autonomy and well-being of workers, teaching students to parse and collectively challenge them should be one of our central concerns. In foregrounding a pedagogy rooted in the critique of workplace logics and collective praxis, this chapter attempts to take a step in this direction.

More research is needed, of course, to understand how the culture of exploitation and productivity acquires individual investment.

Composition scholars must better understand the operation of occupational logics in various areas of social, professional, and university life. With increased corporate presence on college campuses and the number of professional partnerships on the rise,[9] students are being inured to a culture of exploitation and maximal productivity throughout their college experience. The field has yet to substantively investigate how these preprofessional initiatives and corporate partnerships are preparing students for success as "achievement subject[s]" (Han 2015, 11). As we consider what it means to prepare students to enter the working world—acknowledging, of course, that many are already there as contingent workers—in an era marked by increasingly injurious conditions, rising precarity, and the shocks of the 2008 recession and the economic crisis brought about by COVID-19, we must consider our responsibility to students who will inevitably be overworked and undervalued. Regarding these conditions, helping students analyze the logic of work and the potential of collaborative resistance is quickly becoming one of our most important pedagogical tasks.

4
DATA

In recent years, the long-ascendant narrative of digital technology as generally supportive of progressive ends has started to fray.¹ In numerous well-publicized cases, the technology industry has demonstrated a nearly boundless capacity to exploit the most vulnerable and marginalized populations. In 2019, journalists began widely reporting digital profiteering schemes in US prisons in which inmates were charged to read eBooks and make video calls. As Mei-Ling McNamara reported in the *Guardian* on January 13, 2020, the West Virginia Division of Corrections and Rehabilitation, partnering with a technology company, recently launched a program to charge inmates five cents a minute to read, a cost that, as McNamara notes, equates to an hour of prison labor. Prisons have also moved toward phasing out free, in-person visitations and replacing them with a fee-based video chat model. In one instance, a company called Securus Technology charged $12.99 for a twenty-minute video chat (Sims, *Guardian*, December 9, 2017).

Technology companies have additionally been at the forefront of the informal economy, discussed in the previous chapter, enjoying enormous profits while paying their contractors minimal wages (Campbell 2019). Uber and Lyft, in particular, have received a great deal of criticism for their exploitative practices, particularly for fighting attempts to classify their drivers as employees rather than contractors (DeBord 2019).² More significantly, in recent years there have been numerous revelations of far-reaching surveillance programs by both governments and corporations. The Cambridge Analytica scandal of 2018 demonstrated how extensive such efforts could be—leaks by Christopher Wylie revealed how the company used improperly collected data from Facebook to build voter profiles during the 2016 election and, per the admission of the company's chief executive, Alexander Nix, "used seduction and bribery to entrap politicians and influence foreign elections" (Confessore, *New York Times*, April 4, 2018).³

Cumulatively, these various revelations have painted the technology sector in an unflattering light, as politically conservative and aggressively capitalist rather than the partner of progressive activists. Academic discourse around technology has also notably shifted on the subject of technology's relationship to profit. In *The Age of Surveillance Capitalism: The Fight for A Human Future at the New Frontier of Power*, Shoshana Zuboff (2019) traces how technology companies have moved toward data-driven profit models—mining and selling data and, ultimately, modifying human behavior. As she details, following its founding in 1998 by Larry Page and Sergey Brin, Google became aware of "data exhaust" (68) produced from its search engine, such as "the number and pattern of search terms, how a query is phrased, spelling, punctuation, dwell time, click patterns, and location" (67). While this material was initially ignored, the company soon came to understand data's operational and monetary value, and it quickly became a vital resource for the company. First using it to evolve Google's search engine to undertake "a reflexive process of continuous learning improvement" (68), the company would later learn to compile "user profile information" (78) to tailor ad content to users (78). Unbeknownst to most internet users, Google transitioned from being a service provider to a data mining business. As Zuboff argues, "*Users were no longer ends in themselves but rather became the means to others' ends*" (88). In the years since, the rest of the technology industry has uniformly followed suit to the extent that "surveillance capitalism" (9) has become the "default model of information capitalism on the web" (93). This, however, is not the end of the process, as Zuboff explains. Surveillance capitalists additionally strive, in Skinnerian fashion, to modify the behavior of users to meet "revenue and growth objectives" (294). These processes include "tuning" (294), practices that "shape the flow of behavior" (294) or "channel attention" (294); "herding" (295), "controlling key elements in a person's immediate context" (295) such as remotely shutting down a car's engine; and "conditioning" (296), a concept from behaviorism that employs "rewards, recognition, or praise" (296) to influence behavior.

It is, of course, important to acknowledge that what I am referring to as "the technology industry" is not homogenous but, rather, comprised of a vast archipelago of companies with diverse relations to profit. Nevertheless, in many respects, the map of the industry has simplified in recent years due to the efforts of the five most powerful actors (Amazon, Apple, Facebook [now Meta], Alphabet [Google's parent company], and Microsoft), commonly referred to as "Big Tech" (Yglesias 2019), to edge out competition. As Tim Wu and Stuart A. Thompson (*New

York Times, June 7, 2019) clarify, these five companies are "the product of hundreds of mergers," each actively acquiring dozens, and in some cases hundreds, of companies in recent years—Google, as of 2019, had acquired 270, while Facebook had acquired 92. These mergers, Wu and Thompson argue, despite demonstrably stifling competition in the tech world, have gone largely unquestioned by regulators. Big Tech, which is naturally at the forefront of the data economy (Zuboff 2019), hence represents an enormous center of gravity in the world of technology. Benjamin Bratton (2016), however, cautions against reductive constructions when it comes to understanding the influence of technology companies. As he theorizes, contemporary power is an intermingled global architecture of technology, industry, and governance.

> Planetary-scale computation takes different forms at different scales—energy and mineral sourcing and grids; subterranean cloud infrastructure; urban software and public service privatization; massive universal addressing systems; interfaces drawn by the augmentation of the hand, of the eye, or dissolved into objects; users both over-outlined by self-quantification and also exploded by the arrival of legions of sensors, algorithms, and robots. (4–5)

Per Bratton, these are not disconnected intensities but rather form "a coherent and interdependent whole" (5), a hierarchy of systems, processes, hardware, and software he terms "The Stack" (5). One implication of the way this formation sutures the vastness of mechanical, social, and political processes and architectures is that technology (and, by association, technology companies) is deeply and inextricably enmeshed in capitalism. The social world is, likewise, profoundly entangled in techno-capitalist practices.

However one parses it, technology now comprises a $5 trillion industry (A. Levy 2020), with big data set to represent $274 billion of it in 2022 (Marvin 2019). Given these figures, it remains surprising that writing scholars have not extended more attention to the financial processes and logics guiding the digital world or the various behavioral inducements that animate the scene. Virtually all platforms users rely on to communicate, produce, and consume content are for-profit technologies designed to treat the user and their "data exhaust" (Zuboff 2019, 68) as revenue streams.[4] In nearly all additional aspects of internet usage, the extractive project of digital capitalism is no less present—users pay for goods and services; they rent their housing and sell their labor-power using apps like Uber, Airbnb, and TaskRabbit; they consume advertising; and their data are mined. Nevertheless, to date, only a modest number of compositionists have explored the implications of digital technology's financial apparatus for the field of writing or considered how these aspects of the digital world might be taken up in the composition classroom. It is illustrative, for example, that *The Routledge Handbook of Digital Writing and Rhetoric*, edited by Jonathan Alexander and Jacqueline Rhodes (2018), contains only one essay explicitly devoted to economic conditions.[5]

A consequence of this disinterest is that students in conventional multimodal and digital writing courses are typically not approaching the digital world attuned to issues of labor, profit, exploitation, or the attenuation of democratic norms. As pedagogical literature in multimodal composition and digital writing suggests,[6] students in these courses typically learn to communicate effectively in various digital environments, to understand the affordances of specific technologies and platforms, to parse the nuances of HTML, R, or UX design, or even to understand the progressive potential of social media.[7] However, students are not being positioned to consider how the skills and aptitudes honed by standard digital writing curricula are thoroughly managed, anticipated, and commodified by the logics of profit or how digital writing, through its relationship to big data, is subject to extraction, monetization, and behavior modification (Zuboff 2019). On the need for a technological literacy that accounts for economic and social conditions, artist and writer James Bridle (2019) argues, "Learning to code is not enough, just as learning to plumb a sink is not enough to understand the complex interactions between water tables, political geography, ageing infrastructure, and social policy that define, shape and produce actual life support systems in society" (3).

This chapter, with Bridle, considers how a writing class devoted to a critical encounter with digital capitalism could proceed. Students studying digital writing, I believe, should receive a critical introduction to the extensive influence of the digital profit model, specifically one that introduces the political-economic role of surveillance capitalism and big data and explores their threat to progressive ends. In what follows, I begin by characterizing how scholars of digital writing and multimodal composition, having long postponed a substantive engagement with capitalism, are now beginning to address the subject. I subsequently advance a critical anticapitalist approach to digital writing's financial entanglements based in the work of philosopher Bernard Stiegler. Stiegler, as this chapter maintains, is a deeply applicable, though underutilized, theorist for composition insofar as he conceptualizes how capitalism has so comprehensively merged with technology as to render any engagement with contemporary digital technology saturated with capitalist logics.

Naturally, given the breadth and complexity of digital writing and multimodal composition, such a critique cannot hope to be anything more than propaedeutic. I do not, for example, detail an extensive program of digital writing or consider how other scholars might do so. Rather, this critique offers a perspective on how students might be critically oriented to the political economy of the digital world and presents some tentative practices for engaging them in forms of digital writing that strive to resist capitulating to digital capitalist and neoliberal narratives. The context in which I present this material to students, notably, is not a digital writing class, though students did engage in some digital writing, but rather a WAC framework focused on humanities writing. Nevertheless, I contend the following approach is one that can be adapted and repurposed for any number of writing classes, including advanced writing courses explicitly devoted to digital writing. Regardless of context, engaging students in the digital world, whatever the pedagogical occasion, must not neglect the enormous impact of contemporary capitalism or the powerful narratives that have shaped our attitudes about technology companies and the profit model of the digital world. Students, instead, can gain facility with technology while also accruing a critical understanding of its political-economic context.

WRITING WITH DIGITAL CAPITALISM

While multimodal and digital composition's critique of capitalism remains tentative, the subfield has nevertheless offered substantive engagement with a host of social justice issues. Adam J. Banks (2005, 2011) has analyzed the intersections of race and the digital world, Laura Gonzales (2018) has investigated issues of digital accessibility for transnational and multilingual students, and Jacqueline Rhodes and Jonathan Alexander (2015) have explored expressions of queer identity in digital contexts, examining "the simultaneous and often contradictory interplay between digital and traditional writing pedagogies and the author/ed self." These works and others contend the digital world is a site extensively shaped by and relevant to identity, a place of asserting and discovering identity and, likewise, a place of identity-based exclusion. Scholars have also initiated the work of examining the capitalist effects of the digital world, investigating intellectual property (Edwards and Reyman 2018; Hobbs and Donnelly 2011; Howard 2011; Reyman 2009; Rife, Slattery, and DeVoss 2011; Vie and deWinter 2008), online platforms (Dush 2015; Stolley 2008, 2016), and big data (Beveridge 2017; Jarrett 2018; McKee 2011; Reyman 2013) through a political-economic framework.

Kylie Jarrett (2018) offers a valuable critique of data mining and the economic model of the digital world more broadly, criticizing the asymmetrical financial model of digital writing where the extensive forms of content generation offer no remuneration to most internet users but, rather, generate revenue for the tech industry through data extraction. Jarrett equates this profit model to reproductive labor insofar as it is "richly meaningful labor that centrally produces use-values even while structurally embedded within capitalist value creation" (430). Annette Vee (2017) also notably highlights the capitalist valence of the expansion of programming literacy, noting companies like Khan Academy that offer free coding instruction are often funded by "overflow Silicon Valley capital" (75). She argues that while many promote coding literacy as a form of empowerment, its proliferation nevertheless represents the global marketplace dictating the terms of education (90).

A number of scholars have additionally explored the relevance of big data to writing studies, and while some praise the potential of data collection to support new directions for composition research and emerging opportunities for the teaching of writing and argument (Beveridge 2017), others have been critical. In her 2011 article, Heidi A. McKee raises concerns about corporate data mining and its implications for college composition, noting, "We can aim to make ourselves and our students more critically aware of the data mining that is occurring and may occur in the future with the goal, perhaps, of making it harder for corporations to manufacture consent" (284). Jessica Reyman's 2013 article in *College English*, "User Data on the Social Web: Authorship, Agency, and Appropriation," further explores the implications of data mining for writers' agency and ownership of their text. Critiquing the claims surveillance capitalists make to justify their appropriation of user data, namely that user data is "authorless" (525) and created through "aggregation and interpretation" (524), Reyman defends the notion of data as a coagentive excrescence—"the practices of generating, aggregating, and interpreting user data [that] could be understood as collaborative, authorial acts of technological and human agency" (528)—and advocates for more transparency in data mining (531).

Providing the field's most thorough critique of digital capitalism to date, Christian J. Pulver's (2020) *Metabolizing Capital: Writing, Information, and the Biophysical Environment* offers a systematic, object-oriented analysis of the political economy of data mining and presents a responsive writing sequence based in the "*defetishization*" (165) of the digital. As Pulver argues, the internet is in the midst of an epochal transition between Web 2.0, defined by notions of agency, interactivity, and sociality (87), and Web 3.0, a scene of "pervasive data collection by governments worried about terrorism and by corporations determined to commodify every aspect of our lived experience through persistent datafication" (85). As I similarly contend in this chapter, Pulver argues that much of composition's theorization of writing remains locked in a Web 2.0 model and has yet to fully acknowledge the consequences of datafication (88). To amend this inattention, he advocates greater consideration of the historical development of "informational capitalism" (98) and the persuasive aspects of capitalism's digital edge, most critically the technology sector's contribution to "*internet addiction*" (129) that keeps consumers tied to their screens and continually producing data. Given these conditions, Pulver proposes a model of "digital ecological awareness" (158) in the writing classroom, attuning students to the deep enmeshment of material conditions (161) and promoting students' utopian thinking in the promotion of "a more sustainable, just, and ecological world" (165). He likewise promotes assignments like keeping a phenomenological record of disengaging from technology (174) and tracing the life cycle of products (177).

As this brief precis suggests, a number of scholars offer trenchant critiques of the capitalist conditions of the digital world and examine the bearing these conditions have on writing. They nevertheless remain a minority in a subfield that continues to overlook the gravity of digital capitalism. Breaking somewhat with these critiques of digital technology, data mining specifically, I view the most egregious harm of the digital to lie not in the unremunerated nature of data mining, in its lack of transparency, or, necessarily, in internet addiction, though these are certainly significant problems worthy of further disciplinary attention. My critique, rather, is a far more fundamental one concerning the broad consequences of capitalism's threat to the common, namely its capacity to disrupt communities, intervene in the fabric of the social, and thwart activism. I am most significantly concerned with the ways digital capitalism has delimited our capacity to imagine radical political solutions. In the following section, I discuss how Stiegler's work supports this critique and suggests a means of designing digital writing classes that privilege critique and political action.

BERNARD STIEGLER: DATA, DISRUPTION, AND DREAMING

Among contemporary philosophers, Stiegler (1998) has arguably had the most significant influence on the fields of media and technology studies, mostly for his concept of technics, a means of accounting for human development by way of our species' interdependence with and evolution by way of "technical innovations" (21). In Stiegler's view, such innovations are not limited to what we generally refer to as *technology* but comprise rituals, processes, skills, habits, algorithms, shortcuts, and embodied knowledge as well as media and digital communication technologies. Crucial to Stiegler's approach to technology is a vehement critique of capitalism, which Stiegler contends has merged with contemporary digital technology and disrupted human life, particularly our capacity to form connections with others. This merging, as Stiegler contends, occurred during the Industrial Revolution when innovation shifted to become "sufficiently attractive" (38) to investors. The outcome of the financializaton of innovation, in his view, is a system of production now "cut off from productive realities, and functions according to a logic of belief (or credit)" (38). In other words, innovation is now driven by capitalist logics alone. While several scholars in composition studies have addressed Stiegler's relevance to the field, they have mostly overlooked this important aspect of his work.

John Tinnell (2015), for example, has addressed the relevance of Stiegler's notion of grammatization, a concept adapted from Jacques Derrida, to composition. Grammatization, Tinnell argues, "suggests the beginnings of a theoretical framework for orienting rhetorical inquiry" (132) insofar as it "reflects on the history of writing and technology, qua the technics of writing, in order to gain insight into new units of analysis and production emerging across heterogeneous innovations in new media" (142). As Tinnell argues, YouTube, read through such a framework, gives cause for hope insofar as "electronic and digital media have not hopelessly handed over culture to the culture industry" (144). Jonathan S. Carter (2019) has proposed Stiegler's notion of transindividuation as applicable to the study of rhetoric. The term, Carter explains, "considers the tripartite relation between individual, collectivity, and technic that fosters ongoing processes of identity production" (543) as a curative for Bruno Latour's neglect of rhetoricity in his approach to networks. As Carter contends, combining Stiegler's understanding of technics with Latour's actor-network theory offers insight into the interrelation of humans and technology (543). Vee (2017), notably, acknowledges Stiegler's critique of digital capitalism, observing that the philosopher characterizes the latter as "drive[ing] rationalization toward poison" (120). She, however, counters this interpretation, arguing that technologies also "reveal and enable the creation of new kinds of knowledge" (120). Likewise, against Stiegler's uncomplimentary characterization of digital technology's capacity to reduce and transform information from temporal to spatial contexts—what Stiegler (1998) calls "*detemporalization*" (121)—Vee (2017) argues code has the capacity to "*retemporalize* information" (121). As she writes, "When code is written, it translates processes into text. When it runs, it turns text into process, albeit a process that is digitized, rationalized, grammatized" (121). Accordingly, while Vee thoughtfully engages Stiegler's theory of capitalism, she and others in the field who have utilized his theorization of technology have resisted the philosopher's argument regarding technology's disastrous capitalist entanglements.

Stiegler's (2019) critique of capitalism offers composition a means with which to consider the deep rhetorical function (and dysfunction) of the for-profit digital technologies that have transformed the cultural and linguistic landscape. Particularly useful in such a critique is the philosopher's theorization of "disruption" (32), a concept that critiques the destructive effects of digital capitalism and suggests a way forward by means of collective "dreaming" (297). In *The Age of Disruption: Technology and Madness in Computational Capitalism*, Stiegler extends a critique not unlike that of Karl Polanyi, exploring the ways digital technology (and the capitalist logics within it) destabilize the individual and the fabric of the social more broadly. In the text, Stiegler excoriates the conditions of the contemporary digital capitalist landscape for organizing a calamitous, destructive conflict to which the individual has been conscripted. "We are in the midst of a global economic war," he writes, "in which an oligarchy of the lords of economic war sit on boards of directors, and the masses of producers and consumers are its troops" (300). In such a schema, Stiegler revises the Marxian portrayal of antagonism between capitalist and worker, suggesting technological conditions have rendered the individual a militant in the war against the population. This war, for Stiegler, is the coming into being of the barbarism anticipated by Engels and Luxemburg, renovated for an age of technological hagiography. In Stiegler's view, the current state of barbarism acutely menaces the essence and possibility of social relations and political action *tout court*, what theorists discussed throughout this book call *the common*. This new kind of barbarism, for Stiegler, is typified by the hypercapitalist logics that undergirded European austerity during the previous economic downturn: "As for the new barbarian, despite the 2008 collapse and the actions of the European troika that went on to sacrifice Greece, they continue to celebrate the invisible hand as the Providence of God" (51). This unfettered embrace of capitalism, for Stiegler, invites a "war of all against all" (51).

This war hangs on the failure of what Stiegler terms *individuation*, a process resulting from individuals' encounter with technics. As he elaborates in an interview with Irit Rogoff in *e-flux*, "When you are reading a book, you individuate yourself by reading this book because reading a book is to be transformed by the book" (Stiegler and Rogoff 2010). A human's encounter with a book is, for Stiegler, a substantive technical process fundamentally transformative and productive insofar as the individual is *only ever* the result of their technical encounters. *Trans*individuation, relatedly, occurs when this process takes place among a body of individuals. In such a process, the individual and the collective produce one another and are made what they are by technical relations. Transindividuation, Rogoff explains, is "the process of co-individuation within a preindividuated milieu and in which both the 'I' and the 'We' are transformed through one another." Crucially, it is these processes, individuation and transindividuation, that Stiegler contends are at risk from the appearance of digital technology and computational capitalism. The current state of capitalist barbarism, Stiegler (2019) writes, "amounts to a *murderous dis-articulation* of the *I* and the *we*" (5). In other words, in the place of technical relations that produce individuals and communities, capitalism now stands. "Transindividuation," Stiegler further explains, "is replaced by processes of transdividuation that are under corporate control, by corporations that are in turn controlled by shareholders who 'manage' them according to a single criterion: the increase of dividends" (46). Technical innovations, in Stiegler's view, have become corporatized and have imported capitalist logics into individuals and communities, disturbing the essential formation of both.

This endangering of individuation and transindividuation, the key threat capitalism poses, is what Stiegler (2019) calls "disruption" (32).[8] Disruption, as he frames it, engages in "outstripping and overtaking social organizations, and, through that, in short-circuiting collective individuation and transindividuation" (81). Disruption occurs when technical relations take place across digital networks "serving what is referred to today as the 'data economy'" (7), whereby the processes by which individuals and collectives are formed become surveilled, monetized, and transformed. This networked relation, which Stiegler terms "digital reticulation" (7), disrupts transindividuation by becoming intimately involved in its processes. Unlike other contemporary theorists of the common, notably Stengers (2015), who view the network as a potential fulcrum of the common, Stiegler (2019) suggests the digital architecture of the network introduces devastating interruptions or, rather, disruptions. Individuals and groups, he elaborates, "are thus transformed into data-providers, deformed and re-formed by 'social' networks operating according to new protocols of association. In this way, they find themselves disindividuated" (7). Through this process, individuals become disposed of "*their own desires, expectations, volitions, will* and so on" (7).

For Stiegler (2019) there are numerous harmful consequences of disruption, though the most significant is the threat to what he refers to as "*dreaming*," the act of imagining and actualizing an alternative political future, "a *common horizon*" (18). More precisely, dreaming entails the "*protention*"[9] of novel formations to allow for the process of transindividuation to occur. Dreaming, in Stiegler's theorization, "allows not only the generation of new technical organs . . . [but] the generation of works, knowledge and the organizations that these require" (199). In the context of the disruption of the processes of transindividuation by the data industry, dreaming, while imperiled, provides a means of creating new "technical organs" (199) to support the establishment of individuals, groups, and thoughts of the future. At the core of *The Age of Disruption* is Florian, a young person whose alienation under contemporary economic conditions has destroyed his capacity to think of the future: "We no longer have the dream of starting a family, of having children, or a trade, or ideals. . . . we're sure that we will be the last generation, or one of the last, before the end" (9). Dreaming, hence, is what is *at risk* from capitalist conditions—"today's disruption destroys the faculty of dreaming" (201)—but also what makes a way out of the current conditions of disruption possible. Stiegler's chief example of such dreaming is Martin Luther King Jr., a figure who "embodies the dreamer whose dreams, in being realized, become global" (199) and held "the *power to make other adults dream*" (200).

Notably, Stiegler's notion of dreaming resonates with Bettina L. Love's (2019) conception of "*freedom dreaming*" in *We Want to Do More Than Survive: Abolitionist Teaching and the Pursuit of Educational Freedom*. Broadly, the text develops the antiracist conception of "abolitionist teaching" (88) as a means of dismantling forces of disempowerment and liberating minorities. As she writes, "Abolitionist teaching is as much about tearing down old structures and ways of thinking as it is about forming new ideas, new forms of social interactions, new ways to be inclusive, new ways to discuss inequality and distribute wealth and resources" (88). In Love's view, such concomitant creation and destruction in the interest of capacitating freedom entails acts of dreaming or, more precisely, acts of imagination that envision and work toward the actualization of emancipatory worlds. Like Stiegler's concept of dreaming, freedom dreaming is not merely an act of ideation, a fantasy, but a practical act of thinking and working toward achievable social and political change. For Love, a notable example is the Seattle teachers' union strike of 2015, in which teachers made extensive demands of Seattle Public Schools such as pay increases, breaks, a moratorium on standardized testing, and the implementation of antiracist policies (106). While many of the teachers' demands were met, Love locates the success of the strike in both empowering and destructive outcomes: "Teachers and parents found the power of their voices, grassroots organization, a politics of refusal, self-determination, and solidarity" (107). She likewise argues the strike represents "the meticulous, piece-by-piece tearing down of a system of injustice" (107).

The question posed by both Stigler's and Love's conception of dreaming is a practical one—how do we dream when, as Stiegler (2019) contends, the potential of dreaming is opposed by digital disruption? How do we realize our dreams when we dwell in an age of "stupidity" (297)?[10] As Stiegler argues, adversity and impossibility are, in fact, integral components of dreaming: "A true dream is always what presents itself as something that *cannot* be realized" (298). Dreaming of a better world, in other words, only occurs in such contexts in which such possibility seems unattainable. Dreamers, like King, are those who defy impediments to envision worlds that, to others, seem impossible and who work to convince others of their attainability. Stiegler further contends that "on those occasions when [a dream] *is* realized . . . it is because it has become capable of becoming a *desire*— and a *shared* desire" (298). Effectively, dreaming is an act of collective faith that reaches beyond the states of hopelessness modern capitalism has created for us. An attendant task, as Stiegler argues, is for dreams to outpace technological disruption. Stiegler cautions that such outpacing is possible "only on the condition that noesis can move *faster than the algorithms*" (311). Capitalism, he rightly notes, is swift and voracious, constantly expanding to commodify activist dreaming. Dreaming must necessarily evade this force: "*This possibility is precisely that of the bifurcation, which moves infinitely faster than every trajectory pursued in becoming,* since, as its quasi-cause, it reverses this becoming within which it *opens up* the sole motive for hope: the future as improbable possibility" (311–312).[11] The speed to which Stiegler refers is not of the same order as the acceleration of work discussed in the previous chapter or Hartmut Rosa's (2015) conception of "social acceleration" (4) the sociologist claims is an endemic feature of modernization. Rather, this is the speed of *becoming*, of transforming the self into something new. For Stiegler, to accomplish the task of achieving a world liberated from computational capitalism, we must not only dream it, a crucial and imperiled first step, but we must also reimagine ourselves as well.

For the teachers and scholars of writing, Stiegler (2019) offers three key lessons applicable to teaching digital writing and multimodal composition in the anticapitalist classroom:

1. Teaching the culture, logics, conditions, and discourses of the network, specifically with an eye toward how "Californian 'digital business'" (32) disrupts individuals and communities
2. Considering the threat of digital networks to communities, as well as the possibilities and limitations of collaborating by way of reticulated networks
3. Dreaming, that is, thinking and acting beyond the structures of the technology industry and the digital world

This approach, foregrounding the digital scene as one fundamentally of disruption and then following the effects of this disruption from the general contours and logics of the tech scene to its material effects on collectivities, provides both a powerful means of understanding the digital world's persuasive power and a perspective from which to challenge the utopian rhetoric voiced by Silicon Valley evangelists. In many ways, such a perspective is complementary to recent critiques of capitalism in the field—Jarrett's (2018) contention that digital writing is an inherent site of exploitation (423) and Pulver's (2020) understanding of the digital world as a site of pervasive "datafication" (88). One meaningful difference here, however, is that these two critiques maintain the possibility of meaningful interventions in the context of digital technology, while Stiegler calls for a much more substantive reinvention and reimagining of the digital world. The following writing course exhorts students to *dream* of a new technological situation that avoids, or at least reduces, the destabilizing effects of computational capitalism. Through such a model, students learn to counter the prevailing techno-utopianism with an *anticapitalist* utopianism, a perspective that foregrounds the value and potential of gathering.

DIGITAL DREAMING

In the spring of 2020, as the COVID-19 epidemic accelerated across the world and universities took their teaching online, I taught a writing course that foregrounded a critique of the political economy of digital communication. The course, like the one detailed in the previous chapter, was a WAC course focusing on humanities writing, though this version centered on the humanities' critique of digital technology and included a final project that engaged students in digital writing on the future of the internet. I specifically utilized Stiegler's (2019) critique of disruption as a guiding light, organizing the course as an examination of technical logics and culture, an exploration of capitalism's effect on online communities, and an exploration of protential, utopian thinking on the changes needed to remake the digital world for the common good, that is, dreaming. In so structuring the course, I sought to demonstrate the capacities of humanistic critique to intervene in the digital world and, per the collective, anticapitalist focus of my pedagogy, to emphasize the potentialities of the common as a means of resistance, particularly in periods of capitalist hegemony and political authoritarianism. Analogously to Pulver's (2020) pedagogical focus on "*defetishization*" (165), I sought to engage students in the kinds of analyses that would unwind the extensive narratives of technology as a progressive force and allow them to both analyze and reimagine technology. It was, to be sure, a not insignificant irony that a class largely framed as an investigation and a critique of technological capitalism was entirely conducted by way of for-profit technology platforms (Canvas, Panopto, Zoom, Gmail, Google Docs). While certainly not a destabilizing feature, and indeed one that often served to demonstrate to students our extensive reliance on for-profit technologies, the looming presence of these programs was also a reminder of capitalism's utter ubiquity in academic life. As I discuss at the close of the chapter, such technological pervasiveness not only necessitates a nuanced pedagogical response but, more importantly, calls for collective efforts to change the increasing privatization of the university and its reliance on the technology sector.

Beginning broadly with Stiegler's (2019) critique of computational capitalism's intervention in the processes of individuation and transindividuation, I devoted the first part of the class to the culture, logics, and capitalist foundations of the technology industry. In building the introductory readings and assignments, I had two specific goals. First, as with my approach to debt, I wanted students to interrogate the common view of technology and the digital world as rhetorically and politically neutral entities. This notably follows Mark C. Marino's (2006) assertion that "lines of code are not value-neutral and can be analyzed using the theoretical approaches applied to other semiotic systems." In assigning readings and assignments on the persuasive capacities of websites and technologies, I pushed students to consider how technology shapes attitudes and behaviors. Second, I encouraged students to understand that much of this power emanates from the capitalist profit model. Indeed, it is not simply enough that students comprehend they are being tuned, herded, and conditioned (Zuboff 2019, 294–296) by digital technologies; they must understand this process is guided by and in the service of capitalism. Realizing and being able to identify these aspects of the digital world is, to be sure, a worthy goal in itself. However, for this course, political-economic critique of technology also supported students' subsequent exploration of the digital world's threat to collaboration or, per Stiegler's (2019) language, the way individuals are "transformed into data-providers, de-formed and re-formed by 'social' networks operating according to new protocols of association" (7).

In teaching this material, I began by introducing students to Shoshana Zuboff's conception of surveillance capitalism. Beginning the course in such a way gave students a potent counternarrative to the technological apologia offered by tech evangelists like Elon Musk.[12] In an op-ed for the *New York Times* (January 24, 2020), which I asked students to read and respond to, Zuboff critiques the "epistemic inequality" the digital world has created: "Surveillance capitalists exploit the widening inequity of knowledge for the sake of profits. They manipulate the economy, our society and even our lives with impunity, endangering not just individual privacy but democracy itself." Such a statement introduces the notion of a power differential inherent in technology use where surveillance capitalists hold an information advantage over users they exploit for profit. Essential in this critique is the assertion that this extractive mechanism is not simply a passive one, a system in which surveillance capitalists quietly siphon data without any perceptible consequence. Rather, as Zuboff explains, surveillance capitalism also "works its will through the medium of ubiquitous digital instrumentation to manipulate subliminal cues, psychologically target communications, impose default choice architectures, trigger social comparison dynamics and levy rewards and punishments." Students responding to this article begin to approach an understanding, re Stiegler (2019), that the capitalist digital environment has profound, though often unrecognized, effects upon individuals.

It should be noted that students, particularly those who are technologically savvy, which is to say most of them, are already aware of these conditions to some extent and may already be concerned about them. As one student, Ling, wrote in a response paper, "Truly it's scary when I first found out there is a personalized account for all of my searches that is constantly being curated by my interests to exploit me for a company's financial gain." However, despite the fact that many students are apprised of these issues, Zuboff (2020) is a valuable resource for her framing of the structure of digital capitalism and her parsing of the various persuasive outcomes of its dominance, particularly her notion of the digital world's imposition of epistemic inequality. Many students found the concept compelling and were able to identify examples of it in the global political scene. Marjane, for example, saw connections to Brexit: "People don't have the same power to actually understand the intentions of big institutions. As long as people don't have the whole truth, it will be always easier to manipulate the people and gain from them."

I extended this critique by assigning students *The Geek's Chihuahua: Living with Apple* by Ian Bogost (2015), a popular theorist in media and technology studies. The short book gathers a suite of analytical essays on Apple's persuasive power, demonstrating, per the previous point, the rhetoric of seemingly neutral technologies. In one chapter, Bogost analyses several Apple advertisements from the late 1970s, noting computers once were "devices meant to be customized and added onto by their users, who were all assumed to be latent, potential programmers" (21). Today, he continues, "computers are not just devices for everyone but devices *meant to be sold* to everyone" (21), while programming has been transformed into a "lifestyle activit[y]" (26). Another essay analyzes Apple's revolutionary rhetoric, a discourse that promotes the brand as uniquely innovative but, as Bogost argues, offers only "commercial and aesthetic" (30) advances. As Zuboff does (2020), Bogost (2015) challenges the narrative of technology as emancipatory and revolutionary, arguing Apple technologies persuade and influence consumers in often imperceptible ways. As Bogost observes in a chapter likening the smartphone to the cigarette of the twenty-first century, "Technologies like the BlackBerry and its progeny change our social fabric in ways that we often cannot see, and therefore cannot fully reason about" (42). Such a perspective allows students to approach technology critically, not just as a force that organizes occupations and incomes but also one that finds expression in design, software, and, by extension, behavior. Re Stiegler (2019), such an approach also prepares students to understand the *technical* function (and intervention) of digital technology. Insofar as the smartphone changes our gestures and manages our interactions—as Bogost (2015) writes, "The iPhone demands to be touched just right" (3)—it is transforming us as individuals and changing our relation to communities.

To better acquaint students with this idea, I asked them to draft an essay in the style of Bogost's text. Students analyzed the persuasive qualities of various technologies such as Amazon's Alexa, social media platforms like Facebook and Instagram, and video games. In one analysis, Eileen wrote on how Japanese gacha games, games centered around an in-game economy in which players spend currency to obtain various virtual items, engage in "clever manipulation [of] their players" by "colorful animations and catchy sound effects, which further incentivize players to keep rolling for more." In her analysis of Amazon's Alexa, Chris notes how the technology's use of push notifications and constant email reminders about "new updates and 'tricks'" "subconsciously encourages users to spend more money." In both analyses, and in several others, students were attuned not simply to the persuasive aspects of technologies but also to the ways technological persuasion is comprehensively capitalist.

Students' analysis of the culture, logic, and general operation of the current scene of digital technology culminated with a reading and analysis of Anna Wiener's (2020) *Uncanny Valley: A Memoir*, an outsider's perspective on the technology industry. Wiener, as her memoir begins, is underemployed in the New York publishing world. Attracted by the promise of a higher paycheck and a more vibrant working life, Wiener joins the industry, first at an eBook company in New York and then at a series of start-ups in San Francisco, soon discovering the tech scene to be a place of technically mandated conformity, rampant sexism, and unadulterated promotion of digital capitalism's potential. Far more expansively than Bogost (2015) or Zuboff (*New York Times*, January 10, 2020), Wiener (2020) offers a critical reading of the compromised logics of the technology industry in which technology is framed as a utopian force and work is celebrated as a calling and an identity. "Social," she writes of the prevailing ethos, "would bring democracy to the world. Social would redistribute power and set people free, and users would determine their own destinies. Deeply rooted authoritarian governments were no match for design thinking and PHP applications" (229). She likewise describes how a crude and unexplored belief in the value of digital capitalism guided employees' approach to work and, more extensively, their worldview:

> The endgame was the same for everyone: Growth at any cost. Scale at any cost. Scale above all. Disrupt, then dominate. At the end of the idea: A world improved by companies improved by data. A world of actionable metrics, in which developers would never stop optimizing and users would never stop looking at their screens. A world freed of decision-making, the unnecessary friction of human behavior, where everything—whittled down to the fastest, simplest, sleekest version of itself—could be optimized, prioritized, monetized, and controlled. (136)

This pervasive perspective, as Wiener (2020) details, has had extensive and destructive ramifications for social life in the technology scene. In one respect, the belief in efficiency and technological determinism gave cover to the industry's casual and pervasive mistreatment of women. As she writes, "Sexism, misogyny, and objectification did not define the workplace—but they were everywhere" (155). She subsequently recounts how a colleague's comment, "I love dating Jewish women . . . you're so sensual" (166), was brushed off by the company management: "But you know him. That's just how he is" (117). In a separate but related issue, the ubiquitous embrace of technological efficiency paved the way for the eradication of San Francisco's culture and the deepening of economic inequality in the city. As Wiener writes, "In the absence of vibrant cultural institutions, the pleasure center of the industry might have just been exercise: people courted the sublime on trail runs and day hikes, glamped in Marin and rented chalets in Tahoe" (49). She details how the explosion of this individualistic form of achievement culture ran parallel to the development of a growing underclass: "Homeless encampments sprouted in the shadows of luxury developments. People slept and shat and shot up in the train stations, lying beneath advertisements for fast fashion and productivity apps, as waves of commuters stepped delicately around them" (51). Throughout her critique is the forceful contention that Silicon Valley, through its NIMBYism, myopia, and investment in technological determinism, is profoundly remaking both individuals and communities. This, notably, follows Stiegler's (2019) analysis of the death of "local culture and social life" (7) at the hands of digital reticulation.

In teaching the text, I specifically focused on Wiener's critique of digital technology's capacity to remake spaces, cities, interactions, and individuals in the logic of the start-up, and to do so in the spirit of capitalism. In asking students to conduct literary analyses focusing on the text's representation and critique of Silicon Valley culture, my intention was that they consider the broader effects of digital technology on communities and ruminate on remedies to this inherent antagonism. In her analysis, Vigdis analyzed how superficial arguments regarding the "progressive nature" of the technology industry are employed to paper over "the same sexism and hyperproductivity as broader US culture." Regarding the decline of San Francisco as a countercultural haven, she argues the tech scene has "usurped spaces for the systematically oppressed, replacing them with offices that allowed already-privileged people to become even more powerful." She further observes how the mantra of Wiener's (2020) workplace, "Down for the Cause" (64), while it appears to be a rallying cry and a means of deepening solidarity, is, in fact, "masking . . . motivational factors" and subtly permitting sexual harassment. Maxine, in turn, analyzed how, in Wiener's construction, the technology scene's productivity culture threatens the social, and how the "data-driven" nature of the workplace extinguishes "emotions and feeling." Likewise, despite the seemingly liberated culture at one of her places of employment, Wiener, Maxine contends, is positioned such that her life "revolve[s] around work as she constantly thinks about it." As Maxine argues, Wiener, immersed in the profit-driven, efficiency-oriented world, becomes "a part of the ecosystem." For both Vigdis and Maxine, *Uncanny Valley* offers a window into the effects of the technology scene, a world that deploys logics of efficiency to minimize abuse and exploitation while transforming the subjectivity of workers.

The second section of the course investigated reticular networks, following Stiegler's (2019) thesis that digital capitalism "penetrates, invades, parasitizes and ultimately destroys social relations at lightning speed, and, in so doing, neutralizes and annihilates them from within, by outstripping, overtaking and engulfing them" (7). Not necessarily seeking to enforce Stiegler's critical view of social networks, I nevertheless sought to expose students to the internet as a persuasive space and a site of "reticular society" (81) potentially undermined by digital capitalism. Students are themselves constantly communicating on social networks and, at the same time, are mined for their data, advertised to, swayed in many different ways, and exposed to the rhetoric of social media's emancipatory potential. Taking this into account, this section of the course sought to introduce students to the possibility that digital networks' capitalist architecture fundamentally damages social relations and to enhance students' critical capacities with respect to the narratives and discourse of digital capitalism.

I began this phase of the course by introducing three conflicting critiques of digital networks by Zeynep Tufekci (2017), Rafia Zakaria (2017), and Angela Nagle (2016), asking students to analyze an online community using one of the three theories. Tufekci, a leading scholar of technology and social movements, offers arguably the most gentle and conventional perspective on digital networks. The article my students read, "Twitter and Tear Gas: How Social Media Changed Protest Forever," is an excerpt from her subsequently published book *Twitter and Tear Gas: The Power and Fragility of Networked Protest* (2018). In the article, Tufekci (2017) analyzes the capacities of social media to propel social struggles like the Egyptian revolution of 2011 insofar as activists are able "to overcome censorship, coordinate protests, organize logistics, and spread humor and dissent with an ease that would have seemed miraculous to earlier generations." Tufekci, however, offers a nuanced portrayal of these technologies. In one respect, she notes that while they allow for the rapid formation of a vast movement, such a movement can easily falter "because it has sidestepped some of the traditional tasks of organizing."[13] She additionally notes that such technologies can create a crisis of leadership, deepening "the ever-existing tension between collective will and individual expression within movements." Nevertheless, Tufekci presents social media as a vital tool, particularly in its capacity to supplement more traditional forms of organizing. As she writes, these technologies allow people "to find one another, to craft and amplify their own narrative, to reach out to broader publics, and to organize and resist."

Both Zakaria (2017), an attorney and feminist journalist, and Nagle (2016), an academic writer, offer comparatively more critical readings of the potential for social media to abet social struggles. Zakaria (2017) questions the emancipatory potential of social media platforms insofar as they have fundamentally become surveillance tools for regimes around the world. As she details, in 2017, Facebook, Twitter, YouTube, and Microsoft formed a "multi-platform anti-terror initiative" that, far from producing any meaningful means of combatting terror, represented "a sinister expansion of social media and content-sharing platforms into the state-sponsored prosecution of the War on Terror." Zakaria explains that such a shift allowed governments far more agency in tracking users with less transparency than in the past. As she frames the company, Facebook has become an economic and juridical actor of enormous consequence, relying on a business model that "rests on collecting user information and selling it to other platforms—or governments—as the need arises."[14] Nagle (2016), who garnered significant attention for her 2017 book *Kill All Normies: Online Culture Wars from 4Chan and Tumblr to Trump and the Alt-Right*, details the rise of the violent and misogynist "beta culture" on 4chan, an anonymous imageboard website. While Nagle does nothing so dramatic as to credit platforms themselves with responsibility for beta culture or the alt-right, she nevertheless contends such sensibilities are fanned by our technological obsessions as well as our digital capitalist culture. As she argues, "The tastes and values of geeks" have been elevated in the context of our internet-centric culture while, at the same time, "the market ideology of the information society" has become accommodating to various forms of free expression, including hate speech. As with Zakaria (2017), Nagle (2016) regards the networks of the internet not as sites of potential progressive agency but, rather, or at least equally, as permissive of deeply reactionary politics.

Regarding these theories, it must be said students overwhelmingly gravitated towards Tufekci's (2017) position. This parallels similar student behavior reported elsewhere in this book, most specifically the tendency of students to prefer empowering narratives rather than those that expose the complex harm of global capitalism but offer few solutions. While students naturally represent a diversity of opinions and experiences, in this instance, I read these tendencies largely as the consequence of the neoliberal narrative of technological capitalism's capacity to abet progressive social change—by the time they arrive in a college classroom, students have been bombarded with various neoliberal defenses of social media. As a result, students are largely predisposed to find Tufekci's argument compelling insofar as it foregrounds the social over the economic and provides a reading of technology as an asset to progressive ends. In fact, in several cases, students found Tufekci's analysis of social media too critical and sought to counter her reservations. In her analysis of Friday's For Future USA (FFF USA), a climate activism group, Vigdis challenged Tufekci's misgivings regarding the fragility of online movements, writing, "FFF USA's networked activism . . . is much more nuanced than Tufekci's theory allows them to be." Out of nineteen students, none took up Nagle's (2016) article, and only one, Kathy, focused her critique on Zakaria (2017), using the latter's analysis of social media's capitalist surveillance to analyze the discourse of COVID-19 conspiracy theories, arguing that "capitalism may attenuate the efficacy of digital networks." In her critique, she observed numerous instances of dangerous misinformation that, as she understands it, is allowed to stand because Twitter's underlying interest is profit rather than truth. She concludes, "The Internet can be a space for the free exchange of ideas. However, we are fundamentally subjected to the profit capability of that exchange." Such an insightful analysis resonates with Stiegler's (2019) characterization of individuals who are "transformed into data-providers" (7) by reticulated networks. For Kathy, like Stiegler, social networks are not neutral platforms that capacitate the progressive action and connection of users but rather sites of transformation where individuals become sources of profit. While other students found Zakaria's (2017) position compelling—Masha notes, "[The article] opened my eyes to the complications of social media that I had never recognized before. . . . I guess I just thought that the internet was safe from bias"—most ultimately seemed to find her extensive critique of digital capitalism too pessimistic and, perhaps, too bewildering.

The final assignment of the course moved to the subject of dreaming, Stiegler's (2019) proposed corrective to the dominance of computational capitalism. As previously noted, Stieglerian dreaming supports "the future of an improbable possibility" (312) by thinking beyond the strictures of the present and into a future that seems unimaginable. For

Stiegler, such is the only way to gather a body of collaborators seeking "a *shared* desire" (298) in the face of pervasive disruption. In his construction, such an act is one of outpacing capitalism's technological mechanisms of control and bifurcating in the interest of creating a new world (and new subjectivities) not yet commodified by capitalist accumulation. Against the position of those like Tufekci (2017) who view social networks as potentially facilitating progressive action and social change, albeit not without reservation, Stiegler (2019) contends challenges to capitalist control can only take place in the form of substantive reinvention. While I do not wish to dismiss Tufekci and find much to admire in my students' passion for her position, I nevertheless side with Stiegler's comparatively more damning critique of reticular networks and his call for substantive and ambitious action against computational capitalism. Because of this bias, I finished the course in the spring quarter of 2020 with a modified version of the political statement discussed in chapter 1. Asking students to reimagine and propose a *new* internet that would be responsive to the most pressing failures and crises of the current digital world, the task drew from Stiegler's (2019) concept of dreaming (199) by seeking to propel students toward ambitious, inventive critiques of the digital status quo. Rather than simply serving as an occasion for convening the common and introducing students to political comradeship (Dean 2019), which it also certainly aimed to do (despite the physical distance of the students), the assignment additionally asked students to engage in forms of radical invention. With some resonance to Pulver's (2020) promotion of "utopian thinking" (164–165) and Love's (2019) "freedom dreaming" (103), this assignment, notably, was not one pushing students into the logistical weeds (though assignments of this nature can certainly be valuable) but rather an opportunity for them to *dream* and to push against capitalist dominance in envisioning another world.

To prepare students to take on the assignment, I first asked them to review two calls for transforming the digital world by Jaron Lanier, a founding figure in virtual reality and a prominent critic of internet culture, and Wendy Liu, a former software engineer turned tech critic and the author of *Abolish Silicon Valley: How to Liberate Technology from Capitalism*. In his TED Talk aptly titled "How We Need to Remake the Internet," Lanier (2018) recounts that early internet pioneers proceeded from the assumption that "everything on the Internet must be purely public" or, in other words, that the internet should be a commons. As he notes, this drove the internet toward an ad-based model, which allowed broad access without charging consumers. However, Lanier contends that as networks became more sophisticated, technology began to exert more control over consumers, introducing "social punishment and social reward," conditions Zuboff (2019) notably also critiques (294–296). Lanier (2018) argues such behavior modification has had significant negative consequences insofar as advertisers "think all they're doing is advertising toothpaste" and end up feeding what Lanier somewhat ambiguously terms "negative emotions." Lanier's solution, an ultimately unambitious one, is a subscription model, "maybe with micropayments," as an alternative to the vast architecture of surveillance capitalism. As Lanier contends, this would allow people to access "factual information" rather than "a bunch of weird, paranoid conspiracy theories" while presumably maintaining the current structure of the internet without reliance on the data industry. This approach, as Lanier readily admits, is far from an anticapitalist solution but is rather a means of curbing the runaway aspects of the data economy without the chaos of more substantive disruption. He hedges, "I don't believe we need to punish Silicon Valley." Wendy Liu (2019) offers the contrary position in her comparatively more critical and ambitious article "Abolish Silicon Valley," abstracted from her book of the same name (2020). As Liu (2019) argues, the neoliberal narrative of the tech success story, one that often begins in "a garage in California where some enterprising PhDs have hatched a new way to organize information on the web," has become tarnished. What were once sympathetic upstarts have become "a pantheon of faceless multinationals who collectively dominate the world's digital infrastructure, flouting regulations, avoiding taxes, and taking advantage of precarious labour to make a small number of people tremendously wealthy." Unlike Lanier, Liu proposes a drastic solution: "*reclaim* technology: to prevent its capture by capital, and direct it towards creating social value." As Liu asserts, Silicon Valley cannot be tempered but, per the title of her book, must be abolished. More specifically, she defends a variety of proposals for unwinding capitalism's grip on the tech industry, including "shifting away from the return-driven venture capital model, and towards a state-backed social entrepreneurship with public responsibilities. . . . [and] building worker power, within the tech industry and beyond it." By assigning both Liu and Lanier, despite Liu far surpassing Lanier in both analysis and ambition, I aimed to present students with models of bold proposals for transforming the internet resonant with Stiegler's (2019) notion of dreaming.

As with the collaborative work discussed throughout this book, I split students into small groups of three or four and engaged them in brainstorming sessions to generate ideas on the most significant problems plaguing the internet and the solutions that might address them.

As a template, I used Karl Stolley's (2016) "The Lo-Fi Manifesto, v. 2.0." and asked students to divide the text they were creating into three discrete sections: an introduction, an overview, and a list of concrete propositions. Stolley's earlier 2008 "The Lo-Fi Manifesto" notably offers a critique of the "expensive consumer and prosumer software that hinders the extensibility of digital discourse and limits digital production literacy." The text encourages scholars to produce "free and open-source artifacts" to evade both the constraints and the market forces of the technology industry. Defending the argument that digital artifacts should be *open*, that is, "available for inspection, revision, and extension" beyond their initial purpose or producer, the manifesto defends several key positions, including the arguments that software "is a poor organizing principle for digital production" and that digital literacy, accordingly, should "reach beyond the limitations of software." In the subsequent 2016 version, "The Lo-Fi Manifesto, v. 2.0.," Stolley further elaborates upon the kinds of production technologies called for, including plain-text files and plain-text editors. Likewise, I suggested students define the most pressing problems of the digital world in the opening section of their papers, move toward solutions in the second, and then isolate those solutions in a precise, epigrammatic list of statements (with annotations) in the concluding section. Stolley's text not only provided this template but also demonstrated a model of accessible, technologically oriented argumentation that could easily be emulated. However, while Stolley's proposal is ultimately a quite reasonable one, I encouraged students to think somewhat more ambitiously, to "*believe in the possibility of a miracle*" (Stiegler 2019, 303).

Responding gamely to the prompt, students developed collaborative, digital manifestos that engaged what they viewed as the most profound excesses and violations of the technology industry. These followed the trend of the prior assignment in that students, while certainly embracing many of the critical ideas evoked in texts across the course, favored Lanier's (2018) more conventional solution over Liu's (2019). Kathy, Masha, Eileen, and Gary focused on the expansive impact technology has had on "the division of power, society, politics, and culture." They focused on digital technology's threat to the social, contending that the Cambridge Analytica scandal revealed "the true danger of using the Internet is giving ourselves up to these giant corporations who are now manipulating how our society grows." Extending somewhat beyond the remit of the assignment, their solution was not limited to the digital world but had broader aspirations concerning gender diversity in the workplace, a solution I encouraged. Following Lanier's (2018) solution, the group supported a subscription model for online platforms as an alternative to the current paradigm of digital capitalism, noting this solution would "allow for a more private experience for the user because these corporations would be encouraged to protect their customer's privacy." While perhaps an underwhelming thesis given the harms of digital capitalism the course had studied, the group was more ambitious in their treatment of sexism. Using Sweden as a model of gender equality, referencing the voluntary quota system adopted by the country's political parties (Bohlen, *New York Times*, March 8, 2019), the group argued for the mandatory equal representation of women in the tech industry. The group also proposed a wealth tax based on Seattle's "head tax" (Bernstein 2018), a policy that would require technology companies to distribute their wealth to local communities. Chris, Tianlin, Mian, and Vinh also focused on issues of surveillance capitalism and feminism, arguing a new profit model for the internet is needed along with a clear and protected option of opting out of tracking cookies. As the group wrote, "This change would force companies to reconsider a majority of their income sources." The group also defended a far greater emphasis on companies acting upon their hate-speech guidelines—namely removing users like Donald Trump who violate them[15]—and creating more programs to support women in STEM. The group looked to Girls Who Code, a nonprofit organization providing computer education, and Kode With Klossy, a free coding camp started by the model and entrepreneur Karlie Kloss, as their inspiration.

While I consider both manifestos to be ultimately anodyne, particularly regarding their consideration of capitalism, I am nevertheless gratified to see students striving toward imaginative inventions in the context of technology. To be sure, these proposals didn't reach the heights of what Stiegler (2019) suggests is necessary to move "*faster than the algorithms*" (311) and instead largely remained rooted in the immediate and the possible. This was particularly the case with the second group's promotion of coding camps for women and girls. Like the analysis of online networks that largely refrained from questioning the narrative of the utility of networked protest, the project readily capitulated to the exhortations of "learn to code" often thrown at those undone by the unstable economy and the rise of precarity (McHugh 2019). It also indexed the kind of "lean-in" (Sandberg 2013) feminism that encourages women to more aggressively participate in working culture but that does not seek to transform the inherently exclusionary nature of global capitalism. As the late journalist Dawn Foster (2016) writes in her extended critique of Sandberg, *Lean Out*, "Sandberg's corporate feminism doesn't extend to calling for collective rights for women such as state maternity pay, or a stronger welfare safety net, or even encouraging women to unionise" (11). Nevertheless, both student manifestos demonstrated the willingness of students to attempt to step beyond what is merely reasonable and feasible and to consider what is necessary. This, I believe, is the most vital element of anticapitalist composition when it comes to technology—the collective striving toward a better world.

CONCLUSION

I cannot bring this chapter to a close without addressing the thorny contradiction that plagues any course critical of digital capitalism that is also fundamentally reliant on a host of for-profit communication and educational technologies. How, a critic might ask, can an instructor hope to encourage students to interrogate and oppose the unmitigated expansion of capitalism into technology when much of the content of such a course is disseminated over for-profit digital platforms? This issue is notably similar to the problem posed at the end of the previous chapter regarding the capacity of compositionists to oppose capitalism from within the thoroughly capitalist space of the university. The question here is even more acute insofar as the platforms on which our courses rest and the ether through which we extend our pedagogy, particularly in online courses, are entirely within the sphere of the market. How do we find critical ground when capitalism is everywhere?

Some have argued we may not need to insofar as progressive work can be accomplished by way of capitalist technologies. Tufekci (2017), while she discusses certain reservations about social media activism, nevertheless suggests for-profit social media platforms, Twitter specifically, can be an asset to activists. More recently, Tanya Basu (2020), writing on Black Lives Matter for the *MIT Technology Review*, suggests Google Docs, a technology my students use to produce collaborative documents, is the most important digital tool for current progressive movements. Google Docs, she writes, "has emerged as a way to share everything from lists of books on racism to templates for letters to family members and representatives to lists of funds and resources that are accepting donations." For Basu, the accessibility and the collaborative nature of documents "anyone can view and anyone can edit, anonymously" was uniquely valuable to the 2020 BIPOC liberation uprisings.

This perspective is certainly one many of my students support. In the estimation of many of them, as reflected in their papers, while technology companies may have extensive problems, including sexism, racism, and engagement in surveillance capitalism, they can nevertheless be effective tools for activists. This is, at least in part, also the position of Jarrett (2018), who notes that while digital writing amounts to unrecognized and unremunerated labor, akin to unpaid reproductive labor, it is nevertheless "implicated in the development and maintenance of social solidarity" (430). There are certainly countless examples of social media activism that seem to support this thesis. Beyond Basu's (2020) characterization of Google Docs, the Debt Collective, a debt resistance community cofounded by Astra Taylor, has a presence on several for-profit social media sites, including Twitter (@StrikeDebt). However, as I have noted throughout this chapter, I hold deep reservations about the capacity of capitalist technologies to serve progressive, anticapitalist ends in any substantive way because technology companies are not simply deriving profits from activists—and from their mined data—but also because of capitalism's transformation of social relations. I remain persuaded by Stiegler's (2019) contention that the proliferation of digital technology is not engaged in greater unity but rather the opposite, the strengthening of capitalism and the institution of heightening antagonisms, a "war of all against all" (51). In a more surface-level sense, there is the additional problem that many in the technology industry supported Donald Trump and his profoundly reactionary policies and tend toward conservative libertarianism rather than progressivism (DeGeurin 2018; Schleifer 2019). While scholars and critics once celebrated social media platforms, Facebook for instance, as spaces for progressive activism (Vie 2014), in recent years critics like Zakaria (2017) have excoriated it for mining consumer data and refusing to adopt policies to restrict racism and authoritarianism; Facebook, for instance, has been used for doxing, hate speech, voter suppression, and white supremacist organizing (P. Levy 2020). In 2020, it also refused to remove political ads with misleading information (Isaac and Kang, *New York Times* January 9, 2020).

The question, then, is what can be done to avoid the contradiction of teaching an anticapitalist writing course, particularly one concerned with digital communication, while minimizing the effects of digital capitalism. One option is to avoid framing courses as celebratory of certain digital capitalist models and, instead, making explicit the contradictions imposed by capitalism's ubiquity. This, notably, is what I attempted to do by assigning figures like Zuboff (2019), Zakaria (2017), Nagle (2016), and Liu (2019). Another approach is to rely on more progressive, socialist, or anticapitalist platforms and technologies when assigning reading and writing. In my course, the online readings were taken largely from progressive, mostly ad-free publications like the *Baffler* and *Tribune*.

Doing this with online writing, however, is far more difficult due to the ubiquity of for-profit platforms. While there are free, open-source collaborative writing programs that are *not* Google Docs, programs like Etherpad, these are nevertheless part of the internet's broad capitalist apparatus and presumably subject to data mining. The same can be said of publishing platforms like WordPress and Medium. While such a statement risks oversimplification, any writing done online necessarily and unavoidably participates, at least to some extent, in digital capitalism. While this contradiction should certainly not stop us from teaching digital writing and engaging students in public-facing communication on digital platforms, it is a concern we cannot simply ignore.

One consequence of the limited options discussed above is the fact that ultimately little can be done until the university itself becomes a space more supportive of anticapitalist work and less reliant upon for-profit technology companies. While composition instructors can encourage their students to understand, critique, and avoid capitalist technologies, these technologies are everywhere and, ultimately, impossible to avoid entirely. It is important to emphasize, however, that their presence at the university is not by chance but rather the consequence of universities' increasing privatization and participation in public-private partnerships, something universities are actively courting (Renner 2019). Universities, it must also be noted, are often antagonistic to avowed anticapitalist faculty and the kinds of teaching and activism, digital and otherwise, described throughout this book. As noted earlier in this chapter, faculty on the Left, particularly contingent faculty, are frequently censured, fired, and/or not renewed for reasons to do with their politics in the classroom or on social media. Responding to these conditions, the final chapter explores the state of universities' financial entanglements, the various risks and impediments to the work I've described across the first four chapters of this book, and the changes ultimately needed to secure a place for anticapitalist pedagogy at the university.

5
ACTION

Throughout this book, I argue compositionists must take a stronger stance against capitalism and develop teaching practices that support the protection and resuscitation of the common. Were this kind of teaching embraced at the university, or even broadly tolerated, this book might well end here. However, the declining state of academic freedom (Reichman 2019), the commercialization of higher education (Newfield 2016), and the adjunctification of the professoriate (Childress 2019; Kezar, DePaola, and Scott 2019) have troubled the capacity of faculty, particularly contingent faculty, to teach in the ways I've discussed. Of course, the enormity of capitalism's influence and the risk to the teachers who oppose it are not unrelated. As scholars like Bousquet (2008) and Scott (2009) have convincingly argued, the university, and writing programs in particular, are organized by the selfsame policies and economic forces transforming labor worldwide. Just as capitalist shifts have become an acute and irrefutable threat to which all academics must now turn, so has the university undermined our ability to do so, particularly in our teaching and public discourse.

Analogizing progressive actions such as resisting, escaping, or eroding capitalism to moves in a game, Erik Olin Wright (2019) contends the contemporary economic order has defined the rules so as to contain opposition. "The problem," he argues, "is that capitalism's rules of the game specifically restrict the space for such moves" (93). This has long been the case in academia, where many of those who might have served as US society's resources for progressive teaching, thought, and action either remain quiet or are severely censured when they speak out. Certainly, there are some, like Wright himself or other leading Leftist thinkers (many mentioned in this book), who have decried capitalism from within the academy. However, as this chapter details, for many similarly inclined academics, contingent faculty especially, being an anticapitalist is often perilous and, in many cases, grounds for outright dismissal. For Wright, because capitalism limits the possibilities for dissent, the rules of the game must be changed. He advocates "changing the rules of the game that make up power relations of capitalism in such a way as to open up more space for emancipatory alternatives" (93). While Wright's scope is far broader than mine, I similarly contend that instead of simply working within the increasingly restrictive and perilous construct of contemporary higher education, progressive academics must aspire to change the rules of the university if anticapitalist writing pedagogy and anticapitalist faculty are to have a secure home there. In other words, simply teaching along the lines I discuss is ultimately insufficient insofar as larger structural shifts are necessary to protect this work as well as future progressive action.

The following argument, to be clear, is terrifically impractical. I acknowledge that the changes I propose are immense and that I, essentially a "comp droid" (Miller 1999, 96), am in no place to make them. Nevertheless, by making them anyway, I aim, first, to clarify that creating a secure place for anticapitalist teaching is no modest task but rather entails a comprehensive remaking of universities and writing programs along with them. The second purpose of the chapter is to suggest that, despite the immensity of the task, remaking the university in a way that accommodates anticapitalism should be our ambition, however imperiled or unrealistic, because of the extensive cost of inaction. In articulating such an audacious goal, I draw inspiration from Stiegler's (2019) conception of dreaming (312) as I ruminate on what might be possible in the academy even when such aspirations seem like they "*cannot* be realized" (298). In so doing, I do my best to move "*faster than the algorithms*" (311) in the hope that such a vision can be a call to others, that my dreaming can gather some comrades and become "a *shared* desire" (298).

The stance of the common that has guided the approach to pedagogy articulated in this book also offers a means to envision what would be required to transform the university into a more progressive place where anticapitalist teaching and scholarship could occur. This chapter particularly draws from Dardot and Laval's (2019a) theorization of a model of a "common" (10) politics that eschews the exclusionary metrics of membership and ownership and instead prescribes an approach to transform capitalism's "*rules of law*" (305) for the benefit of communities. Their radical and liberatory approach to political work offers to support the transformation of the university in ways that would equitably secure writing pedagogy critical of capitalism while avoiding the logics of ownership and unilateral governance that have led to the privatization of institutions. To follow Dardot and Laval's logic, the common is a site of "instituent praxis" (298), a form of inventive political action that creates new political subjects and novel ways of acting in the world. Applied to the site of the university, Dardot and Laval's intervention supports the contention that no one can truly own the university and that no one has the right to restrict teaching in the interest of profit. Rather, in their view and in the view of similarly aligned political theorists, the common must be a place of freedom and engagement against a political scene marked by division and managerialism. Offering an answer to Wright's (2019) call for a model that creates space for action by changing the rules of the game (93), Dardot and Laval offer the potential for such a revision and a way toward a *(re)commoned* university in the context of an increasingly privatized academy.

In this concluding chapter, I first discuss the extensive limitations the contemporary university has placed on progressive teaching, writing, and discourse. I then historicize these conditions, linking the state of higher education to the long gestation of academic capitalism. I conclude by detailing the immensely ambitious work necessary to secure the place of anticapitalist work at the university, specifically discussing the role of activism in challenging academic capitalism. While, as I acknowledge later in this chapter, activism is itself hazardous and places activists at risk as they seek greater security for their teaching practices and for themselves, safeguarding anticapitalist teaching and scholarship in the academy is a vital task if compositionists believe, as I do, that anticapitalist perspectives are particularly valuable in an era marked by racial and economic inequality, economic exploitation, pervasive technological propaganda, authoritarianism, and devastating climate change.

THE RISK OF RADICALISM

The case of David Graeber, whose theorization of debt (2012) and contemporary work (2018) has undergirded much of this book, is as illustrative as any regarding the perils of progressivism in the contemporary academy. In the spring of 2005, when Graber was an assistant professor at Yale, he was informed his contract would not be renewed (Arenson, *New York Times*, December 28, 2005). A scholar of anarchism and a member of the International Workers of the World, Graeber made little secret of his politics. As he noted in an interview at the time, "So many academics lead such frightened lives. . . . The whole system sometimes seems designed to encourage paranoia and timidity. I wasn't willing to live like that." While members of the campus community protested and more than four thousand people signed a petition critical of Yale, the university refused to reverse or even explain its position (Wilson,

Guardian, October 24, 2005). Despite his attempts to find another job in the US academy, Graeber was unable to secure one (Shea 2013). From 2013 and until his death in 2020, Graeber served as a professor of anthropology at the London School of Economics. As Stanley Aronowitz commented in 2005, "I actually think places like Yale are not for people like David Graeber. . . . He's a public intellectual. He speaks out. He participates" (Arenson, *New York Times*, December 28, 2005).

The more recent case of Steven Salaita[1] is similarly incensing. In the summer 2014, the University of Illinois at Urbana–Champaign revoked its previous offer of a tenured position to Salaita. When he was hired, Salaita had already courted controversy once as an associate professor of English at Virginia Tech with a 2013 op-ed for *Salon* that critiqued compulsory support for the military ("Va. Tech Professor's"). The cause of Salaita's subsequent dismissal from the University of Illinois was a similarly controversial series of tweets critical of the 2014 Israel-Gaza conflict (Pettit 2019b). While he eventually won a $600,000 settlement from the university (Pettit 2019b), Salaita's academic career foundered. Following the rescinding of his employment in 2014, he was briefly hired as the Edward W. Said Chair of American Studies at the American University in Beirut (Zamudio-Suaréz 2018), a position from which he was, in his words, "ousted" (Pettit 2019b) in 2016. While the university denied Salaita's firing was because of his political positions, students nevertheless began a petition in his support, contending his treatment by the university was the result of his previous criticism of Israel (Zamudio-Suaréz 2018). In 2019, no longer employed in academia, Salaita took a job as a school bus driver in the suburbs of Washington, DC (Pettit 2019b).[2]

As the treatment of Graeber and Salaita indicates, being a vocal Leftist in the academy comes with risks.[3] In the context of austerity (Fabricant and Brier 2016; Kalish et al. 2019; Welch and Scott 2016) and the privatized university (Newfield 2016, 30), progressive scholarship, teaching, or public writing on and participation in Leftist causes can thwart job prospects, preclude renewal or promotion, invite harassment, or serve as grounds for dismissal. As Henry Reichman (2019) argues, "Difficult financial straits have afforded college and university administrators specious justifications for assaulting the academic freedom of their faculties" (13). While numerous prominent academics have been penalized for their radical positions, and frequently achieve some degree of notoriety when they are dismissed, countless lesser-known academics' progressivism is often punished with minimal fanfare. In 2017, Georgette Fleisher, a seventeen-year adjunct at Barnard who had been an active union organizer, was not rehired by the university, a move she alleges was retaliation (Flaherty 2017b). In 2019, Jeff Klinzman, a professor at Kirkwood Community College in Cedar Rapids, Iowa, was forced to resign following public outcry over his antifa affiliation (Miller, *Gazette*, August 23, 2019). In a more prominent case from September of 2019, Jamie R. Riley, assistant vice president and dean of students at the University of Alabama, agreed to resign his position after *Breitbart News* published an article that included several of his past tweets (Bolling, *Crimson White*, September 5, 2019). One tweet, expressing a sentiment that later became ubiquitous in 2020, stated that the US flag "represents a systemic history of racism for my people. Police are a part of that system." In late 2020, Garrett Felber, a history professor at the University of Mississippi who studies racism and the carceral state and who publicly accused the university's donors of racism, was given a nonrenewal notice on his contract (Middleton 2020). The cause, which Felber disputes, was that he refused to communicate with his department chair.

It is worth noting that most recent cases of the censure and dismissal of radical faculty follow from public remarks or actions rather than from teaching specifically. However, numerous instances of censorship of progressive teaching demonstrate radical curricula are hardly immune to suppression. In 2016, UC Berkeley suspended a class titled Palestine: A Settler Colonial Analysis because, as UC Berkeley chancellor Nicholas Dirks argued, it "espoused a single political viewpoint and appeared to offer a forum for political organizing" (Sainath 2016). Also in 2016, Steve Nass, vice chairman of the Wisconsin State Senate's higher education committee, announced that a required reading assigned in a University of Wisconsin graduate student's sociology course referring to gay sex could negatively impact the university's budget (Richmond, *Wisconsin State Journal*, July 7, 2016). As Nass asked, "Is this what the people of Wisconsin should expect when paying taxes and tuition to support the UW System?" In 2017, a graduate instructor at the University of Pennsylvania came under attack for "progressive stacking," a pedagogical strategy aiming to redress inequality by calling on racial minorities before white students (Flaherty 2017a). The instructor was attacked by Right-wing groups for her methods and, while the university publicly supported her, Steven J. Fluharty, dean of the School of Arts and Sciences, noted the university was "looking into the current matter . . . to ensure that our students were not subjected to discriminatory practices" (Flaherty 2017a). In another instance from 2018, a professor at Florida Gulf Coast University was attacked and threatened for offering a course titled White Racism (Reilly 2018). Additionally, critical race theory (CRT), the latest bugbear of the GOP, has been aggressively targeted by lawmakers (Smith, *Guardian*, November 3, 2021); while most attempts to ban the perspective have, absurdly, been aimed not at colleges but at K–12 institutions, Texas lieutenant governor Dan Patrick has threatened the tenure of university professors who teach it (Menchaca, *Austin American Statesman*, February 18, 2022). As these various cases indicate, progressive teaching, while often less actionable than public remarks or organizing, can nevertheless place faculty at risk.

While the kinds of incidents I name above are increasingly common, many faculty with whom I've discussed these issues believe, perhaps not unreasonably, in the continued safeguarding of academic freedom and hold that those who are politically active and who organize are legally protected from retaliation. Some have suggested organizing is ultimately safer than keeping quiet. While organizing (as yet) remains a legal right, countless cases of the targeting or dismissal of progressive faculty, specifically contingent faculty engaged in unionization efforts, suggest such confidence may be unjustified. In many instances, such as Graeber's, universities habitually obscure their reasons for dismissing faculty and are often able to plausibly deny their actions are politically motivated. In cases when the faculty member is an adjunct, such as Fleisher's (Flaherty 2017b), the fact that the instructor lacks the protections afforded to tenured or tenure-track faculty often means they may potentially be dismissed as a matter of course without the appearance of retaliation. In my own admittedly anecdotal experience, I know of two highly successful and well-rated contingent faculty members at different institutions who were dismissed after becoming involved in unionization efforts. While either would have been justified in pursuing legal action (and were indeed encouraged to do so by their unions), the inherent tenuousness of contingent employment often entails that claims of retaliation are nearly impossible to prove.

In addition to universities' often shadowy decision-making processes on dismissing contingent workers, there is the added complexity of the public's involvement. In recent years, public outrage, Right-wing attacks, and defamatory websites such as Professor Watchlist have targeted progressive faculty members and have frequently been involved in dismissals. While the university is the ultimate arbiter of a professor's ability to retain their position, public outrage against liberal professors, as in Klinzman's case, can significantly influence a university's decision-making or, perhaps just as likely, serve as the official justification for dismissal. The latter appears to have been the case in the termination of Lisa Durden, an adjunct at Essex Community College in Newark, New Jersey, who was fired in 2017 shortly after a Fox News interview with Tucker Carlson where she defended a Black Lives Matter chapter for holding an event excluding white participants (Schmidt, *Washington Post*, June 26, 2017). In a public statement, the college claimed Durden's dismissal came after the administration was "inundated with feedback from students, faculty and prospective students and their families expressing frustration, concern and even fear that the views expressed by a College employee (with influence over students) would negatively impact their experience on the campus." Yet, as Zaid Jilani (2018) reported in the *Intercept*, an open-records request revealed the university had received just a single complaint.

While there are certainly various explanations for why academics court risk by becoming involved in progressive politics or practicing anticapitalist pedagogy, the neoliberal orientation of the twenty-first-century university is by far the most significant. As scholars of academic capitalism maintain, over the past century, the university has become gradually bound to a capitalist culture and a vast body of typically conservative financial stakeholders including donors, trustees, partner universities, foreign nations, and corporations that limit the freedom, and indeed the security, of faculty. As Reichman (2019) argues, "Academic capitalism—or, as many term it, 'corporatization'—has greatly impacted academic work and the ability of the faculty to unite in defense of professional norms, including academic freedom" (5). Rather than functioning as a site of progressive and pioneering thought, the university has become an increasingly profit-oriented institution whose commitments often lie more with powerful financial stakeholders than with students and faculty. In describing the privatization of the public university, Newfield (2016) details how public institutions increasingly rely on private donors "like wealthy philanthropists indirectly steering research toward their area of interest with a gift" or corporations that press departments "toward applied research or future products with a series of sponsorship agreements" (29). He likewise details how public institutions, in a process of commercialization he terms "the devolutionary cycle" (35), "generally dismiss the public value of educational gains" (29) and "encourage graduates to think of their main purpose as the maximization of their own economic self-interest" (30). Those who voice positions critical of the university's funding model or its donors often become targeted.

Regarding these conditions, writing instruction oriented by a notion of the common, as I argue, is crucial work in a period in which capitalism divides solidarities across the social, political, and academic worlds. Yet it is also potentially unsafe and increasingly incompatible with the financial ethos of the university. As Scott and Welch (2016) note, there is "a felt sense of crisis among those who teach and do research in postsecondary writing education" (4) that follows from "the intensifying sway of neoliberal logics in US higher education, compounded by stepped-up austerity measures in the wake of the 2008–2009 economic crisis" (4). Before I detail the kinds of prescriptive actions I believe are necessary to confront these conditions and to secure the practice of anticapitalist composition, it is important to first review the history of the university's capitalist culture to understand how current conditions have emerged.

A BRIEF HISTORY OF ACADEMIC CAPITALISM

As Henry Heller (2016) contends in his Marxist history of US higher education, *The Capitalist University: The Transformations of Academic Capitalism since 1945*, while the US university has always held a close relationship to financial markets, the postwar period was a time of increasing intimacy between the two and represented a decline in academic freedom. Following the Second World War, universities came more extensively under government control through government-funded research while simultaneously becoming increasingly funded by wealthy philanthropists (18).[4] While Heller acknowledges there were restrictions on academic freedom in the nineteenth and early twentieth centuries, restrictions would become more acute in the postwar period (20) as a managerial culture began to emerge across the US university. He dwells on the example of Stanford in the late 1940s, where the administration pioneered the trend of tracking departments and faculty members, "including reports on research output, numbers of graduate and undergraduate students, and the amount spent on each student" (25), thereby gaining enormous influence over faculty. One notably sees these same practices today with increasingly sophisticated efforts to track and quantify faculty productivity (Patel 2016). Predictably, technological advancements have allowed the culture of surveillance to extend to students as well. In 2014, for instance, it was revealed Harvard had been surreptitiously collecting photographic data on classrooms ("Faculty Tensions I" 2014).

The postwar period also saw the balkanization of university departments, a process that, as Heller (2016) argues, "reinforced a hierarchical and undemocratic organization" (32) that supported the deepening power asymmetries between faculty and administration. This division, he likewise contends, hindered the development of "a holistic understanding of society and culture" (32), an aspiration of Marxist intellectuals, who had been far more prominent prior to the Cold War. Marxists became increasingly pilloried and deprived of academic freedom during this time (38), a trend that only increased with the growing anti-communist movement and McCarthyism. While contemporary universities are generally more tolerant of Leftist professors, particularly those with tenure, than they were during the Cold War, Professor Watchlist and other conservative sites continue the work of identifying, doxing, and defaming liberal academics. In one telling example from 2017, The Daily Caller, a conservative news site founded by Tucker Carlson and Neil Patel, ran a piece critiquing the supposed contradiction between Erik Olin Wright's allegedly high salary and his anticapitalist politics (Owens 2017). In the 1950s and 1960s, Heller notes, the US university system, particularly the humanities and social sciences, responded "almost in lock step" (10) to the procapitalist tenor of Cold War America. While the 1960s were a time of significant protest and radical thought, particularly in the context of the university, these energies were nevertheless ultimately limited by "a combination of concessions and repression" (10). As Seth Rosenfeld (2013) details, the FBI was also involved in the investigation of hundreds of radical students and professors between the 1940s and 1970s (5). The bureau, Rosenfeld further explains, engaged in "a covert campaign to manipulate public opinion about campus events" (5), coordinated with the head of the CIA to "harass students" (5), and orchestrated the firing of radical faculty members (5). As progressive campus energies subsided in the 1970s, the university returned to an increasingly capitalist model with the globalization of education (Heller, 2016, 12).

Beginning around 1980, the fundamental trajectory of academic capitalism shifted as the university became increasingly privatized and financially entangled through an extensive set of initiatives, developments, and corporate partnerships. As Gary Rhoades and Sheila Slaughter (1997) recount, with the advent of neoliberalism, the university became increasingly part-time, managed, and profit driven (9–10). It was during this time that the contemporary model of academic hypercapitalism was born, a system in which, in a "variety of ways . . . markets, states, and higher education are increasingly inter-related" (Heller 2016, 173). Per Heller (2016), this trend notably encouraged the marketability of research (173). Administrative expansion during this period also ensured power remained out of the hands of faculty (174) while universities' efforts to grow their endowments ensured closer ties to the financial industry (175–176). These years also saw the beginning of the regime of permanent austerity that now presides over higher education. As Rhoades and Slaughter (1997) contend, this period has included the "streamlining, downsizing, repositioning, reengineering, and restructuring" (17) of programs. Faculty, they likewise note, are "depending on [their] rhetorical sensibilities, being retrenched, laid off, riffed, or reallocated" (17).

Extending this critique, Adrianna Kezar, Tom DePaola, and Daniel T. Scott (2019) analyze how academic employment has merged with the gig economy, rendering academic employees across the board contingent and disposable. As they note, 70 percent of academic faculty are now non-tenure track (1)—of these, the vast majority are part time (44). On average, non-tenure-track faculty are now paid $22,400 a year (1). These faculty, Kezar at al. further report, have continued to lose status and benefits as their pay and security have declined. Those off the tenure track are "deprofessionalized through a range of material indignities caused or compounded by imposed economic insecurity" (15), are often housing and food insecure, and frequently rely on food and wage supplementation (15). Perhaps most damningly, contingent faculty perform substantial unpaid labor. As Kezar et al. point out, some feel they must do so to fulfill the terms and ethical responsibilities of their position while others perform unpaid work "in the hopes of obtaining a full-time position" (46). These conditions also notably affect academic staff, a group commonly occluded in such discussions. Thirty-two percent of office and administrative staff are part time, and their salaries have contracted over recent years to an average of $16,655 in 2017, a number notably below the national poverty rate (39).

Similarly examining the asymmetrical nature of university finances, Newfield (2016) observes that the funding model of the public university has shifted in recent years with the steady disappearance of state funding and its replacement by a host of private financial revenue streams including private donations and higher tuition. Newfield's insightful thesis regarding this process is that the privatization of universities and the consequent "devolutionary cycle" (35) are not a replacement for the vanishing of public funds, as many have alleged, but the complicit move on the part of universities to become independent of state funding, to "restructure teaching and research" (27), and to turn from public institutions into more profitable private ones. As he argues, "public universities have a *privatization disease*" (27). In other words, per Newfield, the narrative of the university as simply the victim of neoliberal conditions is inaccurate. While the vast populations of university faculty and staff who have been negatively affected by capitalist shifts have long resisted privatization, as the discussion of faculty unions at the close of this chapter bears out, university administrators, in Newfield's account, have often been willing participants in state disinvestment. Newfield describes an extensive process of capitalism's welcomed refashioning of the university, including the shifting of the narrative of higher education from a public good to a form of job training (74), turning to private sources of revenue like philanthropy (115), raising tuition to cover privatization costs (138), defending austerity (169), overpopulating administration (178), turning teaching into a part-time profession (264), and limiting access and opportunity to minority and low-income students (283).

As noted above, a particularly destructive aspect of this cycle has been the way declining state funding has permitted the escalation of crisis rhetoric and the implementation of permanent austerity policies. As Scott and Welch (2016) detail, austerity "describes the shock-therapy intensification" (9) of economic policies following the 2008 crisis and crucially includes "the intensifying cost-shift from public to private" (9). Like Newfield, Michael Fabricant and Stephen Brier (2016) contend such policies are not merely tactical responses to deregulation but "designed to redefine the purposes of higher education" (6). They are particularly censorious of the City University of New York (CUNY) for employing austerity rhetoric to "legitimate bad policies of diminished public support; increased tuition; growing use of part-time faculty paid impoverished wages; and decaying physical facilities" (4). Examples of such austerity are increasingly visible in the contemporary academic world. In 2018, Goucher College announced it would be cutting several majors and minors in the arts and humanities. Curiously, the school reported no financial crisis but, rather, as the president announced, the cuts were merely to keep the college cost competitive: "We are determined to offer the best education for a price more people can afford" (Flaherty 2019b). In 2019, in response to operating losses, the University of Tulsa revealed it would condense its offerings, moving "from 15 departments and 68 degree programs to three divisions with 36 degree programs," cutting majors in philosophy, religion, and other areas of the humanities (Hazelrigg 2019).

When viewed against the continued political assault on universities by exponents of the new neoliberalism (Dardot and Laval 2019b)—attacks such as Victor Orbán's ouster of the CEU (discussed in ch. 1), Scott Walker's undermining of the University of Wisconsin (Savidge, *Wisconsin State Journal*, March 27, 2016), and Trump's charge that US universities engage in "Radical Left Indoctrination" (Graham 2020)[5]—capitalists' efforts to undermine the university are darkly ironic. As this section's historical gloss should illuminate, most US universities are in the mature phase of a nearly century-long capitulation to capitalist interests. Nevertheless, they continue to be aggressively attacked and defunded for their supposed progressive agenda. Rather than a conflict between the radical university and conservative leaders, the tension, instead, lies between two ultimately conservative positions. The neoliberal university expresses an internationalist and ostensibly cosmopolitan sensibility profoundly entangled with industry and the world of finance. This conflicts with the xenophobic and anti-intellectual worldview of new neoliberals like Trump. Both positions, nevertheless, are fundamentally capitalist ones. While it is unclear who will ultimately prevail in this struggle, neoliberal administrators or new neoliberal critics, it should be clear actual radical Leftists are no longer a substantive presence in the world of higher education.

While composition has fared marginally better than other humanities disciplines, it has nevertheless been similarly undermined by academic capitalism and austerity. As Scott and Welch (2016) contend, austerity measures have had a significant impact, removing "the rungs of long-term and secure faculty positions . . . funding for writing programs . . . [and] access and affordability for students" (4). Concerning writing instruction, they argue neoliberal conditions influence "not only writing assessments, curricula, and funding but teacher's agency and philosophies of program administration" (12). They likewise argue the economic conditions transforming the university are also influencing scholarship (12). While, as Welch and Scott point out, these extensive effects have harmed writing programs in both explicit and subtle ways, the shifting of universities' priorities toward greater professionalization can, in fact, account for some of the relative success of writing programs insofar as the latter are seen to provide greater economic value. As a 2018 report on the changing state of the English major concluded, while the major is in general decline, writing-for-new-media courses have "blossomed" (ADE 2018, 13) at several institutions, and technical and professional writing is becoming "well established" (23). As noted in chapter 3, TPC is engaged in a progressive turn. Nevertheless, Wells's (1986) concern that the subfield is acquiescent to capitalism remains relevant today and in need of reflection as capitalism's influence on writing departments continues to expand. Departments as a whole are also becoming increasingly career-oriented (ADE 2018, 13) and faculty members are "enlisted to convince students of the marketability of the English degree" (14).

The economic shifts within academia are the most essential conditions governing our work. Far more than merely limiting progressive or anticapitalist teaching, the financialized state of higher education impacts, often profoundly, nearly every aspect of academic life, from course content to research to decisions on hiring, promotion, and dismissal. As Maximillian Alvarez (2017) contends, "The neoliberalization of higher education is *every* academic's problem." I agree. With Alvarez, I believe the financial state of the university should alarm and incense any who teach there, particularly progressive composition teachers who are active in organizing and social justice and who focus on these issues in their writing courses. However, while a conflict between progressive academics and the university is often unavoidable, it is perhaps not terminal. In what follows, I discuss what I believe is necessary for anticapitalist compositionists, and radical academics more broadly, to conduct their work at the university. As I argue, this effort cannot succeed if critics remain isolated but rather must emerge from our collective engagement in the transformation of the university's capitalist model. Acknowledging the immensity of the challenges facing radical teachers, I rely upon the work of Dardot and Laval to inform a model of (*re*) *commoning* the university resistant to containment by the university's managerial architectures.

THE UNIVERSITY AND THE COMMON

While this book is most centrally concerned with the development of writing instruction capable of confronting, at least modestly, expressions of contemporary capitalism, this task is ultimately inextricable from the more substantive work of challenging the conditions of academic capitalism. Simply put, if teaching critical of capitalism is to thrive at the university, the financial and political structure of higher education cannot remain as it is. To be sure, in many cases, anticapitalist teaching may be practiced by faculty without incident at tolerant institutions. The teaching described in this book, for instance, has so far been uncontroversial. However, as I detail, in the increasingly profit-oriented context of the contemporary university, practicing anticapitalist pedagogy carries increasing risks. Those committed to radical pedagogical approaches might aim to do so quietly and without provoking the ire of institutions or publics, or they might more explicitly work towards changing the nature of the university's entanglements. The former may certainly be more attractive to some, but collectively working to (*re*) *common* the university is, I believe, the only means by which anticapitalist pedagogy and other progressive teaching methods will not place instructors at risk.

Admittedly, this is a monumental undertaking in that, if achieved, it would hold far more consequence than merely enabling a more critical and liberated form of writing pedagogy. Numerous scholars have, of course, addressed such endeavors over the years, proposing a variety of diverse approaches and goals. Kathleen Fitzpatrick (2019), for example, theorizes a remaking of the university by way of the rejection of academic competition and the embrace of "a mode of engagement that emphasizes listening over speaking, community over individualism, collaboration over competition, and lingering with the ideas that are in front of us" (4). In the realm of composition, Holly Hassell and Joanne Baird Giordano (2013) have ambitiously proposed placing open-enrollment institutions and the needs of their students at the center of our profession. The following discussion, while similarly ambitious, is hardly intended as a manifesto on such a scale but, rather, strives to offer a serious assessment of hindrances to and possibilities of offering a collaboratively focused writing instruction critical of capitalism. Acknowledging the impracticalities, limitations, and, indeed, arrogance of such a question, this chapter asks what *would be* necessary to support such teaching, intimating that such a hypothetical is increasingly becoming a necessity. Fundamentally, as with the broad approach of this book, the interventions needed to support anticapitalist teaching at the university are rooted in the common.

Dardot and Laval's (2019a) specific articulation of "the common" (10), based in the work of Marx, Jean-Paul Sartre, and Cornelius Castoriadis, offers a particularly helpful means of challenging the university without appropriating its capitalist norms. The core of their approach is what Dardot and Laval term "instituent praxis" (298), a form of inventive political action with associations to Castoriadis's concept of "radical novelty" (289). With some additional resonance to Stieglerian (2019) dreaming (199), Dardot and Laval (1019a) suggest that instituent praxis functions to "produce new meanings within the social imaginary" (309) and to generate "new conditions and . . . new subjects" (301). In their formulation, instituent praxis is a radical, communal act of transformation—of the self, institutions, and "*rules of law*" (305). The process they describe is ongoing rather than a single decisive action, a continual transformation and reinvention of subjects, logics, and institutions (304). Dardot and Laval leverage this concept to articulate a set of political prescriptions organized against the hegemony of capitalism. These chiefly include a construction of a "politics of the common" (313), a new model of collective political engagement in which property rights are "subordinated to common use rights" (315). While the proposed political model affirms the principle of "co-obligation based on co-decision and co-activity" (318), Dardot and Laval contend this model does not entail the complete subordination of economics to politics but rather the reorganization of the economic sphere as "a self-governing commons" (318). They likewise argue a politics of the common must be founded upon the radical rejection of property rights (328) and the elimination of ownership entirely, whether private or public. In their view, "the 'custody' of the common can only be entrusted to those who are its co-users" (329).

Two aspects of Dardot and Laval's (2019a) approach render it particularly applicable to the university. The first element is their persuasive rejection of conceptions of membership, ownership, and possession (27). This rejection notably differs from the position of many other Leftist critics who have often encouraged teachers and students to reestablish a claim to the university. In a 2007 interview, Henry Giroux defends the need "to reclaim higher education as a democratic public sphere" and "to reclaim those modes of governance, teaching, scholarship, and service that both recognize the promise of the university as a bastion of democracy and are critical of the anti-democratic forces now working to instrumentalize, commodify, and militarize it." While Giroux's position ultimately parallels that of Dardot and Laval (2019a), the latter offer a model of anticapitalism that proposes a rejection of ownership entirely, thereby remaining ultimately untethered to capitalist modes of domination. This model notably avoids such questions as who counts as a member of the university and who can be said to really own an institution. If coactivity, rather, were to serve as the grounds by which to establish a university politics of the common, the fact that faculty, staff, and graduate students are collectively engaged in supporting the flourishing of the institution suggests an inclusive means of developing such a politics and of conceptualizing the university as a radically egalitarian site most fundamentally organized and governed by those who maintain it rather than those who preside over its financial situation. This, moreover, supports the reconceptualization of the university not as a capitalist enterprise but, elementally, as a place of *common work*. Secondly, Dardot and Laval's (2019a) focus on coactivity as a generative site of novel subjectivity, institutions, and laws (305) helpfully answers Wright's (2019) call for strategies of changing the nature of the capitalist game that has limited anticapitalist action (93). Just as Dean (2019) posits the comrade as a site of radical invention (96), Dardot and Laval (2019a) present a novel means of remaking institutions such as the university in ways that liberate progressive action. Such an approach, in particular, entails enabling more vulnerable faculty members currently silenced through fear of dismissal and nonrenewal to join others in progressive action. In other words, extending protections to these individuals would effectively enable junior, more politically radical, and more socially engaged faculty to engage in common struggles.

Following Dardot and Laval's notion of a common politics, I suggest that defending anticapitalist pedagogy must first include resistance to the university's extensive capitalist entanglements. These, as the previous history of academic capitalism illuminates, not only represent institutions' various relationships with corporations but, as in the case of the Koch brothers' involvement in higher education, the ways philanthropy allows donors to purchase control over university operations (Reichman 2019, 108). To work towards the expulsion of the university's capitalist relations would effectively amount to formally rewriting the rules of the contemporary university regarding the kinds of entities and individuals universities can do business with. This change would entail working to recenter knowledge, teaching, and research on campus in lieu of industries and to oppose the various donors and corporations with which the university is involved. An effective means of organizing this work, per Dardot and Laval (2019a), would aim to rewrite the laws of ownership and reassert the right to collective action. As the two contend, the common entails *"the establishment of rules of common use through the exercise of instituent praxis, and its extension into a form of instituent use that is based on the ongoing revision of these rules"* (326). Putting aside for the moment the more substantive issue of university administration and governance, instituent praxis in US higher education would entail the liberation of progressive action on university campuses, namely building coalitions of faculty and students opposing the various capitalist interests that seek to dominate spaces of higher education or limit the action of those who work and study there. Broadly speaking, these coalitions would need to target both those who directly fund the university, including industries, private donors, the technology industry, and those who exploit students directly, namely lenders, the textbook industry,[6] and other industries with a campus presence.

Newfield (2016) offers some helpful suggestions of what would be required to disentangle the university from its extensive financial relations and compromised positions. As he argues, the university must primarily reframe education, more specifically engaging in "accounting reform that quantifies value of indirect effects, nonmarket value, and social benefits with the same dutiful attentiveness that accounting applies to the private market benefit of higher salaries" (311). He additionally advocates placing greater emphasis on education's "network effects" (312) as a public good that includes everything from "greater individual cognitive capabilities to more knowledge about racial conflicts" (312). This emphasis resonates with arguments that compositionists, most notably Bollig (2015), have made regarding the need to offer robust arguments for the nonmarket value of education, writing education specifically. Newfield (2016) also defends publicizing research accounting (315), the federal R&D funds given to industries allocated to universities instead (315), as well as the capping and complete reduction of tuition (to be replaced by public funding) (318). However, while these arguments will certainly be attractive to many academics interested in seeing the de-escalation of academic capitalism, Newfield is less clear regarding how universities might be persuaded to undertake such a de-escalation.

One possibility for this kind of change is common, coalitional opposition to the exploitative corporations and financial relationships on college campuses, akin to what I advocate in the writing classroom. There is, indeed, a precedent for efforts of this kind on campuses, albeit a modest one. In 2014, students at Florida State University protested the financial influence of the Koch brothers on their campus in a campaign called "UnKoch My Campus" (Mulhere 2014). Elizabeth Warren has called for Wells Fargo to be expelled from college campuses due to their exorbitant fees (Levitt 2019). Warren, Bernie Sanders, and others who ran for the 2020 Democratic presidential nomination have also called for the cancellation of student debt (Stein, *Washington Post,* June 24, 2019). Both faculty and students at the University of Washington have opposed the university's reliance on prison labor (Tufel, *Daily*, October 23, 2019). Most significantly, in 2019, the University of California walked away from negotiations with Elsevier, the academic publisher, a move that capped years of rising tensions and protests regarding the monopolistic hold academic publishers have over the intellectual production of the university (Zhang 2019).[7] Examples of such opposition to capitalism's presence on campus, however, are infrequent and have been rarely successful in achieving meaningful change. Nevertheless, as the University of California's interaction with Elsevier suggests, the university holds enormous power to confront corporations when it so chooses, and, indeed, when it is deemed financially advantageous to do so. The task, accordingly, appears to be a persuasive one, namely lobbying the university to respond to campus action and to recognize both the extent to which capitalist entities harm students and what could be gained by adopting a framework of "*common use*" (Dardot and Laval 2019a, 326). Such a contention notably resonates with the argument of James E. Porter, Patricia Sullivan, Stuart Blythe, Jeffrey T. Grabill, and Libby Miles (2000), who maintain that "institutions are hard to change.... But they can be rewritten ... through rhetorical action" (610).

While this work is most critical, and achievable, in public institutions, it is also possible at private universities. Private universities are capitalist by definition and cannot simply be returned to a state-funded model.

Nevertheless, with the explosive growth of university endowments, particularly among the wealthiest private institutions, private universities have become increasingly ensnared in global markets and beholden to an increasing body of financial actors. It is these endowments where significant change could occur and where anticapitalist opposition should rest. Critics have been particularly censorious of Harvard's endowment, by far the largest at $40 billion (Hess 2019a). Divest Harvard has specifically critiqued the university's investment in, and entanglement with, the fossil fuel industry. As Devi Lockwood, a Harvard graduate, wrote in a January 29, 2020, article in the *New York Times*, the university has $5.6 million invested with companies that "produce or own reserves of oil, natural gas and coal, and large electric utilities powered by natural gas and coal." While the number may appear insignificant, Lockwood reports a carbon finance consultancy determined Harvard's endowment was responsible for releasing eleven million tons of carbon dioxide per year. For those such as Divest Harvard, the solution is the withdrawal of funds from problematic industries. More ambitious critics, however, have argued the university should use its endowment to provide free tuition (Saul, *New York Times*, January 16, 2016) or other goods.

A second aspect of liberating radical teaching practices on campus, intimately associated with the first, must be the efforts to democratize the university to allow for the participation of faculty, staff, and students in making decisions affecting the broad campus community. While a crucial means of reducing the power of those who seek to maintain the university's capitalist architectures and shape university operations, including pedagogy, in ways that maintain them, democratizing the university also represents a monumental undertaking given the immense power and connections university administrators now hold. Over twenty years ago, Margaret Baker Graham, Elizabeth Birmingham, and Mark Zachry (1999) argued that greater ties between university administrations and the business world threatened the power of faculty senates (690). In the intervening years, this threat has become fully realized. Heller (2016) explains that at NYU, in many respects the paragon of twenty-first-century neoliberal higher education, the large sixty-five-member board of trustees includes Catherine Reynolds, "who owns a company—Educap—that makes high-interest, predatory loans to students" (180), as well as "some of the city's biggest land developers, Wall Street's wealthy financiers, and a bevy of corporate tycoons" (180). The composition of the board underscores the extent to which the university, in all practical senses, is in the hands of financial actors rather than workers in keeping with trends that have seen public sites become increasingly privatized and financialized over the past four decades (Dardot and Laval 2019a, 64). It also stresses the inherent difficulties of confronting university administrations in which the trustees represent a powerful spectrum of the business world. However, the wealth and power centered on NYU's board also underscores the need for "dismantling" (Wright 2019, 42) the academic capitalist system that views students as little more than revenue streams.

Consistent with Dardot and Laval's (2019a) emphasis on coactivity rather than ownership, a step in this direction, as with opposition to capitalism on campus, ought to be the establishment of collective power through the building of inclusive coalitions to challenge administrative authority, as well as the refusal of WPAs and departmental administrators to capitulate to universities' capitalist positions. Rather than setting a goal as grandiose as *retaking* the university, coalitions of faculty, students, and staff must work to reshape the university as a place of work and collective endeavor instead of an industry in search of maximum profit. Such coalitions must oppose the asymmetrical nature of faculty governance and strive to shift it away from the current factory model, in which financial actors unconnected to the fundamental work of the university govern its operation, and toward a more collective space where those who are coactive in the operation of the university and the production and dissemination of knowledge are substantively involved in the governance of the institution. "Workers," as Dardot and Laval argue, "must take part in the development of the rules and decisions that affect them" (336). As the composition of NYU's board of trustees suggests, an obvious impediment to enacting this change is what Eileen E. Schell (2016) and others have termed "administrative bloat" (177). As Schell evocatively argues, "Universities are now filled with armies of functionaries—vice presidents, associate vice presidents, assistant vice presidents, provosts, associate provosts, vice provosts, assistant provosts, deans, deanlets, and deanlings, all of whom command staffers and assistants—who, more and more, direct the operations of every school" (179). She argues that WPAs should resist their role as enforcers in the managerial structure, acting instead as "change-agents, activists . . . and enactors of a critical discourse" (184). She likewise advocates "interdisciplinary coalitions working toward labor solidarity and action" (185). I believe Schell is right on both counts, particularly in her assertion that cross-campus solidarity and action are necessary for faculty to successfully stand up to administrators. While the outright transformation of an administration is quite rare, there are illustrative cases of coalitional movements and resistance precipitating significant institutional changes.

One of the most significant examples of such struggles in recent years has been the 2015–2016 University of Missouri protests. As Trish Kahale and Michal Billeaux (2016) recount, the protests originated as a response to the university's attempts to cut graduate students' health insurance. While the university quickly reinstated the subsidies, this move did little to quell the long-simmering tensions at the university. Black students, in particular, reported incidents of racist intimidation that were neglected by the administration (Selzer 2018). The coalitional protests that ensued included both a hunger strike and a boycott by the football team, and eventually led to the ouster of the university president and the chancellor (Woodhouse 2015). Some years earlier, the 2012 protests in Québec against austerity, an event some term the "Maple Spring," offered a similar model of coalitional resistance aimed at an ambitious reworking of higher education. As with the protests at the University of Missouri, the protests in Québec began in response to austerity measures, in this case attempts to raise university tuition 75 percent over five years (Fraenkel and Etison 2012). With four hundred and sixty thousand participating, roughly half the province's total student population, the strike was the largest in Québec's history. Notably, educators also joined the protests, forming their own coalition against the tuition hikes, "Profs contre la hausse" (Smith 2019) (see fig. 5.1). Jean-François Venne (2017) contends that while the protests failed to permanently halt austerity measures, they caused a shift in governance that prevented the initially proposed increases. As both examples indicate, large-scale coalitional movements, while unable to guarantee the permanence of their victories, hold the capacity to offer significant resistance to the privatization measures of higher education. Rather than working within the increasingly stymied "normal channels" of university governance, the coalitions of activists at Missouri and in Québec demonstrate the capacity of capitalist rules to be challenged through large grassroots movements that overcome university strictures.

In the spirit of Karen Fitts and William B. Lalicker's (2004) proposal for leveling the disciplinary hierarchies within English departments, the third, and arguably most critical, aspect of securing anticapitalist teaching's place in the contemporary university must be working toward radically leveling the hierarchies and inequalities that render the most valuable academics either unwilling to practice progressive pedagogy and activism or targeted when they do. As Dardot and Laval (2019a) assert, a politics of the common must strive to "'decommodify' private enterprise and redefine it as primarily a 'worker community'" (340). Following this argument, I believe faculty members concerned

Figure 5.1. Profs contre la hausse in Montreal, Quebec. (Photograph by Benoit Rochon. Licensed under the Creative Commons Attribution 3.0 Unported license. https://creativecommons.org/licenses/by/3.0/deed.en.)

with these issues must not only work towards recreating a community of workers against the hierarchies of the privatized university but must also strive to challenge academia's pervasive ideology of hierarchy, what Bousquet (2002) and others have called the discipline's "managerial subjectivity" (494). Bousquet argues the potential of the university to promote activism and social change is inhibited by the narrative of the "heroic WPA" (496) and of singular rather than collective administrative achievements. Moreover, in acquiescing to becoming fields largely staffed by contingent faculty and limiting or simply denying fair pay, security, privileges, leadership roles, and professionalization opportunities to those faculty, departments have tacitly accepted the deskilling of the profession. As Seth Kahn writes (2020), "As long as faculty continue to proclaim to decision-makers that some kinds of teaching are less valuable than others, or than research, we can't be surprised when those decision-makers decide to mistreat faculty who teach" (592). Taking Kahn seriously here means collapsing departmental and institutional hierarchies and redressing the precarity of contingent faculty as to support the needed revision of the university, particularly in ways supportive of anticapitalist composition.

Such flattening must, notably, be a substantive reduction in the status, privilege, pay, and security differential between the vastly unequal ranks of faculty rather than a site of temporary or superficial equality, what Gunner (2012) has critiqued in the WPA-L listserv. As Gunner argues, the listserv dissuades claims to professional hierarchy and instead aims to open a space of professional equality undergirded by colloquial language (630). However, for Gunner, this is hardly a space of parity; it is simply one of occluded professional and economic hierarchy: "The listserv members create a totem of the system that has produced exploitative labor conditions whereby some community members are underemployed, ill paid, and unrecognized, so that any charge of disciplinary shortcoming is reframed and devalued" (630). She contends that the seeming erasure of hierarchy (re)inscribes the capitalist pecking order and poses inequality and exploitation as external problems (631). Crucially, Gunner frames the listserv as a commons, a site "not driven by market logic" (635) that "allows space for debate and controversy unmediated by some representative authority" (635) but that nonetheless can be "made to align with capitalist interests" (635). In illuminating this limitation of the commons, Gunner accords with Dardot and Laval's (2019a) defense of a politics of the common as inhering in action rather than ownership or membership.

I addressed this issue in a *College English* article a few years ago (Daniel 2017), noting how the conditions of the new economy have obviated Lynn Z. Bloom's (1996) claim that first-year composition is a middle-class enterprise. I argued that, unlike the boom years of the late 1990s, the first-year composition of the early twenty-first century is thoroughly destabilized and undercut by the conditions of precarity and inequality that pervade the lives of its students and instructors. To mitigate the worst of these effects, I advocated acknowledgment of the ways material precarity haunts the field and called for increased solidarity between faculty and students. I also called for senior faculty to support stability, benefits, and fair pay for their less fortunate colleagues (76). In a 2019 article in *Philosophy & Rhetoric*, Michael Bernard-Donals (2019) suggests my assertion of the relative stability and power of established academics underestimates the degree of flux, mobility, and vulnerability that both threatens and potentiates all faculty and, indeed, higher education itself. Bernard-Donals advances the concept of rhetorical mobility, a mode of intellectual untethering that resists the "perpetual structural constraint" (15) of higher education that could be utilized to radically remake the university. As he argues, the associations of movement and vulnerability have often been codified in what, drawing on the work of sociologist Guy

Standing (2011), I term *the precariat*, "a category of worker—in this case an academic worker—whose professional identity is insecure because their labor has been devalued and they have been forced to move from job to job and institution to institution without a sense of belonging" (Bernard-Donals 2019, 5). However, Bernard-Donals contends that while my argument for equity and solidarity across the university "forges a link between faculty and students" (5–6), it does so without troubling the logic or structure of the university itself. He hence proposes a more extensive remaking of the university by way of rhetorical mobility such that "the norms that serve as foundations of higher education" (21) can be interrogated.

While we differ in our views of professorial agency, I believe Bernard-Donals and I are after something similar. In defending an extensive intellectual untethering at the university, Bernard-Donals (2019) calls for a thoroughgoing reinvention of higher education. In many respects, this call is not unlike what I call for in this chapter in theorizing a remaking of the university through the concept of the common. A difference between us, however, lies in my contention that a leveling of institutional hierarchies is a crucial first step. Flattening hierarchies, as I see it, can capacitate extensive institutional change by emancipating the political action of silenced and marginalized faculty. While Bernard-Donals critiques the complacency of senior faculty (19), I am concerned with the unwilling silence of contingent and junior faculty, what I see as an expression of self-preservation in an industry that, as Christine Cucciarre (2014) alleges, claims to value equality but insists upon maintaining hierarchy: "We are hypocrites; we betray all the concepts that we teach: open-mindedness, tolerance, inclusivity, diversity, free speech" (62). Deborah J. Cohan (2016), an assistant professor of sociology, recounts such an experience of silence as self-preservation:

> As virtually every tenure-track professor experiences, I, too, have had to make choices about when, where, how and why to speak out and about what, and have had to weigh issues of silence and voice against the hope and need for job security, health insurance, retirement benefits and the like. I have had to decide what is worth it and what is not when I have been on the brink of making my viewpoints clear to the campus community and the larger community. Being untenured is the ultimate manifestation of "You just have to know how and when to pick your battles."

For junior tenure-track academics like Cohan, as well as for contingent faculty like me, the cases of Graeber and Salaita that begin this chapter serve as stark reminders of what contingent and untenured academics risk by becoming politically active. Regarding these conditions, I believe liberating faculty from the fear of censure, dismissal, nonrenewal and impoverishment for political activism (or, indeed, for no reason at all) is a pressing task with respect to supporting the struggle for a common politics of university work. As Dardot and Laval (2019a) suggest, "The common, in the form of concrete cooperation within freely formed groups, is still one of the best ways to counter the effects of hierarchical domination in work and social life, and one of the best ways to allow everyone to freely develop in the context of truly collective work" (336). In the context of higher education, this task must entail working to redistribute some of the rights and privileges currently solely bestowed on research faculty.

Such an initiative could begin with modest interventions, many of which are already common practice in more egalitarian departments. Minimally, departments and WPAs can insist upon hiring full-time faculty members with multiyear contracts rather than relying on a pool of part-time workers. This, of course, is contingent upon the relative power of WPAs, which Shirley K. Rose, Lisa S. Mastrangelo, and Barbara L'Eplattenier (2013) argue has become negligible for many in the position (57). Including contingent faculty, however, has generally been the practice in the Interdisciplinary Writing Program at the University of Washington, my home program, in which directors have prioritized hiring full-time lecturers over adjuncts. Likewise, full-time contingent faculty have been given some voting rights within the department, professionalization opportunities, and are commonly included in departmental operations. This inclusion is notably consistent with Joseph Harris's (2014) position that non-tenure-track faculty must be respected as skilled teachers and as intellectuals: "We need . . . to value in the work of teachers what we claim to value in the writing of students: independence, creativity, responsiveness, surprise" (72). Such efforts, however, cannot simply rest with gestures of inclusion.

Another more substantive action could entail a collective rejection of the probationary nature of junior tenure-stream and contingent faculty's employment or, even more radically, remaking the tenure process in such a way as to protect "political" faculty. Such an argument follows the claims of several scholars within the discipline, notably Bousquet's (2002) prescription of rejecting the university's "market fundamentalism" (510) and granting writing instructors "the chance to govern, enjoy an intellectual life, develop as an instructor, and enjoy better pay, protections, benefits, and security" (516). To be clear, this is not a call for a reversion to the old academy in which the ratio of tenure and tenure-track academics to contingent faculty was far higher[8] but existed within racist, sexist, and otherwise exclusionary contexts. Nor is this a call for greater "flexibility" (Mendenhall 2014) that would seek the continued decline of tenure as a means of growing the disposable class of contingent workers. Rather, following Dardot and Laval (2019a), such a restructuring would entail "the democratic transformation of the workplace in accordance with the cooperative content and social purpose of all workplace activity" (336), more specifically the sharing of rights, privileges, and security among all departmental faculty such that junior faculty could fearlessly engage in the common work of activism and progressive pedagogy.

It should, of course, be acknowledged that any organization, even thoroughly egalitarian ones, will be marked by hierarchy of some kind. As Cucciarre (2014) argues, "Hierarchy is inevitable in other work institutions as well as ours. If we were all tenured or tenure track, the tiers would be created through other criteria" (61). However, few in the field have acknowledged academia's bifurcated (tenure-track versus non-tenure-track) hierarchy is far more vertical than the managerial structure of many companies. If one looks to the technology industry, the trend in recent years has been towards leveling managerial hierarchies and working to create greater equality among employees, a "flat hierarchy" (Spicer, *Guardian*, July 30, 2018). Unsurprisingly, flat hierarchies frequently take place in an environment where racism and sexism are pervasive (Kolhatkar 2017). Nevertheless, companies, institutions, and governments founded upon nonhierarchical ideals are increasingly pervasive (Baron 2018; Rein 2018). Denmark, for example, has recently been touted as the most egalitarian economy in the world, a nation where workers display unparalleled "willingness to delegate authority" (Charlton 2018). Given the growing ubiquity of the flat hierarchy, however flawed, one wonders how it is that academia, an institution purportedly devoted to egalitarian ideals, can continue to defend its vertical model so fiercely.

Returning to the subject of programmatic change, the most significant work regarding leveling faculty hierarchies will need to be accomplished by senior faculty with tenure. While, as Bernard-Donals (2019) rightly contends, having tenure is little defense against many of the threats facing academics today (19), senior faculty are nonetheless comparatively better positioned to use their connections, authority, and security to work toward remaking the rules of the university in favor of vulnerable colleagues. Vulnerable faculty involved in political action and progressive teaching desperately need the support of their senior colleagues, particularly when junior faculty are targeted on political grounds. Naturally, as Bernard-Donals argues, the functional establishment and success of senior academics is precisely what prevents many from embracing intellectual mobility and coming to terms with the material vulnerability of others (19). Nevertheless, having been surprised by the supportiveness of senior colleagues in the course of my own departmental service and union work, specifically tenured faculty willing to mentor and support a contingent colleague, I am guardedly hopeful tenured academics are capable of being persuaded that the existential threats to higher education necessitate changing the status quo of departmental hierarchies and turning towards the common. In the field of composition, some tenured radicals unironically deserve the title for their attention to such issues. Seth Kahn and Sue Doe have displayed exemplary commitment to foregrounding inequality in their scholarship and their efforts to amplify the voices of marginalized faculty in their Precarity and Contingency series at the WAC Clearinghouse and University Press of Colorado. Kahn is also notably the cofounder of Tenure for the Common Good, an organization of tenured faculty striving to improve working conditions for adjuncts and graduate instructors. Marc Bousquet is another scholar who has aggressively exposed the exploitation of academic labor. We need more like them.

THE BARGAINING STAGE

I close this chapter with a word about unions. One of the most important and established means of pursuing improved labor conditions and greater academic freedom regarding progressive pedagogy, though certainly not the only or the final one, is the establishment of a robust faculty union. Unions are the most effective means of securing stable faculty positions, improving salaries, defending intellectual labor, and combatting the university's privatization in ways that offer to provide contingent faculty the foothold they need in the academy. Faculty unions have been crucial in recent years in improving conditions for academic workers, particularly contingent faculty. In October of 2019, the Professional Staff Congress of the City University of New York, the union representing thirty thousand faculty and staff across the university system, agreed to raise adjunct pay by 71 percent (Flaherty 2019a).[9] As Reichman (2019) argues, unions can resist the logics that undermine solidarity and academic freedom (260), among other ends. It is important to note here that while faculty unions have been effective in challenging university administrations, graduate student unions have led the way in acquiring members and organizing labor actions (Anda and Edwards 2018; Houlihan 2021). For the sake of transparency, I should also note my involvement with UW's small, volunteer faculty union. I support the union precisely because I believe unions are the crucial mechanism for reducing academic hierarchies and capacitating the kinds of progressive action by junior and contingent faculty I call for in this chapter. This view of unions, however, is not uncontested, even among progressive faculty.

Horner (2007), for instance, critiques disciplinary discourses on unionization for the ways they occlude both the value and the material reality of labor in the context of teaching writing and writing program administration. As he argues, unionization arguments, by "focusing almost exclusively on questions of hours and pay . . . leave unquestioned, and contribute to, the commodification of work" (176). For Horner, pro-union arguments regarding the value of work effectively acquiesce to capitalist demands by reducing work to an abstract calculus. In a similar argument, sociologist Barry Eidlin (2020) frames unions as occupying an unstable tension between the goals of radical change and compromise.

> They are an essential expression of the working class taking shape as a collective actor and an essential vehicle for working-class action. . . . At the same time, unions are an imperfect and incomplete vehicle for the working class to achieve one of Marxist theory's central goals: overthrowing capitalism.

As Eidlin further argues, unions, while crucial tools of working-class struggle, nevertheless "walk between militancy and bureaucracy." Such an uncomfortable tension is likewise expressed by Bill Lyne (2100), professor of English at Western Washington State University and the president of the United Faculty of Washington State, who notes that "many of us, including me, have had to put our personal political commitments aside, endure the withering looks of our radical friends" (5). With Horner, Eidlin, and Lyne, I certainly contend that unions and the discourse of unionization often offer uncomfortable compromises with capitalists. Unions alone are not enough, not by a mile, to permit the wholesale changes necessary in higher education in the long term. Nor are they sufficient to allow anticapitalist pedagogy to be freely practiced on college campuses or, more ambitiously, to remake the university in order to adequately provide the benefits academic workers need. For this project, more expansive, long-term, and coalitional work is needed to unsnarl the university from its financial entanglements and to allow it to function independently. On this question, Nick Tingle (2007) offers a persuasive and nuanced rebuttal to Horner, acknowledging the concessions unions are forced to make while contending they offer an unquestionable benefit to workers. As he argues, "Unions, to achieve their ends, must to some extent collude with or accept the terms of engagement as these are formulated by the system of capitalism" (766). He nevertheless cautions against rejecting unions simply because of these concessions: "When it comes to unions, don't throw the baby out with the bath water. Sure, the water is dirty. . . . the problems [unions] serve to address are really, really low-down dirty problems. If you throw out that dirty water, you might have clean hands, but you won't have the baby either" (768). I believe Tingle is correct here. Unions, despite their shortcomings, are the organizations best positioned to address the problems that most significantly impact marginalized faculty. They likewise offer a degree of security for faculty, particularly those seeking more ambitious and progressive changes.

It is, of course, important to note that while, as Eidlin contends, unions ultimately represent a compromise with capitalism and, consequently, often fall far short of the radical ambitions of many of their members, they are nevertheless routinely met with naked hostility and well-funded opposition by employers. This is a reflection of the long decline of unions in the public and private sector, having been decimated by right-to-work laws and other policies and legal attacks (Gordon 2019). The vigorous campaign against my own union offers a telling example of the resistance to organized labor on college campuses. From the initial drive in 2015, the administration voiced opposition to the union and used its platform to promote its position. As (then Interim) UW President Ana Mari Cauce and Interim Provost Jerry Baldasty wrote in an open letter to faculty in 2015, "We have grave reservations about the effect collective bargaining would have on our shared governance process. We also have serious concerns about its impact on the freedom we as faculty enjoy to pursue excellence in teaching, research and scholarship, the cornerstones of our success as a university" (Long, *Seattle Times*, September 10, 2015). The letter continues by claiming collective bargaining would "diminish the voice of the faculty, sideline the Faculty Senate and eclipse the collaborative approach we have worked on for generations."[10] Such messaging proved effective—the union, in its initial Washington Public Employment Relations Commission (PERC) card campaign, failed to get the signatures it needed to become a collective bargaining unit. It was also aggressively fought by a grassroots campaign, UW Excellence, which gathered over one thousand signatures of UW faculty members opposed to unionization. Mirroring the forms of antidemocratic rhetoric that have weakened social solidarities in the age of neoliberalism (discussed in ch. 1), the group's website resorts to fear appeals regarding the potential moral and financial hazard of a union strike: "Would you cross picket lines, or skip your graduate student's doctoral thesis defense? Would you cross picket lines, or miss the filing deadline for your grant proposal? Would you cross picket lines, or let down your research collaborators around the world?" (UW Excellence 2015). Notably, similarly fervent opposition to unionization also occurred at the University of New Mexico (Boetel, *Albuquerque Journal*, September 9, 2019) and Marquette University (Pettit 2019a) in 2019.[11]

As these attacks on the UW faculty union demonstrate, union organizing is often aggressively opposed in the context of higher education, often to such an extent that the fight for unionization entirely monopolizes the energies of activists seeking to challenge the neoliberal university. Such opposition might quite rightly dissuade faculty from participating, channeling them toward progressive avenues beyond the university. However, union victories, even modest ones, illustrate how effective unions can be, particularly for marginalized faculty. One of the union's small victories is illustrative. During the 2016–2017 academic year, faculty in the School of Interdisciplinary Arts and Sciences at UW Tacoma recommended replacing two temporary positions with renewable lectureships. Administrators broke with faculty in rejecting the recommendation and refused, when pressed, to reconsider. In response, union leadership drafted a letter (signed by over forty members at UW Tacoma) to the UW president and UW Tacoma chancellor Mark Pagano critiquing the administration's precedent-breaking move of ignoring faculty input in hiring decisions. Following delivery of the letter, the university relented. A minor victory, to be sure, but the example nevertheless demonstrates the capacity of unions to challenge the unilateral actions of administrators. It also demonstrates how faculty unions, even those without bargaining power, can fight to protect teaching positions. It is for these reasons I contend unionization is *the* fight anticapitalists, particularly those in university contexts, must engage in if they hope to challenge corporatism, protect academic freedom, and combat the casualization of academic labor. For many, they also offer a gateway into the world of labor organizing and political solidarity. They also potentiate progressive changes down the road. As Danny Glover (2021) puts it, "Unionization creates citizens, it provides a platform for citizens to take action . . . [unions] strengthen the community itself."

CODA

It is early March of 2020. My Writing in the Humanities course is wrapping things up. The students have been busy—they've read Heike Geissler's (2018) *Seasonal Associate*, accounts of precarious labor, and analyses of social class, and they are finishing their multimodal projects on Natasha Stagg's (2016) novel *Surveys*. None of us know it yet, but the University of Washington will shut its doors within a week in response to COVID-19, sending students and faculty home and moving all classes online. Millions will lose their jobs and be utterly unsupported by their government while others will fall ill and, if they survive, will be stuck with enormous hospital bills they will struggle to pay. At the end of May, in response to the killing of George Floyd by Minneapolis police, activists will pour onto the streets in the United States and cities across the world to protest police violence and systemic racism. White supremacists will guard Targets and Trump will call upon the military to deal with the "thugs" (Scott and Steakin 2020) in the interest of maintaining law and order for all those who profit from the current system. In January of 2020, buoyed by Trump's rhetoric, a mob will storm the US Capitol. Throughout these events, capitalism will thrive. Megacorporations will prosper at the expense of small-business owners and so-called unskilled workers. As Grace Blakeley (2020) illuminates, "Some corporations will not only withstand but even gain from the crisis" (xv). Indeed, billionaires increased their wealth by $1.7 trillion during the pandemic (Zhang 2022).

But for those of us in English 297 A, it is just a typical Thursday. As we begin one of our final discussions, Rhiannon raises her hand. She wants to know *my* take on capitalism. What kind of a life do *I* think people ought to lead in the face of economic inequality, student debt, and spiraling climate change? And, more importantly, is there a way out of capitalism?

While I'm not unprepared for the question, it is one I've purposefully avoided answering. An instructor, particularly one who deals with such explicitly political subjects as I do, doesn't want to dictate actions to students. Rather, I want to provide frameworks so students can formulate their own answers in the contexts of their own lives and act upon them accordingly, which is why much of my time in the classroom is spent asking questions like "What do we do?" and "How do we act?" Of course, I would be lying if I said I didn't have certain hopes regarding what students will do with what I've given them and how they will act in the future. I want my students to be angered by economic inequality. I want them to care more about capitalism's role in global climate change. And while I want them to lead happy, fulfilling, and comfortable lives, I also want them to change the world. Or, more accurately, I want them to want to change the world. Rhiannon's question, then, is particularly difficult to answer, not just because it puts me in the position of telling students what to do but because it addresses two of the most fundamental problems of anticapitalist thought: the limits of capitalism and the necessity of opposition.

On the first issue, many critics argue there is no limit to capitalism. In Heller's (2019) estimation, capitalism is now pervasive: "There is no frontier beyond its reach" (11). Four of my students, Juana, Osman, Blythe, and Rhiannon herself, offered just as precise a critique in their final project when they argued, "There is no way out of our societal framework. . . . Everyone is immersed in capitalism, whether they want to be or not." Others, however, particularly proponents of the commons (Standing 2019), have long tried to assert that there can be spaces outside capitalism and that opening and protecting these spaces should be our task (Gibson-Graham 2006). Communes, notably, have long operated on such a mentality, with Berlin's Kommune 1 (Horvat 2015, 126–146) and the still nominally operating Freetown Christiania in Copenhagen offering prominent examples (Kökerer 2019). Yet, while such spaces have sometimes offered an explicit challenge to the capitalist status quo (Ciccariello-Maher 2016), they have rarely done so in a substantive or lasting way. On this point, I follow Wright (2019) in the contention that escaping capitalism, in most cases, amounts to a "lifestyle strategy" (52).

Rhiannon also seems to ask whether she has to fight. I would, of course, like to be able to say it is enough to simply be conscious of the effects of global capitalism, to avoid relying on supply chains and businesses that exploit precarious workers, to be aware of the capitalist architecture of digital technology, and to understand lenders are actively preying on debtors. I would also like to be able to tell her strong communication and critical thinking skills will allow her to navigate the turbulent conditions of the twenty-first century. I would like to, but I can't. Rather, something much more is necessary. In a sense, this book is an attempt to theorize what that is, at least where the writing classroom is concerned. In these pages, I focus on a core set of capitalist effects in need of intervention—student debt, the scene of work, the internet, higher education—and, likewise, on the kinds of collaborative practices, supported by theories of the common, that offer the potential of collective intervention. To students, these are not abstract matters. Capitalism is the most consequential force shaping their lives. The premise that guides this book is that students will be, at the very least, better served if they have a critical and rhetorical understanding of its operation, its narratives, and its vulnerabilities. More ambitiously, though, my hope in articulating these pedagogical practices is that some students will discover the necessity and, perhaps, the joy (Dean 2019, 88; Stengers 2015, 155) of collaborative resistance, what my student Bobby describes as "the brilliance and color" of activism.

Some, of course, will inevitably ask how any of this will help students such as Rhiannon. How is any of this going to make *her* life any better? As I have argued thus far, adopting an anticapitalist position is an ethical necessity insofar as capitalism is an existential threat that demands our disciplinary acknowledgment and pedagogical response. But while this entails positioning students to encounter, critique, resist, and oppose dominant capitalist logics and pushing the discipline to understand and resist its own capitalist entanglements, the question remains regarding how doing so will be of actual benefit to students and fulfill the basic obligations of the college writing classroom. In responding to this potential criticism, I should note the argument for the value of critical orientations in the writing classroom has been well made. Bruce McComiskey (2017), for example, argues that teaching students "post-truth rhetoric" (6) will help them "understand and counter the Trump effect" (40) and "challenge the manipulative effects of fake news" (41). For McComiskey, these goods are undoubtedly both social and individual. However, in responding myself, I hesitate to answer unreservedly. It is likely the case the pedagogical approach I detail in this book will make students more skilled and critical writers and communicators. But there is another sense that these skills, particularly when it comes to preparing students to parse, critique, and resist capitalist conditions and narratives, are in conflict with the demands and culture of the contemporary working world, at least in the context of the contemporary corporate environment.

The case of WeWork, the coworking company discussed in chapter 3, offers a dramatic illustration of this incompatibility. A documentary on the company, *WeWork: Or the Making and Breaking of a $47 Billion Unicorn*, depicts the extent to which former CEO Adam Neumann utilized utopian and communal rhetoric to secure not only employees' productivity but their devotion as well. Neumann successfully persuaded employees to work long hours for uncompetitive salaries through framing the company as a lifestyle and a cause—workers were told they were part of the "We Revolution," led in chants of the company's name, and treated to mandatory, alcohol-fueled weekends largely devoted to burnishing Neuman's cult of personality (Rothstein 2021). While certainly an extreme case, WeWork nevertheless exposes a palpable current in the contemporary professional world in which companies strive to acquire employees' absolute and ardent devotion. This current is precisely what I want students in my classes to reject. I would like them to see these aspects of contemporary work as escalations of capitalist inducements that falsely promise community while delivering more pernicious forms of control and exploitation. Effectively, the pedagogy I detail in this book aspires to make students *bad* employees insofar as the critical, collective, and confrontational skills and practices of the anticapitalist classroom aim to motivate students to question and take on the capitalist logics that preside over professions and publics. In other words, I hope anticapitalist pedagogy will dissuade students from being "down for the cause" (Wiener 2020, 64). I hope it will make them think twice before wearing their company's t-shirt. What I mean is, I hope to give students reasons to resist, protest, or unionize rather than simply to go to work.

I return to the question, then, Will this help my students? My response is yes, though probably not in the way many university administrators might like. An anticapitalist approach to composition, akin to the goals of critical pedagogy and social-epistemic rhetoric, aims to prepare students to parse the unequal and exploitative conditions and discourses that govern their lives, to understand how these conditions and discourses are sources of profit for corporations, and to challenge, resist, and rewrite dominant conditions. It does not aim, however, to teach students to conform to the ultimately unacceptable conditions of the twenty-first-century working world. This approach, notably, responds to the call of Scott (2009), who argues that writing must be "consequential, immediate, responsive, and sometimes even dangerous" (187) and that our pedagogy must "present hopeful alternatives" to the economic status quo (190).

I can't say precisely what I told Rhiannon back in 2020. It might have been sufficiently direct, though it also certainly would have been couched in careful, institutional language cognizant of the dangers of classroom radicalism for contingent employees. While I couldn't offer her a complete answer then, I offer one here—there is no way "out" of capitalism if what you mean is "escape." Some people will be rich enough to buy themselves an easy life, and there are those who will be simply lucky enough to live well throughout what is inevitably coming. But it will be a life very much within capitalism. And capitalism is becoming more destructive and unequal with every passing day. The only way forward, then, is by facing it. Direct confrontation. Gathering communities. Actualizing the common. Remaking the university. Organizing, protesting, putting up a fight and having some fun while doing it.

This is how we win.

NOTES

INTRODUCTION: MONEY CHANGES EVERYTHING

1. As I discuss later in this introduction, the field is indebted to the pioneering anti-capitalist work of Richard Ohmann (1996, 1978, 1985), John Trimbur (1989, 1997, 2000), and James A. Berlin (2003).
2. For such a history, see Perry Anderson (1976), Michael Harrington (2020), Leszek Kolakowski (2005), or Cedric Robinson (2000).
3. Biden, as Branko Marcetic (2020) points out, "was one of the chief architects of a racist system of mass incarceration and showed a career-long willingness to sacrifice African American communities for political survival" (5). Marcetic further credits Biden as "one of the earliest adopters of neoliberalism" (5).
4. There are, importantly, those in the discipline who attend to material conditions when analyzing social class (Griffiths and Toth 2017).
5. It is nevertheless worth noting that the growing diversity of the working class makes such claims about identity and values increasingly tenuous. Writer and activist Kim Moody (2017) details how the last three decades have seen enormous growth in the racial, ethnic, and gender diversity of the working class as minorities have been drawn into lower-paid occupations (37). In a report for Demos, Tamara Draut (2018) notes that while whites comprised 88.7 percent of the working-class labor force in 1970, that number has fallen to 58.7 percent in 2016. Moody asserts, however, that inequity within the working class stratifies earners along racial and gendered lines—white workers are far less likely than Latin or Black workers to have earnings putting them beneath the poverty line (23.4 percent, 36 percent, and 43.3 percent respectively) (37). Male members of the working class also outearn their female counterparts by more than 20 percent (37). Hence, while the working class has typically been figured as homogenous, its increasing diversity has widened intraclass inequity. Working-class labor is also, notably, diversifying and declining in quality. Mine, mill, and factory workers, once comprising 64 percent of the working class in 1983, now represent only 47 percent, while jobs in logistics, the information sector, service, and sales have grown significantly (38–40).
6. Ibram X. Kendi notably offers a critique of capitalism, arguing that racism and capitalism are "conjoined twins" (2019, 156) that are mutually reinforcing and cannot be adequately addressed through attending to *only* racism or *only* capitalism. "Attributing inequalities solely to capitalism," he continues, "is as faulty as attributing them to racism. Believing these inequalities will be eliminated through eliminating capitalism is as faulty as believing these inequalities will be eliminated through eliminating racism" (158). He likewise critiques those like Elizabeth Warren who claim to be capitalist but decry twenty-first-century forms of predatory capitalism as unacceptable. On Warren's defense, Kendi writes, "history does not affirm this definition of capitalism" (162). It must be said, however, that despite the claim's centralization of capitalism, acknowledgment or criticism of political economy is not prominent elsewhere in Kendi's work.

7. It is crucial to note there are those in the field whose work attends to the entanglement of race and class. Damián Baca (2009), for instance, reframes Wendy Hesford's "global turn" (231) as "a five-hundred-year process by which a capitalist world-system advances across the globe" (231). Questioning the characterization of globalization as a site of greater connection, Baca instead frames globalization as a mechanism of racial capitalism, arguing academics must confront "the underlying rhetorical structures and economies of global colonialism and the correlative emergence of the study of written language as it is understood today" (238).
8. See Gilmore (2007), Reed (2022), and Wang (2018).
9. This relationship is explored by historian Walter Johnson (2020).
10. Elsewhere, Inoue (2015) doubts the utility of the concept of exploitation as a metric with which to analyze inequality. He argues, "I can see how my contract may look like some version of exploitation" (191), subsequently adding that exploitation "is subjective. What I see as fair, my students may see as unfair and exploitative" (191).
11. The term derives from the much more familiar construct of *the commons*, which originally referred to publicly owned lands or resources available to a general population. The concept later came to be central in a variety of fields interested in issues of property, law, and access, particularly economics, urban theory, and, in recent years, climate science. Derek Wall (2014) explains that evidence of public commons as a perennial formation is evident in Roman, Aztec, and Babylonian law (9) and that commons, as land, remain in use in Mongolia and the Middle East, among other sites (10). The standard historical example is medieval Britain, where "common land" (8) was owned by a feudal lord but extended to commoners for such uses as fishing and pasture grazing. Sociologist Guy Standing (2019) traces this lineage to the Charter of the Forest, sealed in 1217 by King Henry III and Regent William Marshall, Earl of Pembroke. The document bestowed rights to common lands, specifically giving people "the right to the means of subsistence, the right to raw materials and, to a limited but substantive extent, a right to the means of production" (4). As Standing details, the Charter recognized "the role of stewardship" and offered commoners protection from "deprivation and homelessness" (9), as well as from "outside surveillance and control" (9). However, the heyday of the commons came to an end through a series of enclosure acts instituted between the sixteenth and nineteenth centuries. As Standing recounts, these acts not only prohibited access to the commons but, as of 1604, also limited the right of land ownership for commoners (12). Commons, according to Standing, now represent 5 percent of British land (14).
12. While the decline of the commons is often exclusively linked to European histories of enclosure, scholars of Indigenous history have recounted how the logic of enclosure has likewise informed the history of settler-colonial appropriation of Native American lands in the United States. As Roxanne Dunbar-Ortiz (2014) contends, many of the British commoners who had been stripped of access to common lands became indentured servants in the new world, exchanging labor for the promise of property (35). She writes, "The traumatized souls thrown off the land, as well as their descendants, became the land-hungry settlers enticed to cross a vast ocean with the promise of land and attaining the status of gentry" (36). In *Braiding Sweetgrass: Indigenous Wisdom, Scientific Knowledge, and the Teachings of Plants*, Robin Wall Kimmerer (2013) shrewdly diagnoses this logic with respect to land and parses its critical difference from Indigenous perspectives. She writes, "In the settler mind, land was property, real estate, capital, or natural resources. But to our people, it was everything: identity, the connection to our ancestors, the home of our nonhuman kinfolk, our pharmacy, our library, the source of all that sustained us" (17).
13. As Elissa Nadworny (2019) reports, at four-year private and public institutions, the six-year graduation rates are 76.1 percent and 65.7 percent respectively, while at

two-year and for-profit schools, the rate is below 40 percent (2019). Unsurprisingly, minority students are most affected, with Hispanic and Black students graduating at 49 percent and 41 percent, far behind white and Asian students. While the rates are slowly improving at every type of institution, the extensive number of students not graduating (many of whom carry debt) is alarming.

CHAPTER 1: GATHERING

1. Republicans have notably sought to enact similar policies in the United States (Migdon, *Hill*, February 28, 2022).
2. In terms of actual economic policy, Orbán, like Trump, has continued to expand Hungary's capitalist project, albeit with greater corruption than in the past several decades (Pogátsa and Fabry 2019).
3. As Martino Comelli and Vera Horváth (2019) contend, "Orbán owes his success to his understanding of popular sentiment and his ability to address the disenfranchised, marginalized, and alienated losers of globalization. He's a liberal smart enough to see that liberalism failed Hungary."
4. As journalist Paul Mason (2015) defines it, neoliberalism is "the doctrine of uncontrolled markets" (xi), a system founded upon the idea "the best route to prosperity is individuals pursuing their own self-interest, and the market is the best way to express that self-interest. It says that the state should be small . . . that financial speculation is good" (xi). In Mason's representative characterization, neoliberalism is not merely a model of capital accumulation but a political and social theory suggesting the deregulation of markets results in an ideal society. Nicole Aschoff (2017) notes how this perspective drove policy in the United States beginning in the 1980s: "It helped free up corporations to restructure operations, fire workers, and demand union givebacks; it deregulated finance, exploding its avenues for profitability; and it greased the wheels through militarism and debt spending." However, while these are commonplace assertions of neoliberalism's posture, its internal logic is the subject of some debate. Historian Quinn Slobodian (2018) presents an alternative view of neoliberalism as a model of economic managerialism deeply skeptical of the notions of self-regulation and the complementarity of democracy to global capitalism. Rather than tracing neoliberalism to the Freiburg School and the Chicago School of Economics, as is more commonly done (Jones 2014), Slobodian (2018) locates its origins in the lesser-known Geneva School of Wilhelm Röpke, Ludwig von Mises, and Michael Heilperin (8). These figures, Slobodian claims, originated the ideas of neoliberalism in articulating a model of economic institutions "of multitiered governance . . . insulated from democratic decision making" (12). The financial world, in such a model, is understood as "an object of constant maintenance, litigation, design, and care" (12). Against common assertions that neoliberals seek the total liberation of markets, thinking such liberation would be inherently complementary to a prosperous, global democratic culture, Slobodian maintains that the neoliberal order long sought "an institutional encasement for the world of nations" (13) that would police the boundary between the political and financial. For neoliberals, he argues, the market is "always an open-ended process of becoming" (269) to which "democracy is a potential threat" (272).
5. The notion of joy is notably also taken up by Isabelle Stengers (2015), whom I discuss in chapter 3. In defending the goods of collaboration against capitalist and authoritarian power, Stengers calls for the "production of a new capacity to act and think" (155), which she links to Spinoza's concept of joy in *Ethics* (1996). As Stengers (2015) details, joy, in Spinoza's conception, denotes "an increase in the

6. The group notably included Bobby, whose work I subsequently discuss in this chapter.
7. A crucial exception to this has been the work of Kshama Sawant (2020) and other Seattle-based socialists. As she writes of her record in 2020, "We spearheaded fights for Seattle to become the first major city to pass a $15 minimum wage, landmark renters' rights victories like the winter evictions ban and the move-in-fees cap . . . the Amazon tax earlier this year for affordable housing and a Green New Deal."
8. The group, referred to by pseudonyms, included a white, queer-identified man; a white transgender man; and a biracial woman.
9. It must be noted that while the group found this experience a valuable one, the Bill and Melinda Gates Foundation exists within the context of capitalist philanthropy, an enterprise that foregrounds identity and inequality but purposefully refrains from critiquing capitalism itself. Zahra Moloo (2018) writes, "By investing vast sums of money in solving complex historical problems, expanding the private sector, and investing in technical fixes, [capitalist philanthropists] advance the idea that capitalism is not the cause, but the solution, to the world's troubles." The centrality of the center in Seattle's activist scene, in part, attests to the inherent difficulties of anticapitalist teaching insofar as the center presents a compelling narrative of activist agency while implicitly lionizing digital capitalism. When I raised this seeming contradiction with students, some were receptive to a deeper critique while others reflexively defended the center and its work. For an in-depth investigation of the foundation's financial dealings, see Schwab (2020).
10. It is important to note that the narrative of Trump's election victory as secured by white working-class voters is incorrect. While Trump enjoyed widespread support among white evangelicals (Gjelten 2020), his strongest support in 2016 came from wealthy white voters (Ogorzalek, Puig, and Piston, *Washington Post*, November 12, 2019).
11. As Daniel Markovits (2019) argues, a regime of meritocracy has become ascendant in contemporary global culture, transforming education into "a rigorous and intense context to join the elite" (5) and altering work "to create the immensely demanding and enormously lucrative jobs that sustain the elite" (5). See also my discussion of Anna Wiener's (2019) critique of meritocracy in chapter 4.

CHAPTER 2: DEBT

1. As of March 2022, Biden has cancelled or promised to cancel $21 billion worth of student loans (Friedman 2022), only a flake of the $1.7 trillion total.
2. Purportedly in response to financial difficulties, dozens of colleges and universities have eliminated programs in recent years, most of them in the humanities. Recently, the University of Wisconsin–Stevens Point announced plans to cut thirteen majors including art, English, history, political science, and sociology (Flaherty 2018b).
3. Several recent lawsuits and journalistic investigations have exposed the extent to which debtors are mistreated by the loan industry. As one lawsuit alleges, Navient provided borrowers with incorrect information regarding their student-loan repayment, coerced many to overpay on loans, and damaged the credit of many veterans and disabled clients (Friedman 2017). It has also been reported that the company extended loans it calculated would have a 92 percent default rate (Cowley and Silver-Greenberg, *New York Times*, April 9, 2017).

4. For a more comprehensive history, see Collinge (2010).
5. This trend, notably, has never ceased. As Christopher Newfield (2016) reports, starting in the 2000s, college tuition increased an average of 3 percent and 5.6 percent per year at private and public colleges respectively (198). I discuss this transition further in chapter 5.
6. Adjusted for inflation.

CHAPTER 3: WORK

1. In March of 2021, Prince Harry, the Duke of Sussex, became chief impact officer of BetterUp, a startup devoted to improving worker performance. As he notes in a company press release, "Being attuned with your mind, and having a support structure around you, are critical to finding your own version of peak performance" (Robichaux and Prince Harry, 2021).
2. As Zoey Poll (2020) reports, conditions of health and safety at Amazon facilities have further declined with the rise of COVID-19. In France, employees with symptoms of the virus were met with a disorganized response, while working conditions inside Amazon facilities reportedly did little to protect frontline workers. Erica Hayasaki (*New York Times*, February 18, 2021) contends similar concerns in the United States led to labor actions and organizing campaigns across the country.
3. See Sara O'Brien (2020).
4. As a 2019 report from the Economic Policy Institute concluded, productivity and hourly pay both rose dramatically at the end of the 1940s. However, beginning in the late 1970s, hourly pay began to stagnate while productivity has continued to rise. According to the report, productivity increased 69.6 percent between 1979 and 2018, while hourly pay increased only 11.6 percent.
5. Notably, Trimbur has also advanced a materialist view of writing deeply critical of late capitalism. In his 2000 essay "Composition and the Circulation of Writing," he reasserts writing's material valence and defends introducing students to "what constitutes the production of writing by tracing its circulation" (2000, 214) to interrogate professional expertise. Writing twelve years later, Trimbur (2012) again advocates investigating the material circulation and unequal distribution of the production of writing, framing writing's contemporary role as "a means of producing wealth and monopolizing profits" (725).
6. See Stengers (2010, 2018).
7. Amazon's union-busting efforts in Bessemer, Alabama, is one example (Leon 2021). The company's firing of Emily Cunningham and Maren Costa for organizing is another (Weise, *New York Times*, April 5, 2021).
8. See Philip Fonser and Robin Kelley (2018).
9. See Elizabeth Redden (2018a).

CHAPTER 4: DATA

1. In the academic world, a wave of publications on the utility of digital tools for grassroots activism emerged following the numerous social and political movements that erupted between 2010 and 2012 (Gerbaudo 2012; Sauter 2014). This narrative has also been ubiquitous in the TED Talk scene, which, while occasionally platforming progressive content critical of digital capitalism, has been a potent site for framing digital technology as utopian (Brown 2009; Morrison 2019).
2. In 2021, following a decision by the British Supreme Court, Uber agreed to reclassify UK drivers as "workers," and thus entitled them to a minimum wage and benefits (Santariano, *New York Times*, March 16, 2021).

3. Jacob Silverman (2020) notably speculates that, in fact, this backlash may be coming to an end. Tech companies, he argues, have begun to occupy a new role in the context of COVID-19, that of "all-purpose savior."
4. There are, some argue, pockets of the internet resistant to capitalist influence. These come in numerous forms, such as free software or sites reliant on user donations or public funds rather than subscriptions, data mining, advertising, and other profit-making strategies. For a more extensive discussion of the potential of teaching writing with such technologies, see Patch (2010) and Gruwell (2015). However, as the prior discussion of Bratton (2016) attempts to illustrate, strict demarcations of "capitalist" and "noncapitalist" platforms and technologies are difficult if not impossible to make given the integration of the technological strata.
5. Kylie Jarrett's (2018) "Exploitation, Alienation, and Liberation: Interpreting the Political Economy of Digital Writing."
6. Characterizing the orientation of multimodal composition, Santosh Khadka and J. C. Lee (2018) contend that because the subfield "includes signifying practices in multiple mediums—print, visual, aural, graphics, animation, and such—writing instruction should consider this plurality of composing mediums and attempt to scaffold students' composing abilities in all possible modalities of expression, hence engaging multimodal theories and pedagogies in writing classrooms" (3).
7. See, for example, Eyman and Davis (2016).
8. Stiegler (2019), to be clear, is not referring to the form of disruption commonly touted by the CEOs of "Californian 'digital business'" (32). Joseph L. Bower and Clayton M. Christiansen (1995), notably, adapted this conventional concept of disruption from Joseph Schumpeter's (2008) notion of "creative destruction," applying it to the digital context. "Disruptive technologies," they contend, "generally make possible the emergence of new markets." Later adopted as the de facto ethic of Silicon Valley entrepreneurs, the term has since become the subject of significant critique, even among those in the technology world. As Hemant Taneja, an investor and managing director of General Catalyst, argues, "I think if we don't build businesses that are broadly good for society, I don't think this entire system really lasts" (Slydell 2019).
9. A term borrowed from Edmund Husserl (2012) referring to one's capacity to anticipate the "presently coming" (150) moment.
10. Stiegler's conception of stupidity, like Stengers's (2015, 119), is rooted Gilles Deleuze's (1995) use of the term (151). For Stiegler, stupidity amounts to the "liquidation of maturity" (2015, 3) ascendant under the reign of modern consumerism.
11. *Bifurcation* is an integral term in Stiegler's (2018) broader theorization of "the Neganthropocene" (34). For the philosopher, the prevailing conditions of the Anthropocene represent a site of entropy. Stiegler argues that rather than acquiesce to these conditions, we must work to resist them and secure a state of *negative entropy*, hence the term "the Neganthropocene" and the associated term "negentropy" (40). This resistance entails an act termed *bifurcation*, which Yuk Hui and Pieter Lemmens (2017) define as "a radical anthropotechnological turn . . . in the anthropic adventure Heidegger calls Dasein" (37). Bifurcation, in other words, is an inflection point for the subject, a shift in being that begins a resistance against entropy. Stiegler (2018) also refers to Deleuze's (1990) concept of the "quasi-cause" (147), a concept adopted from Stoic philosophy to refer to the *becoming* of the event in excess of historical and material causes. As Deleuze writes, the quasi-cause "'give[s] a body' to the incorporeal effect" (147).
12. Musk has made headlines in recent years for a variety of technological projects aimed at solving many of humanity's problems. His Neuralink project strives to, among other ends, offer a means to "repair brain injuries or cancer lesions"

(McFarland 2017) while the Boring Company (n.d.) aims to "solve the problem of soul-destroying traffic."

13. Amber A'Lee Frost (2020) offers the similar, though far more critical, point that social media, while often immediately impactful, simply lacks the capacity for organizing or creating substantive change: "It burns hotly, brightly, and briefly, often with nothing to show in the end but a glut of forgettable, disposable content and the emotional exhaustion of participants (and perhaps a monograph or two)."
14. In 2020, numerous advertisers including Patagonia and Ben and Jerry's boycotted Facebook over the company's inaction with respect to the inaccuracy of Trump's tweets (Hsu, *New York Times*, June 23, 2020).
15. This, of course, was eventually done in response to Trump's role in inciting the riot at the US Capitol on January 6, 2021 (Conger and Isaac, *New York Times*, January 8, 2021).

CHAPTER 5: ACTION

1. The refusal of NCTE and CCCC to condemn Salaita's treatment inspired eleven prominent members to not renew their membership. See Trimbur (2019).
2. For context on the working conditions of school bus drivers, see De La Coeur (2022).
3. In rhetorical studies, Dana L. Cloud, a prominent independent scholar and activist, formerly a professor of communication and rhetorical studies at Syracuse University, was aggressively harassed by extremist groups in 2017 (Parks 2019).
4. Today, philanthropic influence, which began in earnest after the war, has become a vital source of institutional funding and, consequently, of control. Politically motivated private donors have given generously to universities over the past several decades and have often been given considerable influence in return (Reichman 2019, 107). Koch properties alone distributed $50 million to over two hundred institutions in 2016 (108), while George Mason University has received almost $95 million from the Kochs since 2005 (108). Reichman also notes the extent to which this influence determined departmental operations at Florida State University, where outside influence "included the ability to veto tenure hires, or any programming . . . and an annual donor review of curricular/extracurricular programs and non-tenure track hires" (114).
5. Such attacks are becoming increasingly common. In early 2021, Iowa Republicans proposed a bill to eliminate tenure at the state's public schools, citing "the authenticity of tenure review and . . . politicization in higher education" (Miller 2021).
6. See Scott's (2009) discussion of the political economy of the textbook industry (60–107).
7. In 2021, a deal between the two was struck that will allow open access to articles published by UC academics in Elsevier journals (McKenzie 2021).
8. While part-time faculty represented only approximately 30 percent of university teaching staff in 1975, the figure had risen to 73 percent by 2018 (Flaherty 2018a).
9. During COVID-19, the university imposed a new raft of austerity measures that included extensive layoffs and delaying equity raises (Murtagh 2021).
10. It is worth noting that this final argument is not particularly persuasive. As UW historian Moon-Ho Jung noted at the time, "The Faculty Senate is purely advisory" (Bader 2015).
11. In October of 2019, the University of New Mexico faculty voted, by a substantial margin, for faculty representation (Boetel, *Albuquerque Journal*, October 18, 2019).

REFERENCES

Abraham, Matthew. 2016. "Rhetoric and Composition's Conceptual Indeterminacy as Political-Economic Work." *College Composition and Communication* 68 (1): 68–97.
ADE Ad Hoc Committee on the English Major. 2018. "A Changing Major: The Report of the 2016–17 ADE Ad Hoc Committee on the English Major." *Association of Departments of English*, July 18. https://www.maps.mla.org/content/download/98513/2276619/A-Changing-Major.pdf.
Adler-Kassner, Linda. 2017. "2017 CCCC Chair's Address: Because Writing Is Never Just Writing." *College Composition and Communication* 69 (2): 317–340.
Adler-Kassner, Linda, and Elizabeth Wardle, eds. 2015. *Naming What We Know: Threshold Concepts of Writing Studies*. Logan: Utah State University Press.
Alexander, F. King. 2019. "The Reality of State Divestment in Public Higher Education." *Inside Higher Ed*, November 26. https://www.insidehighered.com/views/2019/11/26/recent-studies-state-disinvestment-public-higher-education-are-misleading-opinion.
Alexander, Jonathan, and Jacqueline Rhodes, eds. 2018. *The Routledge Handbook of Digital Writing and Rhetoric*. New York: Routledge.
Alexander, Michelle. 2019. *The New Jim Crow: Mass Incarceration in the Age of Colorblindness*. New York: The New Press.
Alvarez, Maximillian. 2017. "Contingent No More." *Baffler*, May 3. https://thebaffler.com/the-poverty-of-theory/contingent-no-more.
Amazon. 2019. "Our Positions." Who We Are. https://www.aboutamazon.com/our-company/our-positions.
Anda, Ashli, and Adam Edwards. 2018. "Learning on the Job." *Jacobin*, March 15. https://jacobinmag.com/2018/03/uiuc-graduate-union-student-workers-university.
Anderson, Perry. 1976. *Considerations on Western Marxism*. London: Verso.
Arnold, Amanda. 2019. "4 People on Feeling Crushed by Their Student Debt." *Cut*, April. https://www.thecut.com/2019/04/4-people-on-feeling-crushed-by-their-student-debt.html.
Aronowitz, Stanley, Dawn Esposito, William DiFazio, and Margaret Yard. 1998. "The Post-Work Manifesto." In *Post-Work: The Wages of Cybernation*, edited by Stanley Aronowitz and Jonathan Cutler, 31–80. Abingdon: Routledge.
Arruzza, Cinzia, Tithi Bhattacharya, and Nancy Fraser. 2019. *Feminism for the 99%: A Manifesto*. London: Verso.
Aschoff, Nicole. 2017. "The Glory Days Are Over." *Jacobin*, March 20. https://www.jacobinmag.com/2017/03/the-glory-days-are-over-2.
Baca, Damián. 2009. "Rethinking Composition, Five Hundred Years Later." *JAC* 29 (1/2): 229–242.
Bader, Eleanor J. 2015. "As Public Funding of Universities Dwindles, Faculty Are Unionizing." TruthOut, December 20. https://truthout.org/articles/as-public-funding-of-universities-dwindles-faculty-are-unionizing/.
Badiou, Alain. 2005. *Being and Event*. Translated by Oliver Feltham. London: Continuum.
Badiou, Alain. 2009. *Theory of the Subject*. Translated by Bruno Bosteels. London: Continuum.

Badiou, Alain. 2019. *Trump.* Cambridge: Polity.
Banks, Adam J. 2005. *Race, Rhetoric, and Technology: Searching for Higher Ground.* Abingdon: Routledge.
Banks, Adam J. 2011. *Digital Griots: African American Rhetoric in a Multimedia Age.* Carbondale: Southern Illinois University Press.
Baron, James N. 2018. "Can a Company Succeed Without a Hierarchy." Yale Insights, October 23. https://insights.som.yale.edu/insights/can-company-succeed-without-hierarchy.
Basu, Tanya. 2020. "How Google Docs Became the Social Media of the Resistance." *MIT Technology Review,* June 6. https://www.technologyreview.com/2020/06/06/1002546/google-docs-social-media-resistance/.
Baum, Sandy. 2015. "The Evolution of Student Debt in the United States." In *The Evolution of Student Debt in the United States,* edited by Brad Hershbein and Kevin M. Hollenbeck, 11–36. Kalamazoo, MI: W. E. Upjohn Institute.
Bay, Jennifer. 2010. "Writing beyond Writers: Rethinking the Relationship Between Composition Studies and Professional Writing." *Composition Studies* 38 (2): 29–45.
Benjamin, Ruha. 2020. "Essential worker, essential to exploit, essential to sacrifice, essential to expose, essential to gaslight, essential to coerce, essential to romanticize, essential to resist, essential to organize, essential to unionize, essential to protect, essential to pay, essential to care." May 8, 9:01 a.m. https://twitter.com/ruha9/status/1258789223349587968.
Benveniste, Alexis. 2021. "Free Pelotons and iPads: How Wall Street Is fighting Covid Burnout." CNN, March 23. https://www.cnn.com/2021/03/23/business/wall-street-covid-burnout-perks/index.html.
Berardi, Franco "Bifo." 2009. *The Soul at Work: From Alienation to Autonomy.* Translated by Francesca Cadel and Guiseppina Mecchia. Los Angeles: semiotext(e).
Berlin, James A. 2003. *Rhetorics, Poetics, and Cultures: Refiguring College English Studies.* Anderson, SC: Parlor.
Bernard-Donals, Michael. 2019. "Rhetorical Movement, Vulnerability, and Higher Education." *Philosophy & Rhetoric* 52 (1): 1–23.
Bernstein, Susan Naomi. 2016. "Occupy Basic Writing: Pedagogy in the Age of Austerity." In *Composition in the Age of Austerity,* edited by Nancy Welch and Tony Scott, 92–105. Logan: Utah State University Press.
Beveridge, Aaron. 2017. "Writing through Big Data: New Challenges and Possibilities for Data Driven Arguments." *Composition Forum* 37 (Fall). https://compositionforum.com/issue/37/big-data.php.
Bird, Barbara, Doug Downs, I. Moriah McCracken, and Jan Rieman, eds. 2019. *Next Steps: New Directions for/in Writing about Writing.* Logan: Utah State University Press.
Bishop, Wendy. 2001. "Against the Odds in Rhetoric and Composition." *College Composition and Communication* 53 (2): 322–335.
Bizzaro, Patrick. 2001. "Comment: Kostelanetz's Rhetoric of Isolation: Or, Sometimes I Feel Lonely Too." *College English* 64 (2): 237–242.
Bizzell, Patricia, and Stanley Fish. 2009. "Composition Saves the World! [with Response]." *Profession*: 94–104.
Blakeley, Grace. 2020. *The Corona Crash: How the Pandemic Will Change Capitalism.* London: Verso.
Bloom, Lynn Z. 1996. "Freshman Composition as a Middle-Class Enterprise." *College English* 58 (6): 654–675.
Bogost, Ian. 2015. *The Geek's Chihuahua: Living with Apple.* Minneapolis: University of Minnesota Press.
Boice, Robert. 1985. "The Neglected Third Factor in Writing: Productivity." *College Composition and Communication* 36 (4): 472–480.
Bollig, Chase. 2015. "'Is College Worth It?' Arguing for Composition's Value with the Citizen Worker." *College Composition and Communication* 67 (2): 150–172.

Booker, Brakkton, Bill Chappell, David Schaper, Danielle Kurtzleben, and Joseph Shapiro. 2020. "Violence Erupts as Outrage over George Floyd Death Spills into a New Week." NPR, June 1. https://www.npr.org/2020/06/01/866472832/violence-escalates-as-protests-over-george-floyd-death-continue.
Boring Company. n.d. "FAQ." https://www.boringcompany.com/.
Bousquet, Marc. 2002. "Composition as Management Science: Toward a University without a WPA." *JAC* 22 (3): 493–526.
Bousquet, Marc. 2008. *How the University Works: Higher Education and the Low-Wage Nation.* New York: New York University Press.
Bousquet, Marc, Tony Scott, and Leo Parascondola. 2003. *Tenured Bosses and Disposable Teachers.* Carbondale: Southern Illinois University Press.
Boutang, Yann Moulier. 2004. *Cognitive Capitalism.* Cambridge: Polity.
Bower, Joseph L., and Clayton M. Christiansen. 1995. "Disruptive Technologies: Catching the Wave." *Harvard Business Review,* January–February. https://hbr.org/1995/01/disruptive-technologies-catching-the-wave.
Brandt, Deborah. 2008. "When People Write for Pay." *JAC* 29 (1/2): 165–197.
Brandt, Deborah. 2014. *The Rise of Writing: Redefining Mass Literacy.* Cambridge: Cambridge University Press.
Bratton, Benjamin. 2016. *The Stack: On Software and Sovereignty.* Cambridge: MIT Press.
Brey, Jared. 2018. "As Newsrooms Do More with Less, Can Reporters Keep Up?" *Columbia Journalism Review,* September 12. https://www.cjr.org/united_states_project/productivity-stories-news.php.
Bridle, James. 2019. *New Dark Age: Technology and the End of the Future.* London: Verso.
Brown, Gordon. 2009. "Wiring a Web for Global Good." TED video, 16:30. https://www.ted.com/talks/gordon_brown_wiring_a_web_for_global_good.
Brown, H. Claire. 2019. "How Amazon's On-Site Emergency Care Endangers the Warehouse Workers It's Supposed to Protect." *Intercept,* December 2. https://theintercept.com/2019/12/02/amazon-warehouse-workers-safety-cyber-monday/.
Brown, Sherrod, Bernard Sanders, Tammy Baldwin, Kristin Gillibrand, Richard Blumenthal, Elizabeth Warren, Chris Van Hollen, Tina Smith, Richard J. Durbin, Christopher Murphy, Kamala D. Harris, Edward J. Markey, Mazie K. Hirono, Jeffrey K. Merkley, and Cory A. Booker. 2020. "Sanders Demands Answers from Bezos over Amazon Increase in Work-Related Injuries." *Vermont Biz,* February 11. https://vermontbiz.com/news/2020/february/11/sanders-demands-answers-bezos-over-amazon-increase-work-related-injuries.
Brown, Wendy. 2019. *In the Ruins of Neoliberalism: The Rise of Antidemocratic Politics in the West.* New York: Columbia University Press.
Brownstein, Ronald. 2018. "American Higher Education Hits a Dangerous Milestone." *Atlantic,* May 3. https://www.theatlantic.com/politics/archive/2018/05/american-highereducation-hits-a-dangerous-milestone/559457/.
Bruder, Jessica. 2017. *Nomadland: Surviving America in the Twenty-First Century.* New York: W. W. Norton & Company.
Bruffee, Kenneth. 1981. "Collaborative Learning." *College English* 43 (7): 745–747.
Bruffee, Kenneth. 1984. "Collaborative Learning and the 'Conversation of Mankind.'" *College English* 46 (7): 635–652.
Buchanan, Lindal. 2003. "Forging and Firing Thunderbolts: Collaboration and Women's Rhetoric." *Rhetoric Society Quarterly* 33 (4): 43–63.
Bukowczyk, John J. 2016. "California Dreamin', Whiteness, and the American Dream." *Journal of American Ethnic History* 35 (2): 91–106.
Bureau of Labor Statistics. 2021. "News Release: Union Members-2021." January 22. https://www.bls.gov/news.release/pdf/union2.pdf.
Busch, Lawrence. 2017. *Knowledge for Sale: The Neoliberal Takeover of Higher Education.* Cambridge: MIT Press.

Bustillo, Ximena. 2020. "Protests after Floyd's Death Reach Rural America." *Politico*, June 6. https://www.politico.com/news/2020/06/06/protests-after-floyds-death-reach-rural-america-303892.

Caffentzis, George. 2013. "Reflections on the History of Debt Resistance: The Case of El Barzón." *South Atlantic Quarterly* 112 (4): 824–830.

Campbell, Alexia Fernández. 2019. "The Recession Hasn't Ended for Gig Economy Workers." *Vox*, May 28. https://www.vox.com/policy-and-politics/2019/5/28/18638480/gig-economy-workers-wellbeing-survey.

Cantwell, Brendan, and Ilkka Kauppinen, eds. 2014 *Academic Capitalism in the Age of Globalization*. Baltimore: Johns Hopkins University Press.

Carmony, Josh. 2021. "Ground Operations." *Contingent Magazine*, March 22. https://contingentmagazine.org/2021/03/22/ground-operations/.

Carnevale, Anthony P., and Nicole Smith. 2018. *Balancing Work and Learning: Implications for Low Income Students*. Georgetown University Center on Education and the Workforce. https://1gyhoq479ufd3yna29x7ubjn-wpengine.netdna-ssl.com/wp-content/uploads/Low-Income-Working-Learners-FR.pdf.

Carter, Genesea M., and William H. Thelin, eds. 2017. *Class in the Composition Classroom: Pedagogy and the Working Class*. Logan: Utah State University Press.

Carter, Jonathan S. 2019. "Transindividuating Nodes: Rhetoric as the Architechnical Organizer of Networks." *Rhetoric Society Quarterly* 49 (5): 542–565.

Carter, Shannon, Deborah Mutnick, Steve Parks, and Jessica Pauszek. 2019a. "Introduction: What *Does* Democracy Look Like?" In *Writing Democracy: The Political Turn in and Beyond the Trump Era*, edited by Shannon Carter, Deborah Mutnick, Steve Parks, and Jessica Pauszek, 1–22. New York: Routledge Research in Writing Studies.

Carter, Shannon, Deborah Mutnick, Steve Parks, and Jessica Pauszek, eds. 2019b. *Writing Democracy: The Political Turn in and Beyond the Trump Era*. New York: Routledge Research in Writing Studies.

Case, Anne, and Angus Deaton. 2020. *Deaths of Despair and the Future of Capitalism*. Princeton: Princeton University Press.

Cauce, Ana Mari and Jerry Baldasty. 2015. "An Informed Choice About Faculty Unionization." University of Washington, September 10. https://s3-us-west-2.amazonaws.com/uw-s3-cdn/wp-content/uploads/sites/113/2018/07/24113026/Toolkit-An-Informed-Choice-about-Faculty-Unionization.pdf.

Chait, Jonathan. 2017. "Senate Republicans Are Abdicating Their Governing Responsibility." *New York Magazine*, September 20. https://nymag.com/intelligencer/2017/09/republicans-are-abdicating-their-governing-responsibility.html.

Charlton, Emma. 2018. "Denmark Has the Flattest Work Hierarchy in the World." World Economic Forum, October 17. https://www.weforum.org/agenda/2018/10/denmark-has-the-flattest-work-hierarchy-in-the-world/.

Childress, Herb. 2019. *The Adjunct Underclass: How America's Colleges Betrayed Their Faculty, Their Students, and Their Mission*. Chicago: University of Chicago Press.

Chomsky, Noam. 2011. *Profit over People: Neoliberalism and Global Order*. New York: Seven Stories.

Ciccariello-Maher, George. 2016. *Building the Commune: Radical Democracy in Venezuela*. London: Verso.

Clare, Ross. 2020. "How Working-Class Academics Are Set Up to Fail." *Tribune*, October 13. https://tribunemag.co.uk/2020/10/how-working-class-academics-are-set-up-to-fail.

Clark, Taylor. 2020. "University of Alaska Board of Regents Raises Tuition by 5%." KTUU, January 17. https://www.ktuu.com/content/news/University-of-Alaska-Board-of-Regents-raises-tuition-by-5-567096891.html.

Clegg, Geoffrey. 2019. "Sustainable Audiences/Renewable Products: Penn State's Student Farm, Business Writing, and Community Outreach." In *Writing Democracy: The Political*

Turn in and Beyond the Trump Era, edited by Shannon Carter, Deborah Mutnick, Steve Parks, and Jessica Pauszek, 150–161. New York: Routledge Research in Writing Studies.

Cohan, Deborah J. 2016. "Speaking Out as an Untenured Professor." *Inside Higher Ed*, March 16. https://www.insidehighered.com/advice/2017/03/16/advice-how-and-when-untenured-professors-should-speak-their-minds-essay.

Collinge, Alan Michael. 2010. *The Student Loan Scam: The Most Oppressive Debt in U.S. History—and How We Can Fight Back*. Boston: Beacon.

Comelli, Martino, and Vera Horváth. 2019. "What Orbán Knows and His Enemies Don't." *Jacobin*, March 9. https://www.jacobinmag.com/2018/03/viktor-orban-hungary-fidesz-authoritarian-opposition.

Condon, Frankie, and Vershawn Ashanti Young, eds. 2017. *Performing Antiracist Pedagogy in Rhetoric, Writing, and Communication*. Boulder, CO: WAC Clearinghouse.

Connolly, William E. 2017. *Aspirational Fascism: The Struggle for Multifaceted Democracy under Trumpism*. Minneapolis: Minnesota University Press.

Cox, Anicca, Timothy R. Dougherty, Seth Kahn, Michelle LaFrance, and Amy Lynch-Biniek. 2016. "The Indianapolis Resolution: Responding to Twenty-First-Century Exigencies/Political Economies of Composition Labor." *College Composition and Communication* 68 (1): 38–67.

Crary, Jonathan. 2014. *24/7: Late Capitalism and the Ends of Sleep*. London: Verso.

Cucciarre, Christine. 2014. "Happily and Shamefully Non-Tenure Track: Hypocrisy in Academic Labor." *College English* 77 (1): 55–63.

Danberg, Robert. 2011. "On (Not) Making It in Rhetoric and Composition." *Composition Studies* 39 (1): 63–72.

Daniel, James Rushing. 2017. "Freshman Composition as a Precariat Enterprise." *College English* 80 (1): 63–85.

Daniel, James Rushing. 2018. "'A Debt is Just the Perversion of a Promise': Composition and the Student Loan." *College Composition and Communication* 70 (2): 195–221.

Dardot, Pierre, and Christian Laval. 2019a. *Common: On Revolution in the Twenty-First Century*. Translated by Matthew MacLellan. New York: Bloomsbury Academic.

Dardot, Pierre, and Christian Laval. 2019b. *Never-Ending Nightmare: The Neoliberal Assault on Democracy*. London: Verso.

Davies, Tom Adam. 2017. *Mainstreaming Black Power*. Oakland: University of California Press.

Davis, Angela Y. 2003. *Are Prisons Obsolete?* New York: Seven Stories.

Davis, Angela Y. 2020. "Angela Davis on International Solidarity and the Future of Black Radicalism." By Verso Books. *Literary Hub*, August 31. https://lithub.com/angela-davis-on-international-solidarity-and-the-future-of-black-radicalism/.

Day, Meagan. 2020. "Unions Are Essential for Eliminating Racism." *Jacobin*, July 7. https://jacobinmag.com/2020/07/multiracial-solidarity-unions?utm_source=Jacobin&utm_campaign=55f21cecb1-EMAIL_CAMPAIGN_2019_10_01_07_50_COPY_01&utm_medium=email&utm_term=0_be8b1b2846-55f21cecb1-85541154&mc_cid=55f21cecb1&mc_eid=34c851e476.

Deacon, Andrea. 2013. "Launching Curricular Reform in First-Year Composition: Navigating the Terrain between Buy-in and Burnout." *CEA Forum* 4 (1): 3–25.

Dean, Jodi. 2019. *The Comrade: An Essay on Political Belonging*. London: Verso.

DeBord, Matthew. 2019. "Uber and Lyft Are Trying to Make an End Run Around Unionization." *Business Insider*, June 14. https://www.businessinsider.com/uber-and-lyft-opposing-driver-unionization-california-2019-6.

DeGeurin, Mack. 2018. "New Study Indicates Silicon Valley's Elite Are Not as Liberal as They Think." *New York Magazine*, November 21. https://nymag.com/intelligencer/2018/11/study-shows-tech-elites-are-less-liberal-than-they-think.html.

De La Coeur, Nora. 2022. "School Bus Drivers Make School Possible. They Deserve Better." *Jacobin*, February 9. https://jacobinmag.com/2022/02/k12-transporation

-worker-shortage-pay-hours-covid?fbclid=IwAR03lzta6VSnoTTd11-ALVaKLVbndfpKvQ_ydQWwko1O_Qt7DzaFoIzSkcE.
Deleuze, Gilles. 1990. *The Logic of Sense*. Translated by Constantin V. Boundas. New York: Columbia University Press.
Deleuze, Gilles. 1995. *Difference and Repetition*. New York: Columbia University Press.
DeLuca, Kevin Michael. 2003. "Unmoored: The Force of Images as Events." *JAC* 28 (3/4): 663–673.
Denvir, David. 2020. *All-American Nativism: How the Bipartisan War on Immigrants Explains the Politics as We Know It*. London: Verso.
Desan, Mathieu, and Michael A. McCarthy. 2018. "A Time to Be Bold." *Jacobin*, July 31. https://jacobinmag.com/2018/07/socialism-democrats-alexandria-ocasio-cortez.
Dingo, Rebecca, Rachel Riedner, and Jennifer Wingard. 2015. "Disposable Drudgery: Outsourcing Goes to College." In *Transnational Writing Program Administration*, edited by David Martins, 265–288. Logan: Utah State University Press.
Doane, Janice, and Devon Hodges. 1995. "Writing from the Trenches: Women's Work and Collaborative Writing." *Tulsa Studies in Women's Literature* 14 (1): 51–57.
Doebler, Paul D. 1987. "Productivity Improvement through Electronic Publishing." *Technical Communication* 34 (4): 250–251, 254–256.
Dolmage, Jay T. 2017. *Academic Ableism: Disability and Higher Education*. Ann Arbor: University of Michigan Press.
Donnelly, Timothy. 2010. *The Cloud Corporation*. Seattle: Wave Books.
Draut, Tamara. 2018. "Understanding the Working Class." *Dēmos*, April 16. https://www.demos.org/research/understanding-working-class#Defining-the-Working-Class.
Duffy, William. 2014. "Collaboration (in) Theory: Reworking the Social Turn's Conversational Imperative." *College English* 76 (5): 416–435.
Dunbar-Ortiz, Roxanne. 2014. *An Indigenous Peoples' History of the United States*. Boston: Beacon.
Dush, Lisa. 2015. "When Writing Becomes Content." *College Composition and Communication* 67 (2): 173–196.
Dyer-Witheford, Nick. 2005. "Cognitive Capitalism and the Contested Campus." In *Engineering Culture: On "The Author as (Digital) Producer,"* edited by Geoff Cox and Joasia Krysa, 71–93. New York: Autonomedia.
Economic Policy Institute. 2019. "The Productivity-Pay Gap." https://www.epi.org/productivity-pay-gap/.
Ede, Lisa, and Andrea A. Lunsford. 2011. "Collaboration and Concepts of Authorship." *PMLA* 116 (2): 354–369.
Edwards, Mike, and Jessica Reyman. 2018. "Open Access and the Economics of Scholarship in Rhetoric and Composition Studies." *Rhetoric Review* 37 (2): 212–225.
Eidlin, Barry. 2020. "Why Unions Are Good—But Not Good Enough." *Jacobin*, January 6. https://www.jacobinmag.com/2020/01/marxism-trade-unions-socialism-revolutionary-organizing.
Elbow, Peter. 1987. "Closing My Eyes as I Speak: An Argument for Ignoring Audience." *College English* 49 (1): 50–69.
Elbow, Peter. 1999. "Using the Collage for Collaborative Writing." *Composition Studies* 27 (1): 7–14.
Emig, Janet. 1971. *The Composing Process of Twelfth Graders*. Champaign, IL: NCTE.
Epps-Robertson, Candace. 2018. *Resisting Brown: Race, Literacy, and Citizenship in the Heart of Virginia*. Pittsburgh: University of Pittsburgh Press.
Eyman, Douglas, and Andréa D. Davis, eds. 2016. *Play/Write: Digital Rhetoric, Writing, Games*. Anderson, SC: Parlor.
Fabricant, Michael, and Stephen Brier. 2016. *Austerity Blues: Fighting for the Soul of Public Higher Education*. Baltimore: Johns Hopkins University Press.

Fabry, Adam. 2019. *The Political Economy of Hungary: From State Capitalism to Authoritarian Neoliberalism*. London: Palgrave MacMillan.
"Faculty Tensions I: The Sanctity of the Classroom." 2014. *Harvard Magazine*, November 5. https://harvardmagazine.com/2014/11/harvard-professors-object-to-student-monitoring.
Farmer, Frank. 2018. *After the Public Turn: Composition, Publics, and the Citizen Bricoleur*. Logan: Utah State University Press.
Federal Student Aid. n.d. "Federal Student Loan Portfolio." https://studentaid.gov/data-center/student/portfolio.
Fitts, Karen, and William B. Lalicker. 2004. "Invisible Hands: A Manifesto to Resolve Institutional and Curricular Hierarchy in English Studies." *College Composition and Communication* 66 (4): 427–451.
Fitzpatrick, Kathleen. 2019. *Generous Thinking: A Radical Approach to Saving the University*. Baltimore: Johns Hopkins University Press.
Flaherty, Colleen. 2017a. "A Pedagogy Questioned." *Inside Higher Ed*, October 20. https://www.insidehighered.com/news/2017/10/20/penn-grad-student-says-shes-under-attack-teaching-technique-encourage-all-talk-class.
Flaherty, Colleen. 2017b. "An Inconvenient Adjunct." *Inside Higher Ed*, June 9. https://www.insidehighered.com/news/2017/06/09/instructor-who-says-she-brought-adjunct-union-barnard-no-longer-employed-there.
Flaherty, Colleen. 2018a. "A Non-Tenure-Track Profession." *Inside Higher Ed*, October 12. https://www.insidehighered.com/news/2018/10/12/about-three-quarters-all-faculty-positions-are-tenure-track-according-new-aaup.
Flaherty, Colleen. 2018b. "U Wisconsin–Stevens Point to Eliminate 13 Majors" *Inside Higher Ed*, March 6. https://www.insidehighered.com/quicktakes/2018/03/06/u-wisconsin-stevens-point-eliminate-13-majors.
Flaherty, Colleen. 2019a. "CUNY Contract Deal Means Big Raise for Adjuncts." *Inside Higher Ed*, October 24. https://www.insidehighered.com/quicktakes/2019/10/24/cuny-contract-deal-means-big-raise-adjuncts.
Flaherty, Colleen. 2019b. "Cuts to Liberal Arts at Goucher." *Inside Higher Ed*, August 17. https://www.insidehighered.com/news/2018/08/17/goucher-college-says-its-eliminating-liberal-arts-programs-such-math-physics-and.
Fleckenstein, Paul. 2019. "Stopping Climate Change Will Never Be 'Good Business.'" *Jacobin*, July 29. https://www.jacobinmag.com/2019/07/falter-bill-mckibben-350org-review.
Foer, Franklin. 2019. "Victor Orbán's War on Intellect." *Atlantic*, June. https://www.theatlantic.com/magazine/archive/2019/06/george-soros-viktor-orban-ceu/588070/.
Fonser, Philip S., and Robin D. G. Kelley. 2018. *Organized Labor and the Black Worker, 1619–1981*. Chicago: Haymarket Books.
Foster, Dawn. 2016. *Lean Out*. London: Repeater.
Fraenkel, Carlos, and Adam Etison. 2012. "One Hundred Days of Student Protests in Québec: *Printemps Érable* or Much Ado About Nothing?" *Dissent*, May 29. https://www.dissentmagazine.org/online_articles/one-hundred-days-of-student-protests-in-quebec-printemps-erable-or-much-ado-about-nothing.
Fraser, Nancy. 2019. *The Old Is Dying and the New Cannot Be Born*. London: Verso.
Friedman, Zach. 2017. "What the Navient Lawsuit Means for Your Student Loans." *Forbes*, January 20. https://www.forbes.com/sites/zackfriedman/2017/01/20/navient/.
Friedman, Zach. 2019. "Student Loan Debt Statistics in 2019: A $1.5 Trillion Crisis." *Forbes*, February 25. https://www.forbes.com/sites/zackfriedman/2019/02/25/student-loan-debt-statistics-2019/#651bf519133f.
Friedman, Zach. 2020. "Student Loan Debt Statistics in 2020: A Record $1.6 Trillion." *Forbes*, February 3. https://www.forbes.com/sites/zackfriedman/2020/02/03/student-loan-debt-statistics/.

Friedman, Zach. 2022. "Biden Cancels $6.2 Billion Of Student Loans, But Twitter Erupts With These Objections." *Forbes*, March 19, https://www.forbes.com/sites/zackfriedman/2022/03/16/biden-cancels-62-billion-of-student-loans-but-twitter-erupts-with-these-objections/?sh=13ccoa6d3481.

Frost, Amber A'Lee. 2020. "The Poisoned Chalice of Hashtag Activism." *Catalyst*, 4 (2). https://catalyst-journal.com/vol4/no2/the-poisoned-chalice-of-hashtag-activism.

Frymer, Paul, and Jacob M. Grumbach. 2021. "Labor Unions and White Racial Politics." *American Journal of Political Science* 65 (1): 225–240.

Geary, Daniel. 2015. "The Moynihan Report: An Annotated Edition." *Atlantic*, September 14. https://www.theatlantic.com/politics/archive/2015/09/the-moynihan-report-an-annotated-edition/404632/.

Geissler, Heike. 2018. *Seasonal Associate*. Translated by Katy Derbyshire. Los Angeles: semiotext(e).

Gerbaudo, Paolo. 2012. *Tweets and the Streets: Social Media and Contemporary Activism*. London: Pluto.

Gere, Ann Ruggles. 1987. *Writing Groups: History, Theory, and Implications*. Carbondale: Southern Illinois University Press.

Gerstmann, Evan. 2020. "Irony: Hate Crimes Surge against Asian Americans While They Are on the Front Lines Fighting COVID-19." *Forbes*, April 4. https://www.forbes.com/sites/evangerstmann/2020/04/04/irony-hate-crimes-surge-against-asian-americans-while-they-are-on-the-front-lines-fighting-covid-19/#1569b1023b70.

Gibson-Graham, J. K. 2006. *The End of Capitalism (as We Knew It)*. Minneapolis: University of Minnesota Press.

Gilmore, Ruth Wilson. 2007. *Golden Gulag: Prisons, Surplus, Crisis, and Opposition in Globalizing California*. Berkeley: University of California Press.

Giroux, Henry. 2007. "The University in Chains." By Scott Jaschik. *Inside Higher Ed*, August 7. http://www.insidehighered.com/news/2007/08/07/university-chains.

Gjelten, Tom. 2020. "Survey: White Evangelicals See Trump as 'Honest' and 'Morally Upstanding.'" NPR, March 12. https://www.npr.org/2020/03/12/815097747/survey-most-evangelicals-see-trump-as-honest-and-morally-upstanding.

Glover, Danny. 2021. "Danny Glover on Amazon Workers' Struggle to Organize in Alabama." Maximillian Alverez. *Jacobin*, March 9. jacobinmag.com/2021/03/danny-glover-amazon-union-bessemer-alabama.

Goldrick-Rab, Sarah. 2016. *Paying the Price: College Costs, Financial Aid, and the Betrayal of the American Dream*. Chicago: University of Chicago Press.

Gonzales, Laura. 2018. *Sites of Translation: What Multilinguals Can Teach Us about Digital Writing and Rhetoric*. Ann Arbor: University of Michigan Press.

Gordon, Colin. 2019. "State of the Unions." *Dissent*, February 13. https://www.dissentmagazine.org/blog/state-of-the-unions.

Gornick, Vivian. 2020. *The Romance of American Communism*. London: Verso.

Graeber, David. 2012. *Debt: The First 5,000 Years*. New York: Melville House.

Graeber, David. 2018. *Bullshit Jobs: A Theory*. New York: Simon and Schuster.

Graham, David A. 2020 "What a Direct Attack on Free Speech Looks Like." *Atlantic*, 10 July. https://www.theatlantic.com/ideas/archive/2020/07/trump-universities/614038/.

Graham, Margaret Baker, Elizabeth Birmingham, and Mark Zachry. 1999. "A New Way of Doing Business: Articulating the Economics of Composition." *JAC* 19 (4): 679–697.

Gregory, James N. 2015. "Seattle's Left Coast Formula." *Dissent*, Winter. https://www.dissentmagazine.org/article/seattles-left-coast-formula.

Griffiths, Brett, and Christie Toth. 2017. "Rethinking Class: Poverty, Pedagogy, and Two-Year College Writing Programs." In *Class in the Composition Classroom: Pedagogy in the Working Class*, edited by Genesea M. Carter and William H. Thelin, 231–257. Logan: Utah State University Press.

Gruwell, Leigh. 2015. "Wikipedia's Politics of Exclusion: Gender, Epistemology, and Feminist Rhetorical (In)action." *Computers and Composition* 37: 117–131.
Gunner, Jeanne. 2012. "Disciplinary Purification: The Writing Program as Institutional Brand." *JAC* 32 (3/4): 615–643.
Gurley, Lauren Kaori. 2021. "Amazon Workers in Chicago Strike over Ruthless 'Megacycle' Shifts." *VICE*, April 7. https://www.vice.com/en/article/g5gxpb/amazon-workers-in-chi cago-strike-over-ruthless-megacycle-shifts.
Guy, Jack. 2021. "Employees Working from Home Are Putting in Longer Hours Than before the Pandemic." CNN, February 5. https://www.cnn.com/2021/02/05/business /working-from-home-hours-pandemic-scli-intl-gbr/index.html.
Hall, Josh. 2018. "Downward-Facing Capitalist Dogma." *Baffler*, February 27.
Han, Byung-Chul. 2015. *The Burnout Society*. Translated by Erik Butler. Stanford, CA: Stanford University Press.
Hardt, Michael, and Antonio Negri. 2017. *Assembly*. Oxford: Oxford University Press.
Harrington, Michael. 2020. *Socialism: Past and Future*. New York: Arcade.
Harris, Joseph. 2000. "Meet the New Boss, Same as the Old Boss: Class Consciousness in Composition." *College Composition and Communication* 52 (1): 43–68.
Harris, Joseph. 2014. "Places at the Table." *College English* 77 (1): 69–72.
Harvey, David. 2020. *The Anti-Capitalist Chronicles*. London: Pluto.
Hassel, Holly, and Joanne Baird Giordano. 2013. "Occupy Writing Studies: Rethinking College Composition for the Needs of the Thinking Majority." *College Composition and Communication* 65 (1): 117–139.
Hazelrigg, Nick. 2019. "Reorganizing Away the Liberal Arts." *Inside Higher Ed*, June 6. https://www.insidehighered.com/news/2019/06/06/cuts-leave-concerns-liberal-arts -tulsa.
Heller, Henry. 2016. *The Capitalist University: The Transformations of Higher Education in the United State Since 1945*. London: Pluto.
Heller, Henry. 2019. *A Marxist History of Capitalism*. Abingdon: Routledge.
Heller, Rafael. 2003. "Questionable Categories and the Case for Collaborative Writing." *Rhetoric Review* 22 (3): 300–317.
Hershbein, Brad, and Kevin M. Hollenbeck. 2015. "Student Loans and the Dynamics of Debt." In *The Evolution of Student Debt in the United States*, edited by Brad Hershbein and Kevin M. Hollenbeck, 53–116. Kalamazoo: W. E. Upjohn Institute.
Hess, Abigail. 2017. "This Is the Age Most Students Pay Off Their Student Loans." CNBC, July 3. https://www.cnbc.com/2017/07/03/this-is-the-age-most-americans-pay-off-their -student-loans.html.
Hess, Abigail. 2018. "Natty Light Is Giving Away $1,000,000 to Help Grads Pay Off Student Loans." CNBC, February 3. https://www.cnbc.com/2018/02/03/natty-light-is-giving -away-1000000-to-help-grads-pay-off-loans.html.
Hess, Abigail. 2019a. "Harvard's Endowment Is Worth $40 Billion—Here's How It's Spent." CNBC, October 30. https://www.cnbc.com/2019/10/28/harvards-endowment -is-worth-40-billionheres-how-its-spent.html.
Hess, Abigail. 2019b. "Natty Light Is Giving Away Another $1,000,000 to Help Grads Pay Off Their Loans." CNBC, January 31. https://www.cnbc.com/2019/01/31/natty-light-is -giving-away-1000000-to-pay-off-student-loans.html.
Hobbs, Renee, and Katie Donnelly. 2011. "Toward a Pedagogy of Fair Use for Multimedia Composition." In *Copy(write): Intellectual Property in the Writing Classroom*, edited by Martine Courant Rife, Shaun Slattery, and Dànielle Nicole DeVoss, 275–294. Anderson, SC: Parlor.
Hollis, Karyn L. 2004. *Liberating Voices: Writing at the Bryn Mawr Summer School for Women Workers*. Carbondale: Southern Illinois University Press.
Holt, Mara. 2018. *Collaborative Learning as Democratic Practice: A History*. Urbana, IL: NCTE.

Hormel, Leontina, and Lynn M. McAlister. 2017. "'These Are the Choices We've Made': How Professors Turn the Public Issue of Rising Student Debt into a Private Trouble." *Humanity & Society* 1 (3): 313–332.

Horner, Bruce. 2007. "Redefining Work and Value for Writing Program Administration." *JAC*, 27 (1/2): 163–184.

Horner, Bruce. 2012. "Introduction: Economies of Writing." *JAC* 32 (3/4): 453–460.

Horner, Bruce. 2015. "Rewriting Composition: Moving beyond a Discourse of Need." *College English* 77 (5): 450–479.

Horner, Bruce. 2016. *Rewriting Composition: Terms of Exchange*. Carbondale: Southern Illinois University Press.

Horner, Bruce, and Min-Zhan Lu. 2010. "Working Rhetoric and Composition." *College English* 72 (5): 470–494.

Horner, Bruce, Brice Nordquist, and Susan M. Ryan. 2017. *Economies of Writing: Revaluations in Rhetoric and Composition*. Logan: Utah State University Press.

Horvat, Srećko. 2015. *The Radicality of Love*. Cambridge: Polity.

Houlihan, Glenn. 2021. "Columbia Graduate Workers Are on Strike. Other Higher-Ed Workers Should Follow Their Lead." *Jacobin*, March 20. https://jacobinmag.com/2021/03/columbia-graduate-workers-strike-students-nlrb.

Howard, Tharon W. 2011. "Intellectual Properties in Multimodal Twenty-First-Century Composition Classrooms." In *Copy(write): Intellectual Property in the Writing Classroom*, edited by Martine Courant Rife, Shaun Slattery, and Dànielle Nicole DeVoss, 107–129. Anderson, SC: Parlor.

Hu, Jane. 2020. "'Severance' Is the Novel of Our Current Moment—but Not for the Reasons You Think." *Ringer*, March 18. https://www.theringer.com/2020/3/18/21184516/severance-coronavirus-book-ling-ma.

Hudson Yards. n.d. "Edge." https://www.hudsonyardsnewyork.com/discover/edge.

Hui, Yuk, and Pieter Lemmens. 2017. "Reframing the Technosphere: Peter Sloterdijk and Bernard Stiegler's Anthropotechnological Diagnoses of the Anthropocene." *Krisis | Journal for Contemporary Philosophy* 2: 26–41.

Hurlbert, Claude. 2012. *National Healing: Race, State, and the Teaching of Composition*. Logan: Utah State University Press.

Husserl, Edmund. 2012. *Ideas: General Introduction to Pure Phenomenology*. Translated by W. R. Boyce Gibson. Abingdon: Routledge.

Hyman, Louis. 2018. *Temp: The Real Story of What Happened to Your Salary, Benefits, and Job Security*. New York: Penguin.

Inoue, Asao B. 2015. *Antiracist Writing Assessment Ecologies: Teaching and Assessing Writing for a Socially Just Future*. Anderson, SC: Parlor.

Inoue, Asao B. 2017. "Forward: On Antiracist Agendas." In *Performing Antiracist Pedagogy in Rhetoric, Writing, and Communication*, edited by Frankie Condon and Vershawn Ashanti Young, xi–xx. eds. Boulder, CO: WAC Clearinghouse.

Inoue, Asao B. 2019. "2019 CCCC's Chair's Address: How Do We Language So People Stop Killing Each Other, or What Do We Do about White Language Supremacy?" *College Composition and Communication* 71 (2): 352–369.

Inoue, Asao B., and Mya Poe, eds. 2012. *Race and Writing Assessment*. New York: Peter Lang.

Institute for College Access & Success. 2014. "Quick Facts about Student Debt." March. https://ticas.org/files/pub_files/Debt_Facts_and_Sources.pdf.

Jarrett, Kylie. 2018. "Exploitation, Alienation, and Liberation: Interpreting the Political Economy of Digital Writing." In *The Routledge Handbook of Digital Writing and Rhetoric*, edited by Jonathan Alexander and Jacqueline Rhodes, 423–432. New York: Routledge.

Jensen, Kyle. 2010. "The Panoptic Portfolio: Reassessing Power in Process-Oriented Writing Instruction." *JAC* 30 (1/2): 95–141.

Jilani, Zaid. 2018. "New Jersey College Suspended a Professor after Being 'Inundated' With Complaints Over Her Fox News Debate." *Intercept*, January 26. https://theintercept.com/2018/01/26/fox-news-black-lives-matter-essex-county-college/.
Jin, Beatrice, and Andrew McGill. 2020. "Who Is Most at Risk in the Coronavirus Crisis: 24 Million of the Lowest-Income Workers." *Politico*, March 21. https://www.politico.com/interactives/2020/coronavirus-impact-on-low-income-jobs-by-occupation-chart/.
Johnson, Walter. 2020. *The Broken Heart of America: St. Louis and the Violent History of the United States*. New York: Basic Books.
Jones, Daniel Stedman. 2014. *Masters of the Universe: Hayek, Friedman, and the Birth of Neoliberal Politics*. Princeton, NJ: Princeton University Press.
Jones, Natasha N., and Miriam F. Williams. 2020. "The Just Use of Imagination: A Call to Action." Association of Teachers of Technical Writing, June 10. https://attw.org/blog/the-just-use-of-imagination-a-call-to-action/.
Joseph, Miranda. 2002. *Against the Romance of Community*. Minneapolis: Minnesota University Press.
Kahale, Trish, and Michael Billeaux. 2016. "Resisting the Corporate University." *Jacobin*, September 28. https://www.jacobinmag.com/2015/09/graduate-workers-university-missouri-mizzou-scott-walker-wisconsin-unions-labor/.
Kahn, Seth. 2020. "We Value Teaching Too Much to Keep Devaluing It." *College Composition and Communication* 82 (6): 591–611.
Kahn, Seth, William Lalicker, and Amy Lynch-Biniek, eds. 2017. *Contingency, Exploitation, and Solidarity: Labor and Action in English Composition*. Fort Collins, CO: WAC Clearinghouse.
Kail, Harvey, and John Trimbur. 1987. "The Politics of Peer Tutoring." *WPA: Writing Program Administration* 11 (1–2): 5–12.
Kalbfleisch, Elizabeth, and Matthew Abraham, eds. 2016. "The IWP in an Age of Financial Austerity." *College Composition and Communication* 68 (1):173–214.
Kalish, Katie, Holly Hassel, Cassandra Phillips, Jennifer Heinert, and Joanne Baird Giordano. 2019. "Inequitable Austerity: Pedagogies of Resilience and Resistance in Composition." *Pedagogy* 19 (2): 261–281.
Kaste, Martin. 2020. "Seattle Officials Shut Down Police-Free Zone Known as 'CHOP.'" *All Things Considered*. NPR, July 1. https://www.npr.org/2020/07/01/886299176/seattle-officials-shut-down-police-free-zone-known-as-chop.
Kelsky, Karen. 2014. "The Shame of Ph.D." The Professor Is In, January 22. https://theprofessorisin.com/2014/01/22/the-shame-of-ph-d-debt/.
Kendi, Ibram X. 2019. *How to Be an Antiracist*. New York: One World.
Kennedy, Tammy M., Joyce Irene Middleton, and Krista Ratcliffe. 2017. *Rhetorics of Whiteness: Postracial Hauntings in Popular Culture, Social Media, and Education*. Carbondale: Southern Illinois University Press.
Kerschbaum, Stephanie. 2014. *Toward a New Rhetoric of Difference*. Urbana, IL: NCTE.
Kezar, Adrianna, Tom DePaola, and Daniel T. Scott. 2019. *The Gig Academy: Mapping Labor in the Neoliberal University*. Baltimore: Johns Hopkins University Press.
Khadka, Santosh, and J. C. Lee. 2018. *Bridging the Multimodal Gap: From Theory to Practice*. Logan: Utah State University Press.
Kimmerer, Robin Wall. 2013. *Braining Sweetgrass: Indigenous Wisdom, Scientific Knowledge, and the Teachings of Plants*. Minneapolis, MN: Milkweed Editions.
King, Shaka, dir. 2021. *Judas and the Black Messiah*. Burbank, CA: Warner Bros. Pictures.
Kirp, David. 2019. *The College Dropout Scandal*. Oxford: Oxford University Press.
Kökerer, Can Mert. 2019. "Art and Politics in Freetown Christiania: a Benjaminian and Brechtian Utopia?" *International Journal of Politics, Culture, and Society* 34: 359–377.
Kolakowski, Leszek. 2005. *Main Currents of Marxism: The Founders—The Golden Age—The Breakdown*. Translated by P. S. Falla. New York. W. W. Norton.

Kolhatkar, Sheelah. 2017. "The Tech Industry's Gender Discrimination Problem." *New Yorker*, November 20. https://www.newyorker.com/magazine/2017/11/20/the-tech-industrys-gender-discrimination-problem.

Koltai, Mihály Bence. 2017. "Hungary: The End of Democratic Illusions." *Jacobin*, May 7. https://www.jacobinmag.com/2017/05/hungary-central-european-university-george-soros-protests.

Komlosy, Andrea. 2018. *Work: The Last 1,000 Years*. Translated by Jacob K. Watson and Loren Balhorn. London: Verso.

Krull, Robert, and Jeanne M. Hurford. 1987. "Can Computers Increase Writing Productivity?" *Technical Communication* 34 (4): 243–249.

Kuttner, Robert. 2018. *Can Democracy Survive Global Capitalism?* New York: W. W. Norton.

Kynard, Carmen. 2013. *Vernacular Insurrections: Race, Black Protest, and the New Century in Composition-Literacy Studies*. Albany: SUNY Press.

Lamos, Steve. 2011. *Interests and Opportunities: Race, Racism, and University Writing Instruction in the Post-Civil Rights Era*. Pittsburgh: University of Pittsburgh Press.

Lanier, Jaron. 2018. "How We Need to Remake the Internet." April. TED video, 14:39. https://www.ted.com/talks/jaron_lanier_how_we_need_to_remake_the_internet.

Larson, Ann. 2016. "Composition's Dead." In *Composition in the Age of Austerity*, edited by Nancy Welch and Tony Scott, 163–176. Logan: Utah State University Press.

Lazzarato, Maurizio. 2012. *The Making of the Indebted Man: An Essay on the Neoliberal Condition*. Translated by Joshua David Jordan. Los Angeles: semiotext(e).

Lazzarato, Maurizio. 2015. *Governing by Debt*. Translated by Joshua David Jordon. Los Angeles: semiotext(e).

Lederman, Doug. 2006. "A Historical Look at Student Debt." *Inside Higher Ed*, July 6. https://www.insidehighered.com/news/2006/07/06/debt.

LeFevre, Karen Burke. 1986. *Invention as a Social Act*. Carbondale: Southern Illinois University Press.

Lendvai, Paul. 2018. *Orbán: Hungary's Strongman*. Oxford: Oxford University Press.

Leon, Luis Feliz. 2021. "The Amazon Union Vote Is Ending in Bessemer. Workers Are Already Preparing for the Next Fight." *New Republic*, Sold/Short, March 26. https://newrepublic.com/article/161821/amazon-union-vote-results-bessemer-alabama.

Leverenz, Carrie Shively. 1996. "Collaboration, Race, and the Rhetoric of Evasion." *JAC* 16 (2): 297–312.

Levitt, Hannah. 2019. "Elizabeth Warren Demands That Wells Fargo Be Kicked off College Campuses." *Bloomberg*, January 17. https://www.bloomberg.com/news/articles/2019-01-17/elizabeth-warren-takes-aim-at-wells-fargo-over-fees-for-students.

Levitz, Eric. 2019. "We're All 'Socialists' Now." *New York Magazine*, June 13. https://nymag.com/intelligencer/2019/06/bernie-sanders-socialism-speech-gwu.html.

Levy, Ari. 2020. "Big Tech Is Worth Over $5 Trillion Now That Alphabet Has Joined the Four Comma Club." *CNBC*, January 16. https://www.cnbc.com/2020/01/16/big-tech-worth-over-5-trillion-with-alphabet-joining-four-comma-club.html.

Levy, Pema. 2020. "This Week, Mark Zuckerberg Sided with Donald Trump. History Won't Forget It." *Mother Jones*, June 5. https://www.motherjones.com/politics/2020/06/mark-zuckerberg-donald-trump/.

Lieberman, Samuel. 2019. "U.S. Marshals Are Arresting People in Texas Who Have Outstanding Student Loans." *New York Magazine*, February 16. https://nymag.com/intelligencer/2016/02/us-marshals-forcibly-collecting-student-debt.html.

Lindquist, Julie. 1999. "Class Ethos and the Politics of Inquiry: What the Barroom Can Teach Us about the Classroom." *College Composition and Communication* 51 (2): 225–247.

Lindquist, Julie. 2004. "Class Affects, Classroom Affectations: Working through the Paradoxes of Strategic Empathy." *College English* 67 (2): 187–209.

Liu, Catherine. 2021. "Employers Claim They Want to Improve Workers' Wellbeing, but Refuse to Do the One Thing That Will Actually Help: Pay Them More." *Business Insider*,

March 30. https://www.businessinsider.com/employers-refuse-to-pay-workers-more-employee-wellbeing-mental-health-2021-3.

Liu, Wendy. 2019. "Abolish Silicon Valley." *Tribune*, October 1. https://tribunemag.co.uk/2019/01/abolish-silicon-valley.

Liu, Wendy. 2020. *Abolish Silicon Valley: How to Liberate Technology from Capitalism*. London: Repeater.

Longaker, Mark Garrett. 2015. *Rhetorical Style and Bourgeois Virtue; Capitalism and Civil Society in the British Enlightenment*. University Park, PA: The Pennsylvania State University Press.

Lontringer, Sylvère, and Christian Marazzi. 2007. "The Return of Politics." In *Autonomia: Post-Political Politics*, edited by Sylvère Lontringer and Christian Marazzi, 8–22. Los Angeles: semiotext(e).

Love, Bettina A. 2019. *We Want to Do More Than Survive: Abolitionist Teaching and the Pursuit of Educational Freedom*. Boston: Beacon.

Lu, Min-Zhan. 2005. "An Essay on the Work of Composition: Composing English against the Order of Fast Capitalism." *College Composition and Communication* 56 (1): 16–50.

Lu, Min-Zhan, and Bruce Horner. 2009. "Composing in a Global Context: Careers, Mobility, Skills." *College English* 72 (2): 113–133.

Luckel, Madeline. 2021. "Is This the World's New Most Expensive Art Piece?" *Architectural Digest*, January 22. https://www.architecturaldigest.com/story/is-this-the-worlds-new-most-expensive-art-piece.

Lunsford, Andrea. 1991. "Collaboration, Control, and the Idea of a Writing Center." *Writing Center Journal* 12 (1): 3–10.

Lunsford, Andrea A., and Lisa Ede. 1990. "Rhetoric in a New Key: Women and Collaboration." *Rhetoric Review* 8 (2): 234–241.

Lunsford, Andrea A., and Lisa Ede. 2011. *Writing Together: Collaboration in Theory and Practice: A Critical Sourcebook*. Boston: Bedford/St. Martin's.

Lushing, Margaux. 2019. "Equinox Fitness Opens 100th Fitness Club at New York's Hudson Yards." *Forbes*, June 30. https://www.forbes.com/sites/margauxlushing/2019/06/30/equinox-fitness-opens-100th-fitness-club-at-new-yorks-hudson-yards/#6ca7e8932c37.

Lyne, Bill. 2011. "Campus Clout, Statewide Strength: Improving Shared Governance through Unionization." *Journal of Academic Freedom* 2: 1–6.

Ma, Ling. 2018. *Severance*. London: Picador.

Mao, LuMing. 2014. "From the Spread of English to the Formation of an Indigenous Rhetoric." In *Reworking English and Composition: Global Interrogations, Local Interventions*, edited by Bruce Horner and Karen Kopelson, 77–19. Carbondale: Southern Illinois University.

Marazzi, Christian. 2011. *Capital and Effects: The Politics of the Language Economy*. Translated by Giuseppina Mecchia. Los Angeles: Semiotext(e).

Marcetic, Branko. 2020. *Yesterday's Man: The Case against Joe Biden*. London: Verso.

Marino, C. Mark. 2006. "Critical Code Studies." *Electronic Book Review*. https://electronicbookreview.com/essay/critical-code-studies/.

Markovits, Daniel. 2019. *The Meritocracy Trap: How America's Foundational Myth Feeds Inequality, Dismantles the Middle Class, and Devours the Elite*. London: Penguin.

Marvin, Rob. 2019. "The Big Data Market Is Set to Skyrocket by 2022." *PC Magazine*, June 14. https://www.pcmag.com/news/the-big-data-market-is-set-to-skyrocket-by-2022.

Marx, Karl. 1976. *Capital: A Critique of Political Economy, Volume One*. London: Penguin.

Mason, Paul. 2015. *Postcapitalism: A Guide to Our Future*. New York: Farrar, Straus and Giroux.

Mathieu, Paula. 2005. *Tactics of Hope: The Public Turn in English Composition*. Portsmouth, NH: Heinemann.

Matsakis, Loise. 2018. "Why Amazon Really Raised Its Minimum Wage to $15." *Wired*, October 2. https://www.wired.com/story/why-amazon-really-raised-minimum-wage/.

McClanahan, Annie. 2016. *Dead Pledges: Debt, Crisis, and Twenty-First-Century Culture.* Stanford, CA: Stanford University Press.
McClure, Randall, Dayna V. Goldstein, and Michael A. Pemberton, eds. 2017. *Labored: The State(ment) and Future of Work in Composition.* Anderson: Parlor.
McComiskey, Bruce. 2017. *Post-Truth Rhetoric and Composition.* Logan: Utah State University Press.
McFarland, Matt. 2017. "Elon Musk's New Plan to Save Humanity from AI." CNN, April 21. https://money.cnn.com/2017/04/21/technology/elon-musk-brain-ai/index.html.
McGee, Heather. 2021. *The Sum of Us: What Racism Costs Everyone and How We Can Prosper Together.* New York: One World.
McHugh, Molly. 2019. "'Learn to Code': The Meme Attacking Media." *Ringer*, January 29. https://www.theringer.com/tech/2019/1/29/18201695/learn-to-code-twitter-abuse-buzzfeed-journalists.
McKee, Heidi. 2011. "Policy Matters Now and in the Future: Net Neutrality, Corporate Data Mining, and Government Surveillance." *Computers and Composition* 28 (4): 276–291.
McKenzie, Lindsay. 2021. "Big Deal for Open Access." *Inside Higher Ed*, March 17. https://www.insidehighered.com/news/2021/03/17/university-california-reaches-new-open-access-agreement-elsevier.
McNenny, Geraldine, and Duane H. Roen. 1992. "The Case for Collaborative Scholarship in Rhetoric and Composition." *Rhetoric Review* 10 (2): 291–310.
Mendenhall, Annie S. 2014. "The Composition Specialist as Flexible Expert: Identity and Labor in the History of Composition." *College English* 77 (1): 11–31.
Micciche, Laura R. 2002. "More Than a Feeling: Disappointment and WPA Work." *College English* 64 (4): 432–458.
Micciche, Laura R. 2014. "Writing Material." *College English* 76 (6): 488–505.
Middleton, Christian. 2020. "UM Fires History Professor Who Criticizes 'Powerful, Racist Donors' And 'Carceral State.'" *Mississippi Free Press*, December 15. https://www.mississippifreepress.org/7518/um-fires-history-professor-who-criticizes-powerful-racist-donors-and-carceral-state/.
Migdon, Brooke. 2022. "Wyoming Senate votes to end funding for university gender studies program." *Hill*, Feb. 28. https://thehill.com/changing-america/respect/diversity-inclusion/596131-wyoming-senate-votes-to-end-funding-for/.
Milanović, Branko. 2018. *Global Inequality: A New Approach for the Age of Globalization.* Cambridge, MA: Belknap.
Miller, Carolyn R. 1989. "What's Practical about Technical Writing." In *Technical Writing: Theory and Practice*, edited by Bertie E. Fearing and W. Keats Sparrow, 14–27. New York: MLA.
Miller, Richard E. 1999. "'Let's Do the Numbers': Comp Droids and the Prophets of Doom." *Profession*: 96–105.
Minnix, Christopher. 2017. "'Globalist Scumbags': Composition's Global Turn in the Time of Fake News, Globalist Conspiracy, and Nationalist Literacy." *Literacy in Composition Studies* 5 (2): 63–83.
Moloo, Zahra. 2018. "The Problem with Capitalist Philanthropy." *Jacobin*, February 6. https://www.jacobinmag.com/2018/02/charity-philanthropy-howard-buffett-congo.
Moody, Kim. 2017. *On New Terrain: How Capital Is Reshaping the Battleground of Class War.* Chicago: Haymarket Books.
Moore, Jason W. 2016a. "Anthropocene or Capitalocene? Nature, History, and the Crisis of Capitalism." In *Anthropocene or Capitalocene? Nature, History, and the Crisis of Capitalism*, edited by Jason W. Moore, 1–12. Oakland: PM.
Moore, Jason W. 2016b. "The Rise of Cheap Nature." In *Anthropocene or Capitalocene? Nature, History, and the Crisis of Capitalism*, edited by Jason W. Moore, 78–115. Oakland: PM.

Morrison, Darrick. 2019. "Digital Activism: Using Technology to Empower Change." March. TED video, 21:10. https://www.ted.com/talks/darrick_morrison_digital_activism_using_technology_to_empower_change.

Mulhere, Kaitlin. 2014. "UnKoch My Campus." *Inside Higher Ed*, November 4. https://www.insidehighered.com/news/2014/11/04/students-want-koch-corporate-influence-campus.

Murray, Donald. 1968. *A Writer Teaches Writing: A Practical Method of Teaching Composition*. Boston: Houghton Mifflin.

Murtagh, Elliott. 2021. "CUNY Breaks Faculty and Staff Contract, Withholding Promised Pay Raises." World Socialist Web Site, February 19. https://www.wsws.org/en/articles/2021/02/20/cuny-f20.html.

Mutnick, Deborah. 2016. "Confessions of an Assessment Fellow." In *Composition in the Age of Austerity*, edited by Nancy Welch and Tony Scott, 35–50. Logan: Utah State University Press.

Mutnick, Deborah. 2019a. "A Pedagogy for the Political Turn." In *Writing Democracy: The Political Turn in and Beyond the Trump Era*, edited by Shannon Carter, Deborah Mutnick, Steve Parks, and Jessica Pauszek, 82–108. New York: Routledge Research in Writing Studies.

Mutnick, Deborah. 2019b. "Threshold Concepts and Phenomenal Forms." In *(Re)Considering What We Know: Learning Thresholds in Writing, Composition, Rhetoric, and Literacy*, edited by Linda Adler-Kassner and Elizabeth Wardle, 227–243. Logan: Utah State University Press.

Mutnick, Deborah, Shannon Carter, Stephen Parks, and Jessica Pauszek. 2019. "Conclusion: Further Notes on the Political Turn." In *Writing Democracy: The Political Turn in and Beyond the Trump Era*, edited by Shannon Carter, Deborah Mutnick, Steve Parks, and Jessica Pauszek, 261–272. New York: Routledge Research in Writing Studies.

Nadworny, Elissa. 2019. "College Completion Rates Are Up, but the Numbers Will Still Surprise You." NPR, March 13. https://www.npr.org/2019/03/13/681621047/college-completion-rates-are-up-but-the-numbers-will-still-surprise-you.

Nadworny, Elissa, and Claire Lombardo. 2019. " 'I'm Drowning': Those Hardest Hit by Student Loan Debt Never Finished College." NPR, July 18. https://www.npr.org/2019/07/18/739451168/i-m-drowning-those-hit-hardest-by-student-loan-debt-never-finished-college.

Nagle, Angela. 2016. "The New Man of 4chan." *Baffler* 30, March. https://thebaffler.com/salvos/new-man-4chan-nagle.

Nagle, Angela. 2017. *Kill All Normies: Online Culture Wars From 4Chan and Tumblr to Trump and the Alt-Right*. Alresford: Zero Books.

Nancy, Jean-Luc. 2010. *The Truth of Democracy*. Translated by Pascale-Anne Brault and Michael Naas. New York: Fordham University Press.

Nancy, Jean-Luc. 2016. *The Disavowed Community*. Translated by Philip Armstrong. New York: Fordham University Press.

Nancy, Jean-Luc. 2017. "Gratuitousness and Recognition." Translated by Michael Marder and Patrícia Viera. *Philosophical Salon*, March 6. https://thephilosophicalsalon.com/gratuitousness-and-recognition/.

Nelson, Dustin. 2019. "Natural Light Is Bringing Back Its Massive 77-Pack of Beer." *Thrillist*, March 1. https://www.thrillist.com/news/nation/natural-light-77-pack-2019.

Newfield, Christopher. 2016 *The Great Mistake: How We Wrecked Public Universities and How We Can Fix Them*. Baltimore: Johns Hopkins University Press.

Newman, Kathe. 2004. "Newark, Decline and Avoidance, Renaissance and Desire: From Disinvestment to Reinvestment." *The Annals of the American Academy of Political and Social Science* 594: 38–48.

Nonko, Emily. 2018 "Hudson Yards Wants to Become NYC's Next Great Neighborhood." *Curbed*, September 19. https://ny.curbed.com/2018/9/19/17861164/hudson-yards-new-york-development-related-companies.

Nova, Annie. 2018. "Your Student Debt Balance Can Balloon Quickly: Here's How to Prevent That From Happening." CNBC, December 22. https://www.cnbc.com/2018/12/20/your-student-debt-balance-can-grow-quickly-heres-how-to-prevent-that-from-happening.html.

O'Brien, Sara Ashley. 2020. "WeWork's Last Remaining Cofounder Is Leaving." CNN, June 5. https://www.cnn.com/2020/06/05/tech/wework-miguel-mckelvey/index.html.

Ocasio-Cortez, Alexandria. 2021. By Don McIntosh. "TALKING SOCIALISM: Catching up with AOC." Democratic Socialists of America, March 19. https://www.dsausa.org/democratic-left/aoc/.

Ohmann, Richard. 1978. "Questions about Literacy and Political Education." *Radical Teacher* 8: 24–25.

Ohmann, Richard. 1996. *English in America: A Radical View of the Profession.* Hanover, NH: Wesleyan University Press.

Ohmann, Richard. 1985. "Literacy, Technology, and Monopoly Capital." *College English* 47 (7): 675–689.

Oluo, Ijeoma. 2018. *So You Want to Talk about Race.* New York: Seal.

O'Sullivan, Annie. 2018. "Newark Ranks 3rd, NYC Ranks 39th on Neediest Cities in the Country: Study." NBC New York, December 12. https://www.nbcnewyork.com/news/local/newark-ranks-3rd-neediest-city-in-us-homeless-poverty-hunger-children-nyc-39th-rochester-27th/1815792/.

Owens, Eric. 2017. "Marxist Professor Rakes In $170,000 Per Year Teaching about Inequality and Oppression." *Daily Caller*, June 13. https://dailycaller.com/2017/06/13/marxist-wisconsin-professor-rakes-in-170000-per-year-teaching-about-inequality-and-oppression/.

Palmer, Annie. 2019. "Facebook Is Moving into More Than 1.5 Million Square Feet of Office Space in New York's Hudson Yards." CNBC, November 14. https://www.cnbc.com/2019/11/14/facebook-to-lease-office-space-in-new-yorks-hudson-yards.html.

Papandrea, Dawn. 2019. "11 Unexpected Amenities at WeWork Locations around the World." WeWork, November 5. https://www.wework.com/ideas/office-design-space/office-amenities.

Parks, Steve. 1999. *Class Politics: The Movement for the Students' Right to their Own Language.* Champaign, IL: NCTE.

Parks, Steve. 2019. "'I'd Like to Overthrow Capitalism, but Meanwhile, I Would Like the Nazis to be Completely Demoralized': An Interview with Dana L. Cloud." In *Writing Democracy: The Political Turn in and Beyond the Trump Era*, edited by Shannon Carter, Deborah Mutnick, Stephen Parks, and Jessica Pauszek, 111–122. London: Routledge.

Patch, Paula. 2010. "Meeting Student Writers Where They Are: Using Wikipedia to Teach Responsible Scholarship." *Teaching English in the Two-Year College* 37 (3): 278–285.

Patel, Vimal. 2016. "How One University Measured Faculty Productivity—and Nobody Got Hurt." *Chronicle of Higher Education*, February 29. https://www.chronicle.com/article/How-One-University-Measured/235437.

Peckham, Irvin. 2010. *Going North Thinking West: The Intersections of Social Class, Critical Thinking, and Politicized Writing Instruction.* Logan: Utah State University Press.

Pettit, Emma. 2019a. "In Urging Faculty Not to Unionize, Marquette Cites Catholic Identity." *Chronicle of Higher Education*, March 29. https://www.chronicle.com/article/In-Urging-Faculty-Not-to/246022.

Pettit, Emma. 2019b. "'Ousted' From Academe, Steven Salaita Says He's Driving a School Bus to Make Ends Meet." *Chronicle of Higher Education*, February 19. https://www.chronicle.com/article/Ousted-From-Academe/245732.

Piketty, Thomas. 2014. *Capital in the Twenty-First Century*. Translated by Arthur Goldhammer. Cambridge, MA: Belknap.
Piketty, Thomas. 2015. *The Economics of Inequality*. Translated by Arthur Goldhammer. Cambridge, MA: Belknap.
Piketty, Thomas. 2020. *Capital and Ideology*. Translated by Arthur Goldhammer. Cambridge, MA: Belknap.
Plitt, Amy. 2016. "Hudson Yards's First Batch of Condos Will Start at About $2M." *Curbed*, July 22. https://ny.curbed.com/2016/7/22/12256036/15-hudson-yards-pricing-reveal.
Pogátsa, Zoltán, and Adam Fabry. 2019. "Viktor Orbán Is Finally Under Siege." *Jacobin*, February 2. https://www.jacobinmag.com/2019/02/hungary-orban-overtime-slave-law-labor-shortage.
Polanyi, Karl. 2001. *The Great Transformation: The Political and Economic Origins of Our Time*. Boston: Beacon.
Poll, Zoey. 2020. "Antibacterial Wipes, Wigs, Jump Ropes, Vodka: The Fight for Workplace Safety at Amazon France." *N+1*, June 11. https://nplusonemag.com/online-only/online-only/antibacterial-wipes-wigs-jump-ropes-vodka/.
Porter, James E., Patricia Sullivan, Stuart Blythe, Jeffrey T. Grabill, and Libby Miles. 2000. "Institutional Critique: A Rhetorical Methodology for Change." *College Composition and Communication* 51 (4): 610–642.
Porterfield, Carlie. 2020. "White Supremacist Terrorism 'On the Rise and Spreading.'" *Forbes*, June 25. https://www.forbes.com/sites/carlieporterfield/2020/06/25/white-supremacist-terrorism-on-the-rise-and-spreading/?sh=2647f5545a0f.
Pulver, Christian J. 2020. *Metabolizing Capital: Writing, Information, and the Biophysical Environment*. Logan: Utah State University Press.
Ratcliffe, Krista. 2005. *Rhetorical Listening: Identification, Gender, Whiteness*. Carbondale: Southern Illinois University.
Read, Bridet. 2020. "Every Food and Delivery Strike Happening Over Coronavirus." *Cut*, April 28. https://www.thecut.com/2020/04/whole-foods-amazon-mcdonalds-among-coronavirus-strikes.html.
Redden, Elizabeth. 2018a. "As Pathway Market Expands, Enrollment Outcomes Diverge." *Inside Higher Ed*, June 19. https://www.insidehighered.com/news/2018/06/19/more-collegeshire-corporate-partners-international-student-pathway-programs-mixed.
Redden, Elizabeth. 2018b. "Hungary Officially Ends Gender Studies Programs." *Inside Higher Ed*, October 17. https://www.insidehighered.com/quicktakes/2018/10/17/hungary-officially-ends-gender-studies-programs.
Redden, Elizabeth. 2020. "U Alaska Cuts, Reduces More Than 40 Programs." *Inside Higher Ed*, June 8. https://www.insidehighered.com/quicktakes/2020/06/08/u-alaska-cuts-reduces-more-40-programs.
Reed, Adolph L., Jr. 2000. *Class Notes: Posing as Politics and Other Thoughts on the American Scene*. New York: New Press.
Reed, Adolph L., Jr. 2022. *The South: Jim Crow and Its Afterlives*. London: Verso.
Reed, Touré F. 2020. *Toward Freedom: The Case against Race Reductionism*. London: Verso.
Reichert Powell, Pegeen. 2014. *Retention and Resistance: Writing Instruction and Students Who Leave*. Logan: Utah State University Press.
Reichman, Henry. 2019. *The Future of Academic Freedom*. Baltimore: Johns Hopkins University Press.
Reilly, Katie. 2018. "Professor Teaching 'White Racism' Class Gets Hundreds of 'Vile' Calls and Emails." *Time*, January 11. https://time.com/5098776/white-racism-class-fgcu/.
Rein, Raffaela. 2018. "What It's Like to Run a Company with a Truly Flat Hierarchy." *VentureBeat*, March 5. https://venturebeat.com/2017/03/05/what-its-like-to-run-a-company-with-a-truly-flat-hierarchy/.

Renner, Charles G. 2019. "A Few Lessons about Public-Private Partnerships." *Inside Higher Ed*, January 28. https://www.insidehighered.com/views/2019/01/28/advice-institutions-embarking-public-private-partnerships-opinion.

Reyman, Jessica. 2009. *The Rhetoric of Intellectual Property: Copyright Law and the Regulation of Digital Culture*. New York: Routledge.

Reyman, Jessica. 2013. "User Data on the Social Web: Authorship, Agency, and Appropriation." *College English* 75 (5): 513–533.

Rhoades, Gary, and Sheila Slaughter. 1997. "Academic Capitalism, Managed Professionals, and Supply-Side Higher Education." *Social Text* 51: 9–38.

Rhodes, Jacqueline, and Jonathan Alexander. 2015. *Techne: Queer Meditations on Writing the Self*. Logan: Computers and Composition Digital Press. https://ccdigitalpress.org/book/techne/.

Ridolfo, Jim, and Dànielle Nicole DeVoss. 2009. "Composing for Recomposition: Rhetorical Velocity and Delivery." *Kairos: A Journal of Rhetoric, Technology, and Pedagogy* 13 (2). http://kairos.technorhetoric.net/13.2/topoi/ridolfo_devoss/intro.html.

Rife, Martine Courant, Shaun Slattery, and Dànielle Nicole DeVoss, eds. 2011. *Copy(write): Intellectual Property in the Writing Classroom*. Anderson, SC: Parlors.

Roberts-Miller, Patricia. 2017. *Demagoguery and Democracy*. New York: The Experiment.

Robichaux, Alexi, and Prince Harry, the Duke of Sussex. 2021. "Prince Harry, The Duke of Sussex Joins BetterUp as Chief Impact Officer." BetterUp, March 23. https://www.betterup.com/en-us/resources/blog/prince-harry-chief-impact-officer.

Robinson, Cedric J. 2000. *Black Marxism: The Making of the Black Radical Tradition*. Chapel Hill: University of North Carolina Press.

Rogers, Kaleigh, and Geoffrey Skelley. 2021. "How Marjorie Taylor Greene Won, and Why Someone like Her Can Win Again." *FiveThirtyEight*, March 3. https://fivethirtyeight.com/features/how-someone-like-marjorie-taylor-greene-could-win-again/.

Rosa, Hartmut. 2015. *Social Acceleration: A New Theory of Modernity*. New York: Columbia University Press.

Rosalsky, Greg. 2020. "What a 1968 Report Tells Us about Racial Inequality." NPR, June 9.

Rose, Shirley K., Lisa S. Mastrangelo, and Barbara L'Eplattenier. 2013. "Directing First-Year Writing: The New Limits of Authority." *College Composition and Communication* 65 (1): 43–66.

Rosenblum, Jonathan. 2021. "Big Business Goes Up Against Democracy in Seattle." *Nation*, February 9. https://www.thenation.com/article/politics/kshama-sawant-recall/.

Rosenfeld, Seth. 2013. *Subversives: The FBI's War on Student Radicals and Reagan's Rise to Power*. New York: Picador.

Ross, Andrew. 2013. "Mortgaging the Future: Student Debt and the Age of Austerity." *New Labor Forum* 22 (1): 23–28.

Rothstein, Jed, dir. 2021. *WeWork: Or The Making and Breaking of a $47 Billion Unicorn*. Los Angeles: Campfire, Forbes Entertainment, Olive Hill Media.

Rouzie, Albert. 2000. "Beyond the Dialectic of Work and Play: A Serio-Ludic Rhetoric for Composition Studies." *JAC* 20 (3): 627–658.

Russell, Marta, and Ravi Malhotra. 2019. "Introduction: Capitalism and the Disability Rights Movement." In *Capitalism and Disability: Selected Writings by Marta Russell*, edited by Keith Rosenthal, 1–10. Chicago: Haymarket Books.

Ryder, Phyllis Mentzell. 2017. "Democratic Rhetoric in the Era of Neoliberalism." In *Economies of Writing: Revaluations in Rhetoric and Composition*, edited by Bruce Horner, Brice Nordquist, and Susan M. Ryan, 252–268. Logan: Utah State University Press.

Sainath, Radhika. 2016. "The Real Free-Speech Threat." *Jacobin*, April 6. https://www.jacobinmag.com/2017/04/israel-palestine-free-speech-college-campuses-occupation-bds.

Samuels, Robert. 2016. "Contingent Labor, Writing Studies, and Writing about Writing." *College Composition and Communication* 68 (1): A3–A9.

Sandberg, Sheryl. 2013. *Lean In: Women, Work, and the Will to Lead*. New York: Knopf.
Sano-Franchini, Jennifer. 2016. " 'It's Like Writing Yourself into a Codependent Relationship with Someone Who Doesn't Even Want You!' Emotional Labor, Intimacy, and the Academic Job Market in Rhetoric and Composition." *College Composition and Communication* 68 (1): 98–124.
Sauter, Molly. 2014. *The Coming Swarm: DDOS Actions, Hacktivism, and Civil Disobedience on the Internet*. London: Bloomsbury Academic. https://madison.com/wsj/news/local/education/university/changes-to-tenure-budget-and-regents-show-extent-of-scott-walkers-impact-on-uw/article_90954155-df31-5fdb-bb93-dd93a0f81225.html.
Sawant, Kshama. 2020. "Kshama Sawant: Democrats and the Right Are Attacking Me—And Left Movements Everywhere." *Jacobin*, November 24. https://jacobinmag.com/2020/11/kshama-sawant-seattle-socialist-city-council-recall-campaign-tax-amazon.
Schaffner, Katharina. 2016. *Exhaustion: A History*. New York: Columbia University Press.
Schell, Eileen E. 2016. "Austerity, Contingency, and Administrative Bloat: Writing Programs and Universities in an Age of Feast and Famine." In *Composition in the Age of Austerity*, edited by Nancy Welch and Tony Scott, 177–190. Logan: Utah State University Press.
Schleifer, Theodore. 2019. "Silicon Valley Is Throwing Trump a Fundraiser. They'd Just Rather Not Talk about It." *Vox*, September 17. https://www.vox.com/recode/2019/9/17/20869679/donald-trump-silicon-valley-fundraiser-2020.
Schumpeter, Joseph. 2008. *Capitalism, Socialism, and Democracy*. 3rd ed. New York: Harper Perennial.
Schwab, Klaus. 2019. "Davos Manifesto 2020: The Universal Purpose of a Company in the Fourth Industrial Revolution." World Economic Forum, December 2. https://www.weforum.org/agenda/2019/12/davos-manifesto-2020-the-universal-purpose-of-a-company-in-the-fourth-industrial-revolution/.
Schwab, Tim. 2020. "Bill Gates's Charity Paradox." *Nation*, March 17. https://www.thenation.com/article/society/bill-gates-foundation-philanthropy/.
Scott, Rachel, and Will Steakin. 2020. "Trump Again Stokes Racial Divides, a Reality at Odds with His Efforts to Court Black Voters." ABC News, May 30. https://abcnews.go.com/Politics/trump-stokes-racial-divides-reality-odds-efforts-court/story?id=70957826.
Scott, Tony. 2009. *Dangerous Writing: Understanding the Political Economy of Composition*. Logan: Utah State University Press.
Scott, Tony. 2016a. "Subverting Crisis in the Political Economy of Composition." *College Composition and Communication* 68 (1): 10–37.
Scott, Tony. 2016b. "Writing Enacts and Creates Identities and Ideologies." In *Naming What We Know: Threshold Concepts of Writing Studies*, edited by Linda Adler-Kassner and Elizabeth Wardle, 48–49. Logan: Utah State University Press.
Scott, Tony, and Nancy Welch. 2016. "Introduction: Composition in the Age of Austerity." In *Composition in the Age of Austerity*, edited by Nancy Welch and Tony Scott, 3–17. Logan: Utah State University Press.
Seitz, David. 2004. "Making Work Visible." *College English* 67 (2): 210–221.
Selzer, Rick. 2018. "Missouri 3 Years Later: Lessons Learned, Protests Still Resonate." *Inside Higher Ed*, September 12. https://www.insidehighered.com/news/2018/09/12/administrators-students-and-activists-take-stock-three-years-after-2015-missouri.
Sharp-Hoskins, Kellie, and Amy E. Robillard. 2012. "Narrating the 'Good Teacher' in Rhetoric and Composition: Ideology, Affect, Complicity." *JAC* 32 (1/2): 305–336.
Shea, Christopher. 2013. "A Radical Anthropologist Finds Himself in Academic Exile." *Chronicle of Higher Education*, April 19. https://www.chronicle.com/article/A-Radical-Anthropologist-Finds/138499.
Shor, Ira. 1977. "Writing about 'Work': A Sequential Syllabus." *Radical Teacher* (4): 21–24.
Shor, Ira. 1997. *When Students Have Power: Negotiating Authority in a Critical Pedagogy*. Chicago: University of Chicago Press.

Shwartz, Alexandra. 2019. "Hudson Yards Is the Hotel California of New York." *New Yorker*, March 23. https://www.newyorker.com/culture/cultural-comment/hudson-yards-is-the-hotel-california-of-new-york.

Silverman, Jacob. 2020. "The End of the Backlash to Big Tech." *New Republic*, May 28. https://newrepublic.com/article/157834/end-backlash-big-tech.

Simmons, W. Michele, and Jeffrey T. Grabill. 2007. "Toward a Civic Rhetoric for Technologically and Scientifically Complex Places: Invention, Performance, and Participation." *College Composition and Communication* 58 (3): 419–448.

Simpkins, Neil. 2018. "Towards an Understanding of Accommodation Transfer: Disabled Students' Strategies for Navigating Classroom Accommodations." *Composition Forum* 39. https://compositionforum.com/issue/39/accommodation-transfer.php.

Skinnell, Ryan, ed. 2018. *Faking the News: What Rhetoric Can Teach Us about Donald J. Trump*. Exeter, NH: Societas.

Slobodian, Quinn. 2018. *Globalists: The End of Empire and the Birth of Neoliberalism*. Cambridge, MA: Harvard University Press.

Slydell, Laura. 2019. "Tech Industry Confronts a Backlash against 'Disruptive Innovation.'" NPR, January 28. https://www.npr.org/sections/thetwo-way/2019/01/28/689198803/tech-industry-confronts-a-backlash-against-disruptive-innovation.

Smit, David. 2007. *The End of Composition Studies*. Carbondale: Southern Illinois University Press.

Smith, Ashley. 2019. "A Maple Fall in Quebec?" *Jacobin*, October 9. https://www.jacobinmag.com/2015/10/quebec-classe-asse-student-strike-ftq-daniel-boyer-austerity-fae-couillard/.

Smith, Trixie G. 2019. "Writing Is/As Communal." In *Explanation Points: Publishing in Rhetoric and Composition*, edited by John R. Gallagher and Dànielle Nicole DeVoss, 103–106. Logan: Utah State University Press.

Solanas, Valerie. 2016. *SCUM Manifesto*. London: Verso.

Spinoza, Baruch de. 1996. *Ethics*. Translated by Edward Curley. London: Penguin Classics.

Standing, Guy. 2011. *The Precariat: The New Dangerous Class*. London: Bloomsbury Academic.

Standing, Guy. 2019. *Plunder of the Commons: A Manifesto for Sharing Public Wealth*. London: Pelican Books.

Stengers, Isabelle. 2010. *Invention of Modern Science*. Minneapolis: University of Minnesota Press.

Stengers, Isabelle. 2015. *In Catastrophic Times: Resisting the Coming Barbarism*. Translated by Andrew Goffey. London: Open Humanities.

Stengers, Isabelle. 2018. *Another Science Is Possible: A Manifesto for Slow Science*. Translated by Stephen Muecke. Cambridge, MA: Polity.

Stiegler, Bernard. 1998. *Technics and Time, 1: The Fault of Epimetheus*. Translated by Richard Beardsworth and George Collins. Stanford, CA: Stanford University Press.

Stiegler, Bernard. 2015. *States of Shock: Stupidity and Knowledge in the Twenty-First Century*. Translated by Daniel Ross. Cambridge: Polity.

Stiegler, Bernard. 2018. *The Neganthropocene*. Translated by Daniel Ross. London: Open Humanities.

Stiegler, Bernard. 2019. *The Age of Disruption: Technology and Madness in Computational Capitalism*. Translated by Daniel Ross. Cambridge, MA: Polity.

Stiegler, Bernard, and Irit Rogoff. 2010 "Transindividuation." *e-flux journal* 14 (March). https://www.e-flux.com/journal/14/61314/transindividuation/.

Stimilli, Elettra. 2016. *The Debt of Living: Ascesis and Capitalism*. Translated by Arianna Bove. Albany: SUNY Press.

Stolley, Karl. 2008. "The Lo-Fi Manifesto." *Kairos: A Journal of Rhetoric, Technology, and Pedagogy* 12 (3). http://kairos.technorhetoric.net/12.3/topoi/stolley/.

Stolley, Karl. 2016. "The Lo-Fi Manifesto, v. 2.0." *Kairos: A Journal of Rhetoric, Technology, and Pedagogy* 20 (2). https://kairos.technorhetoric.net/20.2/inventio/stolley/.

Strickland, Donna. 2007. "Caring About the Dismal Science." *JAC* 27 (1/2): 211–222.
Strike Debt/Occupy Wall Street. 2012. *The Debt Resisters' Operations Manual.* http://strikedebt.org/The-Debt-Resisters-Operations-Manual.pdf.
Students for a Democratic Society. 1962. "The Port Huron Statement." June 15. https://history.hanover.edu/courses/excerpts/111huron.html.
Taylor, Astra. 2019. *Democracy May Not Exist but We'll Miss It When It's Gone.* New York: Metropolitan Books.
Taylor, Keeanga-Yamahtta. 2016. "What About Racism?" *Jacobin*, March 16. https://www.jacobinmag.com/2016/03/black-lives-matter-slavery-discrimination-socialism/.
Taylor, Keeanga-Yamahtta. 2017. "Why Women Should Strike." *Jacobin*, February 25. https://www.jacobinmag.com/2017/02/womens-strike-march-8-march-protest-trump/.
Taylor, Keeanga-Yamahtta. 2019. *Race for Profit: How Banks and the Real Estate Industry Undermined Black Homeownership.* Chapel Hill: University of North Carolina Press.
Therborn, Göran. 2012. "Class in the Twenty-First Century." *New Left Review*, November/December. https://newleftreview.org/issues/ii78/articles/goran-therborn-class-in-the-21st-century.
Thier, Hadas. 2020. "The Pain of Pandemic-Induced Unemployment in America Is Brutal and Unceasing." *Jacobin*, December 15. https://www.jacobinmag.com/2020/12/pandemic-covid-19-unemployment-benefits-workers.
Tiffany, Kaitlyn. 2018. "In Amazon We Trust—But Why?" *Vox*, October 25. https://www.vox.com/the-goods/2018/10/25/18022956/amazon-trust-survey-american-institutions-ranked-georgetown.
Tingle, Nick. 2007. "We Can't Work It Out: The Alienated Labor of the WPA and the WI." *JAC* 27 (3/4): 759–770.
Tinnell, John. 2015. "Grammatization: Bernard Stiegler's Theory of Writing and Technology." *Computers and Composition* 37: 132–146.
Trimbur, John. 1989. "Consensus and Difference in Collaborative Learning." *College English* 51 (6): 602–616.
Trimbur, John. 1997. "Berlin's Citizen and First World Rhetoric." *JAC* 17 (3): 500–502.
Trimbur, John. 2000. "Composition and the Circulation of Writing." *College Composition and Communication* 52 (2): 188–219.
Trimbur, John. 2004. "Keeping the World Safe for Class Struggle: Revolutionary Memory in a Post-Marxist Time" In *The Private, the Public, and the Published: Reconciling Private Lives and Public Rhetoric Book*, edited by Barbara Couture and Thomas Kent, 47–58. Logan: Utah State University Press.
Trimbur, John. 2012. "Writing after Print Capitalism." *JAC* 32 (3/4): 723–773.
Trimbur, John. 2019. "Composition's Left and the Struggle for Revolutionary Consciousness." In *Writing Democracy: The Political Turn in and Beyond the Trump Era*, edited by Shannon Carter, Deborah Mutnick, Stephen Parks, and Jessica Pauszek, 27–50. New York: Routledge.
Trotter, William Joe Jr. 2019. *Workers on Arrival: Black Labor in the Making of America.* Berkeley: University of California Press.
Tufekci, Zeynep. 2017. "Twitter and Tear Gas: How Social Media Changed Protest Forever." *Wired*, May 22. https://www.wired.com/2017/05/twitter-tear-gas-protest-age-social-media/.
Tufekci, Zeynep. 2018. *Twitter and Tear Gas: The Power and Fragility of Networked Protest.* New Haven, CT: Yale University Press.
United States Census Bureau. n.d. "QuickFacts: Newark city, New Jersey." https://www.census.gov/quickfacts/newarkcitynewjersey.
UW Excellence. 2015. "The Case Against Unionization." http://www.uwexcellence.org/the-case-against-unionization.html.
Varoufakis, Yanis. 2018. *Talking to My Daughter about the Economy, Or How Capitalism Works—And How It Fails.* New York: Farrar, Straus, and Giroux.

"Va. Tech Professor's Military Op-Ed Sparks Outcry." CBS DC, August 30. https://washington.cbslocal.com/2013/08/30/va-tech-professors-military-op-ed-sparks-outcry/.

Vee, Annette. 2017. *Coding Literacy: How Computer Programming Is Changing Writing*. Cambridge: MIT Press.

Venne, Jean-François. 2017. "The Dubious Legacy of Quebec's Maple Spring." *University Affairs/Affaires universitaires*, March 1. https://www.universityaffairs.ca/features/feature-article/dubious-legacy-quebecs-maple-spring/.

Vie, Stephanie. 2014. "In Defense of 'Slacktivism': The Human Rights Campaign Facebook Logo as Digital Activism." *First Monday* 19 (4). https://doi.org/10.5210/fm.v19i4.4961.

Vie, Stephanie, and Jennifer deWinter. 2008. "Disrupting Intellectual Property: Collaboration and Resistance in Wikis." In *Wiki Writing: Collaborative Learning in the College Classroom*, edited by Robert E. Cummings and Matt Barton, 109–122. Ann Arbor: University of Michigan Press.

Wall, Derek. 2014. *The Commons in History: Culture, Conflict, and Ecology*. Cambridge: MIT Press.

Walton, Rebecca, Kristen R. Moore, and Natasha Jones. 2019. *Technical Communication After the Social Justice Turn: Building Coalitions for Action*. New York: Routledge.

Walwema, Josephine, and Felicita Arzu Carmichael. 2020. "'Are You Authorized to Work in the US?' Investigatin' 'Inclusive' Practices in Rhetoric and Technical Communication Job Descriptions." *Technical Communication Quarterly* 30 (2). https://doi.org/10.1080/10572252.2020.1829072.

Wang, Jackie. 2018. *Carceral Capitalism*. South Pasadena, CA: Semiotext(e).

Wardle, Elizabeth, and Doug Downs. 2011. *Writing about Writing*. Boston: Bedford/St. Martin's.

Weber, Max. 2002. *The Protestant Ethic and the Spirit of Capitalism and Other Writings*. Translated by Peter Baehr. London: Penguin Classics.

Weeks, Kathi. 2011. *The Problem with Work: Feminism, Marxism, Antiwork Politics, and Postwork Imaginaries*. Durham, NC: Duke University Press.

Weiss, Hadas. 2019. *We Have Never Been Middle Class*. London: Verso.

Welch, Nancy. 2008. *Living Room: Teaching Writing in a Privatized World*. Portsmouth, NH: Heinemann.

Welch, Nancy, and Tony Scott, editors. 2016. *Composition in the Age of Austerity*. Logan: Utah State University Press.

Wells, Susan. 1986. "Jurgen Habermas, Communicative Competence, and the Teaching of Technical Discourse." In *Theory in the Classroom*, edited by Cary Nelson, 246–269. Champaign: University of Illinois Press.

Wiener, Anna. 2020. *Uncanny Valley: A Memoir*. New York: MCD.

Williams, Jeffrey. 2014. *How to Be an Intellectual: Essays on Criticism, Culture, and the University*. New York: Fordham University Press.

Wilson, Valerie. 2020. "Racial Disparities in Income and Poverty Remain Largely Unchanged amid Strong Income Growth in 2019." Economic Policy Institute, September 16. https://www.epi.org/blog/racial-disparities-in-income-and-poverty-remain-largely-unchanged-amid-strong-income-growth-in-2019/.

Wirthman, Lisa. 2018. "NYC's Hudson Yards Looks towards the Future of Smart Development." *Forbes*, October 3. https://www.forbes.com/sites/nuveen/2018/10/03/nycs-hudson-yards-looks-towards-the-future-of-smart-development/#161c02b346b4.

Wolff, Michael. 2018. "Trump's Failing War on Green Power." *Politico*, January 24. https://www.politico.com/story/2018/01/24/trumps-failing-war-green-power-307281.

Woodhouse, Kellie. 2015. "Activists Oust Two Leaders." *Inside Higher Ed*, November 10. https://www.insidehighered.com/news/2015/11/10/u-missouri-leaders-resign-amid-student-concerns-over-racism-and-diversity.

Wright, Erik Olin. 2016. "But at Least Capitalism Is Free and Democratic, Right?" In *The ABCs of Socialism*, edited by Bhaskar Sunkara, 22–29. New York: Verso.

Wright, Erik Olin. 2019. *How to Be an Anti-Capitalist in the Twenty-First Century*. London: Verso.
Yglesias, Matthew. 2019. "The Push to Break Up Big Tech, Explained." *Vox*, May 3. https://www.vox.com/recode/2019/5/3/18520703/big-tech-break-up-explained.
York, Lorraine. 2002. *Rethinking Women's Collaborative Writing: Power, Difference, Property*. Toronto: University of Toronto Press.
Zakaria, Rafia. 2017. "The Military-Messaging Complex." *Baffler* 36 (September). https://thebaffler.com/salvos/military-messaging-complex-zakaria.
Zaloom, Caitlin. 2019. *Indebted: How Families Make College Work at Any Cost*. Princeton, NJ: Princeton University Press.
Zamudio-Suaréz, Fernanda. 2018. "Professor's Criticism of Israel Is Condemned as 'Hate Speech.'" *Chronicle of Higher Education*, December 2. https://www.chronicle.com/article/Professor-s-Criticism-of/245242.
Zebroski, James T. 2007. "The Turn to Social Class in Rhetoric and Composition: Shifting Disciplinary Identities." *JAC* 27 (3/4): 771–793.
Zebroski, James T. 2017. "An Afterword to *Class in the Composition Classroom*: First-Year Writing as a Social Class Enterprise." In *Class in the Composition Classroom: Pedagogy and the Working Class*, edited by Genesea M. Carter and William H. Thelin, 320–335. Logan: Utah State University Press.
Zhang, Charlie. 2021. "'Da Vinci of Debt' Is Now the World's Most Expensive Artwork, Valued at $470 Million USD." *Hypebeast*, January 21. https://hypebeast.com/2021/1/da-vinci-of-debt-470-million-usd-worlds-most-expensive-artwork-info.
Zhang, Sarah. 2019. "The Real Cost of Knowledge." *Atlantic*, March 4. https://www.theatlantic.com/science/archive/2019/03/uc-elsevier-publisher/583909/.
Zhang, Sharon. 2022. "Billionaires Have Gotten $1.7 Trillion Richer Over the Pandemic, Report Finds." *Truthout*, March 14. https://truthout.org/articles/billionaires-have-gotten-1-7-trillion-richer-over-the-pandemic-report-finds/.
Zuboff, Shoshana. 2019. *The Age of Surveillance Capitalism: The Fight for a Human Future at the New Frontier of Power*. New York: Public Affairs.

INDEX

The ABCs of Socialism (Sunkara), 116
ableism, 8, 10, 41. *See also* disability
Abolish Silicon Valley: How to Liberate Technology from Capitalism (Liu), 142
academic capitalism, 65, 151, 155–161, 164–165. *See also* austerity
academic freedom, 27, 149, 152, 155, 174, 177; decline of, 27, 149, 156–157; preserving, 154
activism, 6, 33, 35, 40, 45, 50, 53–54, 56–57, 83, 127, 181; on climate change, 141; on debt, 78, 84; in higher education, 151, 168, 169, 172–173; on racial justice; 19; in Seattle, 51; social media, 146, 147–148, 189$n1$; workplace, 24, 117. *See also* unions
adjuncts. *See* contingent workers
Adorno, Theodor W., and Max Horkheimer, 106
Adler-Kassner, Linda, 7
The Age of Disruption: Technology and Madness in Computational Capitalism (Stiegler), 129–133
The Age of Surveillance Capitalism: The Fight for A Human Future at the New Frontier of Power (Zuboff), 122
Against the Romance of Community (Joseph), 59–60
Alexander, Jonathan, and Jacqueline Rhodes, 124, 125
Alexander, F. King, 67
Alexander, Michelle, 11–12
Alvarez, Maximillian, 161
Amazon, 51, 188$n7$; CamperForce, 92–93, 105; pedagogy on, 109–112, 114; technology, 122, 136–7; unionization, 14, 52, 189$n7$; working conditions at, 96, 189$n2$
American Communist Party, 13
American Dream, the, 54
antiracism, 19–24, 47, 131–132. *See also* racism
Apple, 119, 122, 136
Arca, 3
Aronowitz, Stanley, 152

Arruzza, Cinzia, 46
austerity, 5, 15, 64, 87, 92, 117, 152; COVID-19, 191$n9$; in Europe, 129; in higher education, 156, 157, 159–160; in Québec, 168. *See also* academic capitalism
Autonomia Operaia, 102

bad employees, 182
Badiou, Alain, 41–42
Baldwin, Tammy, 109
Balk, Gene, 51
Banks, Adam J., 125
Battistoni, Alyssa, 53
Bay, Jennifer, 98–118
Being and Event (Badiou), 42
Benjamin, Ruha, 89
Berardi, Franco "Bifo," 102
Berlin, James A., 14, 185$n1$
Bernard-Donals, Michael, 170–171, 173
Basu, Tanya, 146
Bezos, Jeff, 109, 110
Bhattacharya, Tithi, 46
Biden, Joe, 14, 185$n3$, 188$n1$
Big Tech. *See* tech industry
Bill and Melinda Gates Foundation Discovery Center, 53, 56, 188$n9$
Bishop, Wendy, 97
Bizzell, Patricia, 87
Black Lives Matter (BLM), 146, 155
Black Panther Party, 14, 41
Blake, Daniel, 85
Blakeley, Grace, 179
blogging, 51, 84, 115, 116
Bloom, Lynn Z., 170
Bogost, Ian, 136–137
Boice, Robert, 97
Bollig, Chase, 68–69, 164
Bourdieu, Pierre, 17
Bousquet, Marc, 15, 174; academic labor, 16, 149; critique of the WPA, 8–9, 169, 172; student debt, 68, 69
Brandt, Deborah, 99
Bratton, Benjamin, 123, 190$n4$
Bridle, James, 124

218 INDEX

Brown, Sherrod, 109
Brown, Wendy, 30, 40
Bruder, Jessica, 92–93
Bruffee, Kenneth, 34–35, 37, 38, 44, 48
burnout, 26, 99, 101, 112
Buchanan, Lindal, 39, 40
Bullshit Jobs (Graeber), 90, 93–94

Caffentzis, George, 84–85
Cambridge Analytica scandal, 121, 144
Can Democracy Survive Global Capitalism? (Kuttner), 30
The Capitalist University: The Transformations of Academic Capitalism since 1945 (Heller), 156–157
Capital Hill Autonomous Zone (CHAZ), 51
Capitalocene, 12
Carmony, Josh, 9–10
Carter, Jonathan S., 128
Case, Anne, and Angus Deaton, 11
Central European University (CEU), 29–33, 159
Chicago teacher's strike (2019), 60
Chomsky, Noam, 78
citizen juries, 106–107
class, 7, 12, 15, 20, 60, 64, 78, 173, 179, 185n4; Bloom, Lynn Z., 170; class consciousness, 9, 72; class difference, 19, 57; class system, 24; middle class, 61–65, 72, 79, 81–83, 85, 90, 116; precarity, 170–171; race, 24, 108 186n7; underclass, 31, 68, 138; working class, 8, 11, 15, 17–18, 23, 39, 50, 61, 87, 175, 185n5, 188n10
Clegg, Geoffrey, 6
Clinton, Bill, 66
The Cloud Corporation (Donnelly), 80
coding, 124, 126, 129, 134, 145
Cohan, Deborah J., 171
collaborative writing, 25, 26, 33–40, 47, 53, 57, 84, 148, 187n5; anti-capitalist, 33, 43–45, 50; community, 58–59, 86; technology, 148. *See also* composition
College Composition and Communication (CCC), 97, 99
common, 142, 150, 170, 171, 181, 183; composition, 32, 33, 62, 65, 155; Dardot, Pierre and Christian Laval, 25, 27, 150–151, 161–165, 168, 172–174; Dean, Jodi, 33–34, 40–41, 42–43, 44; debt, 70, 73, 75, 83, 85; instituent praxis, 25, 26; Stengers, Isabelle, 105–107, 111, 114; Stiegler, Bernard, 129, 130–131, 134; technology, 127; work, 90, 104
COVID-19, 14, 88, 92, 95, 141; austerity, 191n9; remote learning, 52, 133, 179;

tech companies, 190n3; working conditions during, 119, 120
commoning. *See* common
commons, 105, 142, 162, 170, 180; history of, 186n11; internet, 142; non-Western, 186n12; WPA-L listserv, 170. *See also* common
community, 7, 34, 100, 110, 162, 182; collaborative writing, 39, 48, 51, 53, 56; Dardot, Pierre and Christian Laval, 168; Dean, Jodi, 33, 40, 43, 45; endangerment of, 32, 58; higher education, 166, 169, 171; Joseph, Miranda, 59–60; Nancy, Jean-Luc, 63, 73, 76, 85; online, 139, 170; protest, 151; Stengers, Isabelle, 104, 108; unions, 177
composition, 10, 44, 52, 119, 128–129, 160, 162, 164, 170, 174; anti-capitalist, 5–9, 17–19, 24–28, 30, 31, 32, 33, 43, 44, 56, 113, 117–118, 146, 149, 151, 156, 161, 169, 182; anti-racist, 19–22; collaborative writing, 34–40, 57, 62; debt, 63–65, 68–70, 73, 74, 83–84, 85, 86; digital writing and multimodal composition, 123–127, 133, 148; disability, 12; writing about work, 89–91, 96–101, 103–104, 107
comrade. *See* Dean, Jodie
Comrade: An Essay on Political Belonging (Dean), 40
Condon, Frankie, and Vershawn Young, 20
Conference on College Composition and Communication (CCCC), 7, 20, 21, 191n1
contingent workers: in academia, 3, 9, 28, 149, 158, 170–172, 173, 182; retaliation against, 152–153, 154; unionizing, 174–175
corruption, 3, 5, 29, 187n2
Crary, Jonathan, 102–103
Cucciarre, Christine, 171

Dangerous Writing: Understanding the Political Economy of Composition (Scott), 15
Da Vinci of Debt, 85
data economy, 123, 130, 143
data exhaust, 27, 122, 123
data industry. *See* tech industry
data mining, 122, 190n4
Dardot, Pierre, and Christian Laval, 173; coactivity, 167; common, 25, 27, 150–151, 161–165, 168, 172–174; instituent praxis, 27, 152, 162, 164; new neoliberalism, 31, 58, 159
Davis, Angela Y., 21, 41
Davos. *See* World Economic Forum

Day, Meagan, 24
Deacon, Andrea, 100
Dean, Jodi, 55, 105, 115; collaboration, 54, 58, 59; comrade, 26, 33, 40–48, 50, 51, 54, 56, 60, 106, 163; joy, 57
Deaths of Despair (Case and Deaton), 11
debt, 134; cancellation, 14; Graeber, David, 151; pedagogy, 75–85; resistance, 147; student debt, 26, 28, 60, 61–87, 165, 179, 180–181, 186*n13*, 188*n3*
Debt Collective, 147
The Debt Resisters' Operations Manual (Strike Debt), 78
Deleuze, Gilles, 106, 190*n10*, 190*n11*
democracy, 36, 38, 135, 137; in decline, 10, 44; neoliberalism, 17, 31–34, 187*n4*; universities, 163
Democracy in Europe Movement 2025 (DiEM25), 78
Derenoncourt, Ellora, and Claire Montialoux, 23
Desan, Mathieu, 5
Dewey, John, 38
deWinter, Jennifer, 36
digital writing, 27, 124–125, 127, 148; Jarrett, Kylie, 126, 147; Stiegler, Bernard, 133
Dingo, Rebecca, 16
Dirks, Nicholas, 153
disability, 12–13
disruption, 27, 130, 134, 142, 143, 190*n8*
Divest Harvard, 166
Doane, Janice, and Devon Hodges, 39
Doe, Sue, 174
Doebler, Paul D., 97
Donnelly, Timothy, 80–81, 125
Downs, Doug, 7–8
dreaming: Love, Bettina, 131–132, 142; Stiegler, Bernard, 27, 129, 131–133, 134, 141–143, 150, 162
The Dropout, 14
Duffy, William, 37
Dunleavy, Mike, 67

economic inequality, 5, 28, 47, 69, 70, 87, 90, 151, 179–180; effects, 10–11; gig labor, 92; pedagogy, 9, 45, 49, 54, 78; race, 21, 22; San Francisco, 138; social class, 18, 19
Economies in Writing: Revaluations in Rhetoric and Composition (Horner, Nordquist, and Ryan), 17, 64
Ede, Lisa, 36, 38, 39, 48–49
Eidlin, Barry, 175, 176
Elbow, Peter, 35, 43, 57
El Barzón movement, 84–85

enclosure acts, 104, 105, 186*n11*, 186*n12*
Engels, Friedrich, 80, 129
English in America: A Radical View of the Profession (Ohmann), 15
Epic Systems, 99

Fabricant, Michael, and Stephen Brier, 159
Facebook, 121–123, 136, 140, 147, 191*n14*
Faculty governance, 5, 167. *See also* faculty senates
faculty senates, 166, 176, 191*n10*
Farmer, Frank, 84
Feminism for the 99%: A Manifesto (Arruzza, Bhattacharya, and Fraser), 46
Fidesz, 29, 59
Fitts, Karen and William B. Lalicker, 168
Fitzpatrick, Kathleen, 162
Fleckenstein, Paul, 12
Fleisher, Georgette, 152, 154
Fleming, Peter, 95
Flint, Michigan, 3
Floyd, George, 14, 52, 179
Foster, Dawn, 145–146
Fraser, Nancy, 31, 46
Freetown Christiania, 180

Gaia, 104
The Geek's Chihuahua: Living with Apple (Bogost), 136–137
Geissler, Heike, 111–114, 116, 179
gender, 23, 46, 54, 60, 116; diversity, 144–145, 185*n5*; inequality, 11, 47; genderism, 10, 41, 42; gender roles, 17; gender studies, 29; politics, 103; unions, 24
gender studies, 29
genderism. *See* gender: genderism
General Strike of 1919, 51
Gere, Anne Ruggles, 36
Giroux, Henry, 78, 163
globalism, 16, 32, 102
Glover, Danny, 53, 177
Goldrick-Rab, Sara, 65–67, 76
Goldstien, Dayna V., 9
Gonzales, Laura, 125
Google, 122–123, 134, 146–147, 148
GOP, 14, 33, 67, 153, 187*n1*, 191*n5*
Governing by Debt (Lazzarato), 72
Grabill, Jeffrey T., 38, 165
Graeber, David, 151–152, 154, 171; bullshit jobs, 90, 93–94; debt, 70–72, 73, 74, 76, 77, 79
"Gratuitousness and Recognition" (Nancy), 63, 73–75
The Great Transformation: The Political and Economic Origins of Our Time (Polanyi), 30

220 INDEX

Greene, Marjorie Taylor, 33
Green New Deal, 14, 188n7
Gregory, James N., 51
Grumbach, Jacob M., 24
Gunner, Jeanne, 99, 170
Gurley, Lauren Kaori, 96

Hall, Josh, 94
Harvey, David, 6
Hampton, Fred, 14
Han, Byung-Chul, 103
Hardt, Michael, and Antonio Negri, 48
Harris, Joseph, 15, 172
Hassell, Holly, and Joanne Baird Giordano, 162
Hayden, Tom, 47
Heller, Henry, 156–157, 166, 180
Higher Education Act of 1965, 65
Hollis, Karyn L., 39
Holt, Mara, 33, 34, 38, 39, 43
homophobia, 10, 45
Hormel, Leontina, and Lynn M. McAlister, 64
Horner, Bruce, 8, 13, 15, 64, 97; on unions, 175; on work, 89
Horvat, Srećko, 78
How the University Works (Bousquet), 16
Hu, Jane, 88
Hudson Yards, 3–4
Hyman, Louis, 91, 92

Ignatieff, Michael, 29, 30
inequality. *See* economic inequality
Inoue, Asao B., 20–22, 186n10

Jacobin, 24, 53
Jarrett, Kylie, 126, 133, 147, 190n5
Jefferies, 119
Jelinek, Elfriede, 113
Jim Crow, 12, 24
Joseph, Miranda, 59–60
joy, 44, 57, 115, 181, 187n5
Judas and the Black Messiah, 14

Kahn, Seth, 9, 15, 169, 174
Kail, Harvey, 37
Kezar, Adrianna, Tom DePaola, and Daniel T. Scott, 158
Kill All Normies: Online Culture Wars from 4Chan and Tumblr to Trump and the Alt-Right (Nagle), 140
King, Martin Luther, Jr., 131, 132
Kirp, Robert, 77
Klein, Naomi, 78
Koch brothers, 164, 165, 191n4
Komlosy, Andrea, 91, 93

Kommune 1, 180
Krull, Robert, and Jeanne M. Hurford, 97
Kuttner, Robert, 30

Lanier, Jaron, 142–144
Larson, Ann, 117
Latour, Bruno, 104, 128
Lazzarato, Maurizio, 71–72, 73, 74, 77, 86
Lean Out (Foster), 145–146
LeFevre, Karen Burke, 36, 43
Leipzig, Germany, 111
Leverenz, Carrie Shively, 37–38, 57
Liberating Voices: Writing at the Bryn Mawr Summer School for Women Workers (Hollis), 39
Liu, Catherine, 119
Liu, Wendy, 142–144, 147
Living Room: Understanding the Political Economy of Composition (Scott), 16
Longaker, Mark Garrett, 52
Love, Bettina L., 131–132, 142
Lovelock, James, 104
Lu, Min-Zhan, 16
Luckel, Madeline, 85
Lunsford, Andrea, 36, 38, 39, 48–49
Lyne, Bill, 175

Ma, Ling, 88
Maple Spring (2012), 168
McNamara, Mei-Ling, 121
Macron, Emmanuel, 32
The Making of an Indebted Man (Lazzarato), 71
manifestos, 31, 45–47, 144–146
de Man, Paul, 80
Mao, LuMing, 16
Margulis, Lynn, 104
Marx, Karl, 22, 98, 162
Marxism, 15, 17, 102, 129, 156–157, 175
McCarthy, Michael A., 5
Malhotra, Ravi, 12
Manning, Chelsea, 60
Marino, Mark C., 134
McClanahan, Annie, 72, 74, 80, 86
McClure, Randall, 9
McComiskey, Bruce, 181
McGee, Heather, 23, 24
McKee, Heidi A., 126
McKinsey, 92
McNenny, Geraldine, and Duane Roen, 59
minimum wage, 11, 20, 23, 108, 188n7, 189n2
Medicare for All, 14
Metabolizing Capital: Writing, Information, and the Biophysical Environment (Pulver), 126–127

Micciche, Laura R., 36, 100
Microsoft, 51, 122, 140
Miller, Carolyn R., 100, 101
Minnix, Christopher, 16
Modern Language Association (MLA), 15
Moore, Jason W., 12
Moynihan, Daniel Patrick, 21
multimodal composition. *See* digital writing
Musk, Elon, 135, 190*n12*
Mutnick, Deborah, 9, 15, 50

Nadworny, Alyssa and Claire Lombardo, 61
Nagle, Angela, 139, 141, 147
Nancy, Jean-Luc, 26, 81; debt, 63, 65, 70, 73–75, 77, 78, 82, 83, 84, 85; gratuitousness, 74, 78; recognition, 74, 85, 106
National Defense of Education Act of 1958, 65
Natural Light, 85–86
neoliberalism, 17, 30, 64, 68, 101, 102–103, 176, 187*n4*; Biden, 185*n3*; debt, 69, 72, 76, 78, 84; fantasy, 40; higher education, 6, 15, 117–118, 143, 155–156, 157, 158, 160–161, 166, 177; new, 31–34, 40, 43, 58, 59, 60, 159; pedagogy, 50–51; technology, 141; workplace, 26–27, 91, 92. *See also* Dardot, Pierre, and Christian Laval: new neoliberalism
Neumann, Adam, 182–183
Newfield, Christopher, 66, 155, 158–159, 164–165, 189*n5*
New Left Review, 18
Next Steps: New Directions for/in Writing about Writing (Bird, Downs, McCracken, and Rieman), 7
Nix, Alexander, 121
Nixon, Richard, 66
Nomadland: Surviving America in the Twenty-First Century (Bruder), 92
Nordquist, Brice, 64

Obama, Barack, 66
Ocasio-Cortez, Alexandra, 14, 25
Ohmann, Richard, 14–15, 185*n1*
Oluo, Ijeoma, 58
Omar, Ilhan, 15
Orbán, Victor, 29, 31, 42, 187*n3*, 187*n3*

Patrick, Dan, 154
peak performance, 89, 189*n1*
Peckham, Irvin, 17, 18, 87
Pell Grants, 65–66
Pemberton, Michael A., 9
Performing Antiracist Pedagogy in Rhetoric, Writing, and Communication (Condon and Young), 20

Piketty, Thomas, 10–11, 32, 67
podcasting, 51, 53–55, 84
political economy, 8, 10, 31, 50, 64, 99, 103; antiracism, 19–22, 24, 185*n6*; composition, 10, 15, 17, 18–19, 68, 117, 191*n6*; surveillance capitalism, 124; technology, 27, 125–126, 133, 135; twenty-first century, 13
Polanyi, Karl, 30, 129
"The Port Huron Statement" (Students for a Democratic Society), 46–47
precariat, 171. *See also* precarity
precarity, 7, 44, 69, 102, 119, 120, 145; higher education, 9–10, 27, 170; in the working world, 90–91, 93, 110–111
Pressley, Ayanna, 14
Professor Watchlist, 154, 157
prisons, 21, 53, 62, 121, 165
privatization, 5, 15, 25, 123, 150, 167; higher education, 65–66, 134, 148, 151, 157–159, 160, 168, 169, 174; student debt, 79
productivity, 60, 96, 119, 189*n4*; composition theory, 97–101; critical theory, 102–103; higher education, 117, 120, 156; technology, 138; workplace, 88, 89, 90–91, 93, 95, 96, 104, 109, 111, 112, 182
protest, 51, 56, 139, 157, 165, 182, 183; against police violence, 179; El Barzón movement, 84–85; Bessemer (Alabama), 52; BIPOC liberation protests, 14; Florida State University, 165; Graeber, David, 151–152; Hungary, 27; Maple Spring, 168; networked, 145; University of California, Berkeley, 72; University of Missouri, 168; WTO protests, 51. *See also* activism
The Protestant Ethic and the Spirit of Capitalism (Weber), 21
Pulver, Christian J., 126, 127, 133, 134, 142

Race for Profit: How Banks and the Real Estate Industry Undermined Black Homeownership (Taylor), 19
racism, 5, 10, 42, 45, 47; academic freedom, 153; and capitalism, 19–24; critique of, 47; flat hierarchies, 173; Kendi, Ibram X., 185*n6*; legal, 12; solidarity, 41; systemic, 179; technology, 146, 147. *See also* antiracism
Ratcliffe, Krista, 42–43
Reagan, Ronald, 66
Reed, Adolph, Jr., 23–24, 186*n8*
Reed, Touré F., 23
Reichert Powell, Pegeen, 68–68, 86
Reichman, Henry, 152, 155, 174, 191*n4*
Republicans. *See* GOP

retirement, 88, 92, 171
Reyman, Jessica, 126
rhetoric and composition. *See* composition
rhetorical listening, 42
Rhoades, Gary, and Sheila Slaughter, 157
Ridolfo, Jim, and Dànielle Nicole DeVoss, 98
Riedner, Rachel, 16
Rogoff, Irit, 130
Rosa, Hartmut, 132
Rosenfeld, Seth, 157
Ross, Andrew, 76
The Routledge Handbook of Digital Writing and Rhetoric (Alexander and Rhodes), 124
Rouzie, Albert, 98–99
Russell, Marta, 12
Ryan, Susan, 64
Ryder, Phyllis Mentzel, 33

Salaita, Steven, 152, 171, 191*n1*
Sallie Mae, 66
Samuels, Robert, 117, 118
Sanders, Bernie, 13, 72, 109, 165
Sasaki, Betty, 38
Savage, Azure, 53
Schaffner, Anna Katharina, 89, 95
Schwab, Klaus, 31
Schell, Eileen E., 167
Scott, Tony, 9, 109; austerity, 156, 159, 160; criticism, 109, 118; critique of capitalism, 13, 15; dangerous writing, 182; student workers, 90; textbook industry, 191*n6*; threshold concepts, 7; writing programs, 149
SCUM Manifesto, 47
Seasonal Associate (Geissler), 111–114, 179
Seattle, 53, 57, 109, 188; head tax, 145; history, 51; teachers' union strike, 132
Sawant, Kshama, 188*n7*
Seitz, David, 108
Severance (Ma), 88
sexism, 41, 45; flat hierarchies, 173; in the tech industry, 137–138, 145, 146; at work, 108
Sharma, Versha, 14
Sharp-Hoskins, Kellie, and Amy E. Robillard, 45
Shor, Ira, 46, 47
Silicon Valley. *See* tech industry
Simmons, W. Michele, 38
Smit, David, 6, 8
Smith, John, 3
Snowden, Edward, 60
social class. *See* class
Solanas, Valerie, 47
Soros, George, 29, 33

So You Want to Talk about Race (Oluo), 58
Sperling, Gene B., 62
Squid Game, 14
Stafford Loans, 66
Stagg, Natasha, 114, 116, 179
Stengers, Isabelle, 104–108, 110, 115, 116, 189*n6*; joy, 188*n5*; stupidity, 26, 91, 105–106, 107, 111, 114, 190*n10*
Stiegler, Bernard, 124, 127–133, 134–136, 138, 139, 141–145, 147; bifurcation, 132, 190*n11*; disruption, 27, 130, 134, 142, 190*n8*; dreaming, 27, 141–142, 143; capitalism, 129, 134, 135; dreaming, 131–133, 150, 162; reticular networks, 139, 142; stupidity, 190*n10*; technics, 128, 136
Stolley, Karl, 144
student debt. *See* debt
Stimilli, Elettra, 64
strikes, 14, 51, 60, 132, 168, 177
The Sum of Us: What Racism Costs Everyone and How We Can Prosper Together (McGee), 23
supply chain, 89, 180
Surveys (Stagg), 114–116, 179

Talking to My Daughter about the Economy, or How Capitalism Works—And How It Fails (Varoufakis), 78
Taylor, Astra, 45, 147
Taylor, Keeanga-Yamahtta, 19, 57
Taylorism, 93, 107
Teen Vogue, 14
tech industry, 27, 92, 99, 122–123, 126, 143, 145
technical and professional communication (TPC), 100, 160
Theory of the Subject (Badiou), 42
Therborn, Göran, 18
threshold concepts, 7–8
Tinnell, John, 128
Tingle, Nick, 175–176
Tlaib, Rashia, 14
"To His Debt" (Donnelly), 80
Tovey, Josephine, 96
transgender, 53, 56, 188*n8*. *See also* gender
Trimbur, John, 14, 26, 33, 39, 185*n1*, 191*n1*; collaborative writing, 34, 37, 43–44, 45, 56; consensus, 47
Trotter, Joe William, Jr., 117
Trump (Badiou), 42
Trump, Donald, 42, 51, 147, 179, 181, 191*n14*, 191*n15*; materialism, 189; policies, 14, 32–33, 187*n2*; racism, 29, 145; supporters, 59, 188*n10*; university, 159–160
The Truth of Democracy (Nancy), 73

Tufekci, Zeynep, 139–142, 146
Twitter and Tear Gas: The Power and Fragility of Networked Protest (Tufekci), 139

Uber, 91, 121, 123, 189
Uncanny Valley: A Memoir (Wiener), 137–139
unions, 60, 158, 174; Amazon, 52; declining, 96; faculty, 27, 174–177; feminism, 146; opposition, 89, 91; retaliation, 152, 154; strike, 132
university administration, 64, 66, 156–161, 182; conflict with faculty, 52–53, 118, 152, 166–168, 174–177; neoliberalism, 160
University of Alaska, 67
University of California, Berkeley, 72
University of Missouri protests, 168
University of Washington, 28, 46, 52, 53, 119, 165, 172, 179; prison labor, 53, 165; union, 176–177

vanden Heuvel, Katrina, 13
Varoufakis, Yanis, 78
Vee, Annette, 126, 128, 129
Vie, Stephanie, 36
violence, 19, 23, 51, 102, 117, 179

Wagner, Lindsay Peoples, 14
Walker, Scott, 159
Walton, Elizabeth, Kristen Moore, and Natasha Jones, 100–101
Wardle, Elizabeth, 7–8
Warren, Elizabeth, 165, 185*n*6
We Have Never Been Middle Class (Weiss), 82–83
West Coast Waterfront Strike (1934), 51
We Want to Do More Than Survive: Abolitionist Teaching and the Pursuit of Educational Freedom (Love), 131–132, 142
WeWork. *See* work
Weber, Max, 21–22, 88, 101–102
Weeks, Kathi, 103
Weiss, Hadas, 82–83
Welch, Nancy, 15, 50; austerity, 156, 159, 160; critique of capitalism, 13; labor, 9; privatization, 15; working-class action, 50

Wells, Susan, 100, 101, 160
Welteroth, Elaine, 14
white racial habitus, 8, 19, 21
Wiener, Anna, 137–139, 188*n11*
Williams, Jeffrey, 68
Wingard, Jennifer, 16
Wing Luke Museum, 53
work, 26–27, 60, 70, 151, 163, 164, 167, 168, 173; conditions, 26, 68, 89, 91, 100, 107–108, 109, 111, 114, 117, 118–119, 174, 189*n2*, 191*n2*; contingent, 28, 154, 158, 170–172, 180; culture of work, 82, 145; debt, 71; meritocracy, 188*n11*; pedagogy, 86, 89–120; performance, 189*n1*; tech industry, 137; unions, 175–176; WeWork, 94–95, 105, 181–182; work ethic, 88; workplace, 68, 69, 77, 138–139, 144
Work: The Last 1,000 Years (Komlosy), 91
working learners, 90. *See also* work
World Economic Forum (WEF), 31
World Trade Organization (WTO) protests, 51
Wright, Erik Olin, 6, 149–150, 151, 163; conservative attacks, 157; escaping capitalism, 180; resistance, 116
writing. *See* composition
Writing About Writing (WAW), 7, 8
Writing-Across-the-Curriculum (WAC), 45, 49, 107, 125, 133
Writing Democracy: The Political Turn in and Beyond the Trump Era (Carter, Mutnick, Park, and Pauszek), 17
writing program administration (WPA), 8–9, 100, 167, 169, 172
WPA-L, 170
Wylie, Christopher, 121

York, Lorraine, 39
Young, Iris Marion, 101

Zakaria, Rafia, 139–141, 147
Zaloom, Caitlin, 62, 83
Zebroski, James T., 18
zines, 51, 84, 115
Zuboff, Shoshana, 136, 137, 143, 147; surveillance capitalism, 27, 122, 135

ABOUT THE AUTHOR

James Rushing Daniel is an associate teaching professor at the University of Washington–Seattle.

www.ingramcontent.com/pod-product-compliance
Lightning Source LLC
Chambersburg PA
CBHW020525080526
44583CB00013B/747